Blood and Culture

Politics, History, and Culture
A series from the International Institute at the University of Michigan

Series Editors
George Steinmetz and Julia Adams

Series Editorial Advisory Board
Fernando Coronil
Mamadou Diouf
Michael Dutton
Geoff Eley
Fatma Müge Göçek
Nancy Rose Hunt
Andreas Kalyvas
Webb Keane
David Laitin
Lydia Liu
Julie Skurski
Margaret Somers
Ann Laura Stoler
Katherine Verdery
Elizabeth Wingrove

Sponsored by the International Institute at the University of Michigan and
published by Duke University Press, this series is centered around cultural and
historical studies of power, politics, and the state—a field that cuts across the
disciplines of history, sociology, anthropology, political science, and cultural
studies. The focus on the relationship between state and culture refers both to
a methodological approach—the study of politics and the state using culturalist
methods—and a substantive one that treats signifying practices as an essential
dimension of politics. The dialectic of politics, culture, and history figures
prominently in all the books selected for the series.

Blood and Culture

Youth, Right-Wing Extremism,
and National Belonging in
Contemporary Germany

Cynthia Miller-Idriss

Duke University Press
Durham and London 2009

© 2009 Duke University Press
All rights reserved
Printed in the United States
of America on acid-free paper
Designed by Christina Pelech
Typeset in Adobe Caslon
by Tseng Information Systems, Inc.
Library of Congress Cataloging-in-Publication
data and republication acknowledgments appear
on the last printed pages of this book.

For Shamil, Aniset, and Nura
for bringing laughter and light
to every single day

contents

One afternoon in the late summer of 2008, as this book was already going to the publisher, I was strolling along the docks of the Granville Public Market in Vancouver when I passed a young woman with a strong German accent emphatically explaining to her companion, "and that was the *first* time that one could say I am proud to be a German. That was the *first* time . . ." Just the day before, driving out of the same market, I saw a young man wearing a German flag on his backpack.

These two incidents suggest that much has changed since I began the research for this book nearly a decade ago and subsequently wrote a story about two generations of Germans struggling with their relationship with the nation. My time in Berlin came before the flag-waving and nationalism of the 2006 World Cup, when Chancellor Angela Merkel told a national newspaper that the flag-waving German fans were merely displaying a "relaxed pride in their country . . . without having to justify themselves" (Landler and Longman 2006). Just five years earlier, while I was living in Berlin, President Rau had publicly stated that German pride was an impossibility. In a short span of years, it seemed, Germans had set aside the automatic association of flag-waving with negative expressions of nationalism (Bernstein 2006a) and displayed what one newspaper reporter called "a sort of unembarrassed patriotism" (Bernstein 2006b).

For the youngest Germans—today's children and teenagers—this book may already seem, then, like an odd artifact from another era. Indeed, cultural phenomena are ephemeral and trying to capture them on paper is inevitably a risky endeavor. The story I tell of German culture in the early part of this century, in other words, would likely look somewhat different today, less than a decade after I first began researching it.

But it is an important story nonetheless, and not just as a cultural artifact. Setting aside the exceptional circumstances of national sporting events, many Germans continue to struggle with their relationship with the nation. The kinds of generational clashes that I observed were likely taking place in schools and other settings where generations interact throughout Germany during the time that I was there. The stories here, therefore, will ring true to many Germans born in the postwar era who continue to feel compelled to reject the nation, as they will to many members of a younger generation who resent the insistence of their elders that they can never be proud to be German.

The words of the Germans in this book will not resonate with all Germans, of course. National cultures are not homogeneous; rather, they are fluid and multivocal (Benhabib 2002), and there is tremendous variation among national populations in political opinions, attitudes, and relative emotional attachment to their collective national identities. I do expect, though, that these stories will ring true to other readers, too, even if they have never been to Germany and have little interest in it. The story I tell here of the clash of generations around a shared collective value—the nation—is an instance of generational difference that I contend happens in other places and at other times. Whenever a younger generation is striving to redefine a collective identity—whether national, ethnic, or religious—in ways that an older generation resists— I would expect a similar kind of pattern to emerge.

Overview of the Book

In chapter 1, I place the German case in the context of theories of national identity and nationalism, setting up the exploration of generational changes in Germany that will follow in subsequent chapters. I explain how academic and popular understandings of Germanness assume it is determined by "blood" and briefly review recent scholarship on nations and nationalism. Because these questions are impossible to investigate ahistorically, particularly in the German case, I turn in chapter 2 to a historical overview of citizenship, naturalization, and national belonging and identity in Germany. I focus on the periods leading up to and after World War II in order to provide a context within which current debates and contemporary understandings of Germanness can be investigated.

In chapters 3, 4, 5, and 6, I turn to the ethnographic research I conducted in three schools in Berlin. I begin in chapter 3 with debates about national pride in Germany, drawing on interviews with students and teachers to compare an older generation of teachers' views on pride with students' reactions to a prevailing public discourse about national pride in unified Germany, which has presented national pride as an illegitimate emotion that is directly linked to right-wing activities. In chapter 4 I turn to the radical right-wing. Drawing on school and classroom observations, interviews with students and teachers, participant-observation in teacher-training workshops on right-wing extremism, research on curriculum and school-based interventions in Berlin, and life narratives from a selected group of self-identified radical right-wing and former radical right-wing young men, the chapter details the nature of the radical right and the challenges posed to teachers who are trying to address these youth in their classrooms. In chapter 5 I turn to the school-based ethnography, first addressing the context of civic education in German vocational schools before shifting to an account of the months I spent observing school and classroom practice in three schools, examining how conceptions of citizenship and national identity are addressed by state actors and in particular by public vocational school teachers in civics classrooms. In the final part of the chapter, I examine students' responses to what they perceive as a hegemonic classroom discourse about national identity. Finally, chapter 6 takes up the question of generational change in conceptions of citizenship and national belonging, revealing how a younger generation of working-class Germans constructs their understanding of citizenship and national belonging based on cultural rather than blood-based criteria, and showing how this redefines prevailing understandings that many outsiders (including academics) have of Germanness. In the concluding chapter, I return to the discussion about the constructed nature of nations, arguing that a younger generation of Germans is actively re-imagining the German nation as their relationship to the nation and their understandings of who can be a German evolve. I point out the ways in which these findings illustrate both the success and the failure of the German state's project to create "democratic" and "tolerant" citizens. I also suggest that educators, parents, and other adults who are concerned about adolescents' participation in extremist movements would do well to consider whether generational shifts in the meaning of collective identity are playing a role in the appeal of such groups.

acknowledgments

This book has been nearly a decade in the making, and the list of people who helped shepherd it through its various stages reminds me that even the isolation of academic work is deeply dependent on the generosity, good will, and support of so many others. I am thankful to all who helped this project to completion. First and foremost, I am incredibly grateful to the students, teachers, principals, and administrators who welcomed me into their schools and classrooms and shared their opinions and feelings with me. Without their voices, this book would not have been possible. I am keenly aware of the potential for misinterpretation or misrepresentation inherent in any effort to depict the cultural and political landscape of a country other than the one in which one was raised, and it is my sincerest hope as I complete this project that I have done the participants in this research project justice in my analysis of their words and actions.

I am deeply indebted to Michael Kennedy and George Steinmetz, along with Fatma Müge Göçek, David K. Cohen, and Steve Hamilton, whose deep commitment as advisors of this work during its first life as a dissertation at the University of Michigan launched this project. The conversation among these five scholars at my dissertation defense remains one of the most intellectually interesting of my life and set the stage for my return to Berlin to conduct new research in order to reframe the book around the notion of generational transformation. The generosity of my new colleagues at New York University and their deep commitment to mentoring junior scholars has had a significant impact on this project as well. Rene Arcilla, Floyd Hammack, and Phil Hosay were thoughtful and conscientious in their efforts to protect my time for writing. Sally Franson, Nick Gozik, Nina Pessin-Whedbee, and especially Christian Bracho provided key research assistance at various stages of writing and editing. Various scholars, colleagues, and friends read parts of this manuscript or had conversations with me about the work that helped refine my thinking in important ways; for this, I am especially grateful to Richard Arum, Craig Calhoun, Anne Esacove,

Jon Fox, Andreas Glaeser, Darcy Leach, Nicole Lucier, Jeffrey Jurgens, Edward McDonald, Ann Morning, Doug Ready, Bess Rothenberg, Ari Sammartino, Janelle Scott, Jeff Shook, Mitchell Stevens, Lisa Stulberg, Jon Zimmerman, and the members of workshops and writing groups at New York University and the University of Maryland.

For research assistance in Berlin, I thank Hendrike Bake, Geraldine Gardner, and especially Katharina Börner, without whom this project would have taken years longer. For advice in the field and help with access to schools and materials, case selections, translations, housing needs, and other issues, I am indebted to Manfred Bergmann, Jürgen van Buhr, Brigitte Geisel, Christa Händle, Steve Hamilton, Georg and Ulrike Kirschniok-Schmidt, Darcy Leach, Wolfgang Lempert, Heike Lühle, Michaela Orizu, Hanns-Fred Rathenow, Klaus Schweikert, Hermann Schmidt, Barbara Sheldon, and Stephanie Wilde. I am particularly grateful to Mary Agnes and Steve Hamilton for granting me permission to adapt and use for this project an interview question that Mary Agnes Hamilton had designed for another research project. At Duke University Press, I am tremendously grateful for the enthusiasm and support of its senior editor Reynolds Smith, and to Pam Morrison, the production editor, to the series editors George Steinmetz and Julia Adams, and to the reviewers Mabel Berezin and Christian Joppke.

None of this would have been possible without the generous support of various funders. For field research funding, I am grateful to the Social Science Research Council, the Alexander von Humboldt Foundation, the National Science Foundation under Grant No. 0202017, the University of Michigan Sociology Department and Rackham Graduate School, and the New York University Steinhardt School of Culture, Human Development, and Education. For writing fellowships and residential or visiting scholar support at various stages of this project, I am indebted to the German Academic Exchange Service and the American Institute for Contemporary German Studies (DAAD/AICGS), the German Historical Institute in Washington, D.C., the German-American Center for Visiting Scholars (GACVS) in Washington, D.C., the Institute for Social Sciences and Education in History and Politics at the Technical University of Berlin, and the Department of Economic and Adult Education at Humboldt Universität in Berlin. New York University generously provided me a semester's leave to complete the final revisions.

While the primary data in this book is ethnographic and qualitative data that I gathered myself, I compare these findings in selected areas to data from the Allgemeine Bevölkerungsumfrage der Sozialwissenschaften (ALLBUS)—German General Social Survey (GGSS) 1996. From 1980 to 1986 and in 1991, the ALLBUS-program was funded by the German Research Foundation (Deutsche Forschungsgemeinschaft, DFG). For all other surveys, state and federal funding has been made available through GESIS (Gesellschaft sozialwissenschaftlicher Infrastruktureinrichtungen). ALLBUS/GGSS is accomplished by the Center for Survey Research and Methodology (Zentrum für Umfragen, Methoden und Analysen e.V., Mannheim, ZUMA) and the Central Archive for Empirical Social Research (Zentralarchiv für Empirische Sozialforschung, ZA, Cologne) in cooperation with the ALLBUS scientific council. Data and documentation are obtainable through the Central Archive for Empirical Social Research (ZA, Cologne). Any opinions, findings, and conclusions or recommendations expressed in this book, however, are mine and do not necessarily reflect the views of any of these agencies or organizations, and therefore the institutions and persons mentioned above bear no responsibility for the use or interpretations of the data in this book.

On a personal note, my parents' support during the whole process—from forwarding mail and adopting my cat when I moved overseas to abandoning many of the more relaxing things they could have done with their retirement to become part-time nannies—made everything possible. Friends and colleagues in Ann Arbor generously offered a place to stay during multiple trips to Ann Arbor—for this I am especially thankful to Nadia Kim, Nicole Lucier and Dana Shea, Doug Ready, Karen Ross, George Steinmetz and Julia Hell, and Mina Yoo. I owe special thanks to Sean Shahida, a Washington, D.C., landlord who rescued irreplaceable boxes of research materials from a basement flood. Laura Kogel helped me let go of the quest for perfection. Lupei "Lulu" Mei, Bibi Ali, Erin Cocke, and my parents took care of my most precious "projects" so that I could focus on writing. Last but not least, I am so fortunate to have tremendous intellectual, motivational, and emotional support from wonderful friends and family: Gary and Lynn Miller, Jon Miller, Zee Miller and Michael O'Brien, Havva Idriss, Reed Idriss and Meredith Renda, Erin McMonigal, Sonja Plesset, and Laurel Spindel. I can't even begin to thank Shamil, who has done all this and more as a true partner in this project from beginning to end—and whose love, patience, and support across multiple time zones, borders, and oceans motivated me and kept me grounded. Together with our beautiful daughters Aniset and Nura, who joyously entered our lives as this project was nearing completion, our expanding family is a constant reminder to me of the most important things. Everything else pales in comparison.

I, of course, take full responsibility for any errors or omissions in the text.

abbreviations

CDU   Christian Democratic Union

DGB   The German Federation of Trade Unions

FDP   Free Democratic Party of Germany

FRG   Federal Republic of Germany

GDR   German Democratic Republic

Greens   The Green Party (Alliance 90/The Greens)

NPD   National Party of Germany

NSDAP   National Socialist German Workers Party

PDS   Party of Democratic Socialism

SPD   Social Democratic Party of Germany

SS   Schutzstaffel (Protective Squadron)

Citizenship and National Belonging as Cultural Practices

Once best known for its dividing wall—perhaps the most famous symbol of the Cold War—Berlin today is best described as a city in transition. Unified Berlin has a population of 3.4 million, 466,500 of whom are foreigners (Statistische Bundesamt Deutschland 2007). Home to the federal government since 1999, the city has undergone massive transformations and is still struggling to define its identity. By 2000, whole city districts were fully unrecognizable to visitors who had come to Berlin even five years earlier: construction cranes stretched across nearly every horizon in the center city, and the neon signs of international clothing chains and restaurants lit up the ground floors of modern skyscrapers that had sprouted in the former "no-man's land" between east and west. Berliners experience more interaction between east and west Germans than their fellow citizens, and while the percentage of ethnic minorities is lower than in many other west German cities, such as Frankfurt or Cologne, young Berliners still experience a great deal of interaction with people of other ethnicities and backgrounds. Like other European citizens, Berliners today are learning to navigate a new European currency, vote in European elections, and live and work with ease across borders. And they do so in a country that has experienced nearly constant political change over the course of the past century, making Germany an ideal place to study nations and nationalism (Lepsius 2004, 481).

Berlin, in other words, is an excellent place to look for transformations in conceptions of citizenship and national belonging. But the changes happening in Berlin are not entirely unique, especially when compared with the rest of Europe. Increasing migration, coupled with higher birth rates among many immigrant groups, is changing the cultural and ethnic landscape of most European countries. Streetscapes that used to be peppered with church steeples now make room for the minarets of mosques, as the largely secular but staunchly Christian nature of many cities and towns in Europe is gradually shifting to include significant Muslim populations. In many parts of Germany, young people today are as likely to snack on a Turkish *Dönerkebab* as they are a traditional German *Bratwurst*.

The influence of immigrant groups aside, globalization processes have introduced cultural products, languages, and practices far removed from traditional national customs. The proliferation of multinational corporations, global markets, and the spread of fast food restaurants, pop music, hotel chains, and brand-name clothing have taken capitalism beyond national borders, as anyone who has popped into a Starbucks in Zurich for a mocha latte or shopped at a Benetton store in Berlin can readily testify. Meanwhile, the European Union is growing in power and prominence, as a European currency gains in strength and national citizens become used to the idea of living, working, and traveling across borders with ease. Questions of national culture, religion, diversity, and belonging, in other words, have been forced into the public eye throughout Europe, as Europeans learn to negotiate new ways of thinking about citizenship and national belonging during a period of historic and unsettling change.

The transition to a multicultural Europe has not been an easy one. The murder of a Dutch filmmaker and subsequent anti-Muslim violence in Holland, deliberation about the proposed entrance of a predominantly Muslim nation (Turkey) to the European Union, debates about Muslim headscarves in German and French schools, and increasing neo-Nazi violence in Germany and elsewhere have all been the subject of dinner table conversations and civic classroom discussions throughout Europe and across the globe. At the heart of these conversations are several questions. How should national (and transnational) communities be defined and understood? Who counts as a German, or a Frenchman, or a European? What does it mean to belong?

Violent incidents in many parts of Europe illustrate the potential consequences of failing to adequately attend to these questions. The potential for youth—whether immigrant or native born—to become disaffected and disconnected from the nation was illustrated all too well by the recent "home-grown" terrorism in the United Kingdom.

The violent reactions of skinhead and neo-Nazi groups to immigrants and racial or religious minorities in a variety of European countries are equally troubling. Yet there has been no unitary response to these challenges. Political parties running on antiforeigner platforms have gained significant percentage points in several European countries. Prime minister Tony Blair responded to the terrorist attacks in London with a newfound assertion of British values, arguing that living in Britain means agreeing to "share and support the values that sustain the British way of life" (Manji 2005). In France, policymakers have taken a protectionist stance, turning to the legal system to find ways to protect the French language and prohibit the display of Muslim headscarves and other religious symbols in schools (Bowen 2006). Macedonians utilize the media, crafting a new popular children's television program featuring a cast of Albanian, Macedonian, Turkish, and Gypsy children to confront challenges of ethnic difference and conflict. Throughout Europe, policymakers, educators, politicians, and others are being forced to make decisions about how to balance the ethnic, racial, religious, or ideological differences of minority groups with the national identities and claims of the broader community.

In some ways, of course, these challenges are nothing new. National populations have likely always been less homogenous than they have imagined themselves to be. As Edward Said (1993, 331) argued, "We are mixed in with one another in ways that most national systems of education have not dreamed of." Centuries of migration and immigration have blended populations across borders such that the creation of national identities, as is now widely recognized, is based not on actually existing ethnicities, but on an imagined sense of community with others who share customs, language, traditions, culture, or residence within a given set of borders (Anderson 1991). But in other ways, new patterns of diversity are posing a different set of challenges from those which national populations have confronted in the past. This is especially clear in Europe, where immigrants today are more likely to be from outside of Europe and from predominantly Muslim societies than has been the case in the past.

In Germany, reactions have been polarized. Declining birth rates, coupled with increased immigration and naturalization of foreigners from non-European countries, have transformed both the national and local communities throughout the country. German youth today are growing up in a nation in which Germanness has become difficult to define. About 8 percent of the German population—6.8 million people—are foreigners, over half of whom have lived in Germany for a decade or more. Nearly two million are Turkish, almost six hundred thousand of whom were born in Germany but are Turkish citizens (Statistische Bundesamt Deutschland 2007). Unlike other guest workers and immigrants from southern Europe, most (but not all) of Germany's Turkish community is Muslim, adding a new cultural and religious dimension to immigration and integration. Tensions are not only between "ethnic" Germans and "non-ethnic" Germans, however.[1] Hundreds of thousands of Turks in Germany are of Kurdish descent (Canefe 1998, 533), for example. Continuing cultural and ethnic conflicts between Kurds and Turks in Turkey are often reflected in patterns of tension and conflict within Germany's foreign population.

Like many other European countries, the German population will become more and more multicultural over the next several decades, even if immigration is severely restricted. Germans are aging rapidly, and the foreign population in Germany is significantly younger, on average, than Germans (Statistische Bundesamt Deutschland 2007). In addition to the sizeable Turkish population, a large number of refugees fleeing violence in the former Yugoslavia and elsewhere sought asylum in Germany during the 1990s, until a reform in the German Basic Law led to a reduction in applicants (Heiderich and Rohr 2000, 14; Hogwood 2000, 130–31; O'Brien 1992, 380; also see Isoplan 2002, 12). But it is not just ethnic minorities who are complicating the notion of Germanness. The fall of the Soviet Union and the transformations in the rest of Eastern Europe prompted a major influx of "ethnic" German returnees from Eastern Europe and the former Soviet States, as hundreds of thousands arrived at the German border seeking citizenship and a better economic future (O'Brien 1992, 380; Rotte 2000). Meanwhile, however, millions of second- and third-generation Turks and other immigrants whose families had come to Germany in the 1960s as guest workers were living in Germany as noncitizens. It was this paradox that fed public debate about the reforms in citizenship and naturalization law in the late 1990s discussed later in this chapter.

Of course, statistics and trends can't even begin to tell the entire story of who is considered to be "German" today. The numbers don't indicate how many millions of Germans have foreign ethnic backgrounds, are multiracial or multiethnic, or have more than one citizenship (legally, this is forbidden in Germany, but in practice, many people hold more than one passport and citizenship). Moreover, "ethnic" Germans are dispersed well beyond the borders of Germany. As Peter O'Brien (1992, 378) points out, no other "state in Europe has so many of its people (perhaps 8 million) living in so many foreign countries." The complex layers of German national identity are further complicated by the indelible mark that the Holocaust and World War II have left on German national identity. Discussions of German identity are so fraught with the past that it is difficult for Germans to talk unselfconsciously about issues of diversity and difference in contemporary Europe. What could a multicultural Germany look like? How might it take shape?

While some have been outspoken advocates for minority rights and eased restrictions on naturalization, others have rejected the notion of a multicultural national community, clinging instead to an ethnically restrictive definition of national belonging. Antiforeigner attacks and violence from skinheads, neo-Nazis, and hooligans have persisted. But there have also been vocal counterprotests from anti-right-wing groups and broad citizen coalitions who have been horrified by the violence. In the early 1990s, hundreds of thousands of Germans across the country poured into the streets for candlelight vigils after several violent and deadly attacks against foreigners.

This book is about how a younger generation of Germans is learning to negotiate conceptions of citizenship and national identity in changing historical circumstances. Although many of these changes are not unique to Germany, the particular constellation of transformations in Germany makes it an especially good place to study these changes. Since Germany is a core part of the European Union, the changes Germany is experiencing are indicative of the transformations in Europe as a whole. But Germany is an ideal location to study citizenship and national identity for reasons peculiar to Germany, too. National identity and, in particular, national pride have been extremely difficult issues for Germans. In post-unification Germany, national pride has been largely perceived as illegitimate, in large part because pride is inextricably linked to Germany's role in World War II and the Holocaust. Efforts to invalidate national pride through the school system are deeply intertwined with educators' concerns about rising right-wing violence over the past decade, as well as increases in right-wing extremist participation among working-class youth in particular (Miller and Ready 2002; Paul 1995, 40; Steinmetz 1997). The growth of the extreme right-wing among German adolescents is particularly troubling because the education system has made explicit efforts to create a tolerant, engaged, democratic citizenry in the post–World War II era. Because of this, German schools are a site well suited for the examination of the cultural processes involved in the shifting negotiations of national identity across generations.

Generations as Agents of Change in Citizenship and National Belonging

Scholarship on national identity is in complete agreement that national identities are powerful forms of membership. They incite wars and revolutions and inspire individuals to sacrifice their lives in battle, or at least to care about the welfare of fellow citizens whom they have never met. In contrast to earlier scholars who believed that nations and national identities were based on primordial or natural attachments (Geertz 1973), most scholars today recognize that these powerful attachments do not exist automatically. Instead, they must be imagined by the individuals living within a given set of borders. This "imagining" of the national community gets help from institutions such as the state, the public school system, and the media, of course, but in the end, individuals must collectively agree to the notion that they belong together under one national umbrella. This collective agreement is what we refer to as the "imagined community" (Anderson 1991) of the nation. Although the idea that nations are imagined communities has been widely recognized by scholars, however, we have paid less attention to the ways in which nations can be "re-imagined."

What happens when nations are faced with transformative change — such as that taking place in Europe today? How do individuals recreate and re-imagine their national identities to incorporate transnational memberships or new patterns of national diversity? I believe that nations are not only imagined, but that they are also continually re-imagined by successive generations. But to understand how this takes place, we need to add a cultural dimension to the study of citizenship, which has been dominated by the study of structures and institutions — examinations of laws, policies, and official parliamentary debates. This means studying citizenship and national belonging as *practices* in addition to *statuses* (C. Miller 1999). While the study of policies and laws about citizenship is important, we also need to investigate how citizenship and national belonging are understood and practiced by ordinary citizens. Only by examining citizenship and national belonging as cultural practices can we account for change in the conceptions of nationhood across generations.

To do this, I talked to 119 working-class youth and 31 of their teachers, in interviews and focus groups in three vocational schools in Berlin, primarily during an intensive thirteen-month period in 2000–2001, a two-month period in 2002, and a two-month period in 2004. I observed over 170 hours of classroom instruction in these schools and spent countless hours hanging around school cafeterias, faculty meetings, teachers' lounges, and other school social and academic spaces. I examined the schools' curriculum, textbooks, and instructional materials, read the daily German newspapers, and analyzed public and political debates about citizenship, nationhood, foreigners, and the radical right.

The story that I set out to uncover, as I began this research, was not about generational differences. As is so often the case in ethnographic field research, what I found in Berlin—that a younger generation is actively transforming the meaning of being German—occurred to me gradually. When I first began talking to teachers and principals about the possibility of conducting case studies in their schools, what interested me most were the differences among three groups of students. The three schools I ultimately selected for case studies—a construction school, an information technology school, and a school for hotel and cooking trades—were chosen to create maximal variation among the students on some variables, such as future position in the global economy, while maintaining as much constancy as possible on others, such as blue-collar versus white-collar occupations (see appendix A). But by the time I was halfway through the research, it became clear that the similarities among these groups of students were much more intriguing than their differences. Even more fascinating, though, was an apparent divergence between students' conceptions of national belonging and those of their teachers. Gradually, it began to dawn on me that I might be observing generational transformations in the meaning of being German.

Vocational schools provide a unique opportunity to study differences in conceptions of citizenship and national identity—and the teaching of citizenship education—for groups of young people with significantly different employment prospects and relationships to the "new" global economy. At the time, I was interested in knowing whether young people training for global occupations, such as information technology, differed in their views about European and national identity when compared to their peers who were studying for occupations with clear local connections, such as construction. There is no better place to investigate these comparisons than in the German vocational system, which likely has the most highly structured occupational credentialing system in the world.

Vocational schools in Germany educate two-thirds of German youth aged sixteen to twenty for one of 356 state-certified occupations. The schools are clustered by career field (such as banking, hospitality, information technology, or construction), and academic classes are further structured by occupation. In other words, students attend all of their academic classes with other students training for their exact occupation. Due to the fairly structured and rigid nature of the German economic and occupational system, they have a reasonable expectation of remaining in that career field for the better part of their lives, although the system recently has made efforts to become more flexible (see Miller-Idriss 2002). This structure makes it possible to observe classroom instruction among groups of adolescents who are all training to be masons, chimney-sweeps, bank tellers, hotel clerks, or any one of the 356 occupations in the system. In effect, this creates a unique opportunity to observe classrooms—and interview students from those classrooms—where all of the students not only generally share similar social class backgrounds, but who are, by design, destined for similar social classes and share similar employment prospects.

I was particularly interested in the comparison between future information-technology workers and future construction workers. Information technology fields experienced a major growth period in the 1990s. Desperate for skilled employees, German companies began calling for relaxed immigration policies for computer specialists. This led to the implementation of the so-called "Green Card," an American-style work visa designed to grant faster immigration and work permits to foreign computer and information technology specialists. The national vocational school system has added new occupational specializations in information technology fields to respond to industry demands. Employment prospects are strong in most of the fields offered, especially in the information technology (IT) branches. Many apprentices report they expect to have their choice of job offers upon graduation. With job opportunities fueled in part by a global and transnational economy, I expected these apprentices to express European and transnational identities.

The field of construction, on the other hand, was faced with a startling paradox by the time I began my research. Despite its rank as the city in Europe with the most on-going construction, an astonishing decline in employment left some forty thousand German construction workers unemployed in Berlin by the end of the decade. A swelling pool of illegal workers from eastern and southern Europe, combined with an influx of foreign firms, has drastically limited the chances for German workers in construction. Although their peers a decade earlier had been virtually guaranteed jobs, by 2000 most of the young men (and the few women) in the construction school were headed straight for unemployment. The impact of the job market on students' and teachers' moods and motivation at the school was tangible. Many of the youth I observed in the hallways, the cafeteria, the courtyard, and later, in classrooms, displayed the shaved heads that often signify right-wing radical membership. Even when employed, construction workers are, by design, grounded in fairly local contexts. Combined with the threat to their livelihood from foreign firms and workers, I expected these youth to express strongly local and national identities, rejecting global and transnational memberships.

But by the time I returned to Berlin in the late summer of 2000 to study these comparisons in greater depth, unemployment was second to another, more pressing, concern for teachers at the construction school and other schools throughout Berlin and Germany. My arrival coincided with a wave of press coverage and public discussion about an increase in right-wing violence in Germany that year (*Berliner Zeitung* 2001; Homola 2001; Hops 2001; Krupa 2001; Schwennicke 2001; *Süddeutsche Zeitung* 2001; *Tagesspiegel* 2001a, b, c).[2] Day after day, as I traveled around the city on the subway searching for an apartment and waited in the myriad of bureaucratic lines that accompany a move to Germany—police registration, visa and residence permits, health insurance applications—the headlines in the daily papers I read warned of the growing problem of right-wing extremism among Germany's adolescents.

Although some critics argued that the increased media attention to right-wing extremism and radicalism was due to a *Sommerloch*—literally, a summer "hole" in other news to report—the racist and xenophobic violence nonetheless raised obvious concerns for educators, who have struggled to respond to the growth of right-wing subcultures among young people born well after the end of National Socialism.[3] With several studies reporting higher rates of violence in the east, accusations flew, as fingers were pointed at socialization processes in families, at social and economic conditions, and at schools. Although it likely came as no surprise to them, the teachers at the construction school had particular cause to be concerned. Construction apprentices exhibit some of the highest antiforeigner sentiments of all apprentices (Schnabel and Goldschmidt 1997).

At times, it was difficult to separate the media and public discussions of the right wing from a series of other debates that erupt periodically in Germany about who belongs in the German nation. As the twenty-first century dawned, public outrage about the waves of right-wing violence and brutal hate crimes against foreigners that took place in the early and late 1990s was still close to the surface. But this outrage was accompanied by nearly constant political and public debate about proposed legal and constitutional reforms in citizenship, naturalization, immigration, and asylum-seeking policies.

Citizens and Foreigners: Who Belongs in the German Nation?

The public debates about Germanness, national identity, and diversity revolve around the question of how Germanness should be determined—and reveal the multiple narratives which coexist in Germany around the contested terrain of nationhood. Are blood and ethnic heritage more important, or is culture and cultural assimilation? Who is a German citizen, and who is eligible for membership in the community of citizens? Like any other highly politically charged topic, there is a range of responses to such questions. Two positions in particular have emerged as especially vocal and polarized in Germany (Räthzel 1990, 45).

Conservatives and right wingers, on the one hand, talk about the need for a "guiding" German culture (*Leitkultur*) in assimilation processes and call for reduced immigration, increased assimilation among those immigrants already in the country, and a protection of national languages, among others. German national culture and identity are to be protected against the threat of linguistic, ethnic, and cultural dilution. Conservative politicians argue that the immigration "boat" is already full and that German jobs should go to German workers. At its most extreme, radical right-wing groups who call for an end to immigration argue that Germans will end up like Native Americans, as foreign immigrants take over the country and force native Germans onto reservations.

Leftists and social liberals, on the other hand, argue against the notion of any form of national identity, linking it with the rampant nationalism and fascism of the Third Reich. Huyssen (1995, 77) calls this view the "leftist taboo on nationhood, the antinationalist consensus so central to the self-understanding of the Federal Republic of Germany since the 1960s." In this view, there can be no common German culture, no national pride, and no unifying sense of Germanness (see Räthzel 1990). At its most extreme, this position "reject(s) any notion of national identity" and holds that "only that which is not-German is 'free of an ideological taint,' worthy of admiration" (Peck 1996, 488).[4] Elements of this taboo on nationhood coalesced, by the turn of the century, in a prevailing national narrative interdicting pride, which I describe in greater detail in chapter 3 by tracing a heated public debate that emerged in the spring of 2001 in Germany about whether it is acceptable to be proud of being German.

In fact, for the vast majority of Germans, neither of these claims to the future of Germany (and Germanness) is adequate. But this dynamic—between the antiforeigner right and the antinationalist left—turns out to have striking parallels in the dynamic I observed between young, working-class vocational school students and an older generation of teachers.

The fact that such broadly different responses to the question of Germanness and immigration exist illustrates the ways in which multiple versions of the nation coexist and potentially compete for dominance. Nationhood, in other words, is dynamic and contested. For ordinary Germans trying to navigate these questions of Germanness in their daily lives, understandings of who belongs in Germany—and indeed, of what a "German" is—have become increasingly complicated in the past decade. During the 1990s, a linguistic transformation in discussions about foreigners took place in Germany. In a meeting at a research institute early on in my preliminary research in 1999, I used the word for foreigner and was quickly interrupted by my host. "The whole question of who is a foreigner," he argued, "is complicated." He described the contradictions present in calling a third-generation Turk who was born and raised in Germany, who speaks fluent German and may have little or no connection to Turkish culture, a "foreigner," while "ethnically German" immigrants arriving with no German language skills and little or no connection to Germany can essentially pick up a German passport at the border (also see Bade 1996; White 1997).

In the course of less than a decade, in fact, a new vocabulary had emerged to talk about "foreigners" in Germany. Instead of the term *"Ausländer,"* which implies a belonging to another land, many Germans increasingly use the term *"ausländische Mitbürger"* —foreign cocitizen— to refer to second- and third-generation immigrants.[5] But distinctions among foreigners and Germans are even more complicated than this; Germans distinguish between discussions of *Aussiedler* (Germans who had settled out, mostly immigrants with "ethnic" German heritage from Eastern Europe and the former Soviet States), *Volksdeutsche* (ethnic Germans), *Spataussiedler* (late resettlers), *Übersiedler* (generally used to refer to former East Germans who had emigrated to West Germany), *Ausländer* (foreigners), *Mitbürger ausländischer Herkunft* (fellow-citizens of foreign ethnic heritage), or even *einheimische Ausländer* (native foreigners).[6]

As these semantic distinctions illustrate, by the late 1990s, discussions about Germanness and foreigners had become complicated enough that the stage was set for reform in citizenship and naturalization law.[7] Although changes in German citizenship law had begun soon after the fall of the Berlin Wall (Baumann 1999, 69; Räthzel 1990, 43), by the end of the decade German citizenship law continued to be largely based on the Reich Citizenship Law of 1913, which firmly established German citizenship along *jus sanguinis* (based on blood) principles (Bade 2001, 29–35). This law automatically granted citizenship to anyone with proven German "blood," regardless of where they were born. This policy can be contrasted with citizenship and naturalization policies based on *jus soli*, or principles of birthplace or territory, such as those of France and the United States.

A reform in 1999 in Germany made a decisive move toward a jus soli policy (Miller-Idriss 2006a). The new law automatically grants eligibility for German citizenship to all children born in Germany after the first of January 2000, provided that one parent has legally resided in Germany for at least eight years and has a secure resident status. The reforms also reduced the required legal residency for naturalization applications from other immigrants from fifteen years to eight, among other changes (Ausländerbeauftragte des Senats von Berlin 2000). Although the reforms made a notable step away from a jus sanguinis–based citizenship policy toward one rooted in the principles of jus soli, significant elements of the blood-based version of citizenship still remain in German law. Article 116 of the German constitution continues to define a "German," not only as someone who holds German citizenship, but also as someone who "belong[s] to the German *Volk*" (Storz and Reisslandt 2002, 27). It is still much easier for "ethnic" German returnees or other individuals of ethnic German heritage to gain German citizenship than it is for "non-ethnic" Germans. Nonetheless, the reforms marked a clear shift in official German narratives about national identity, formally rejecting a conception of Germanness based on descent or ethnicity. As minister of the interior Otto Schily (SPD) detailed in a 1999 press release:

> With the reform of the citizenship law, Germany acknowledges a realistic conception of the nation. It was always an illusion to think it possible to found the idea of the nation on the basis of ethnic homogeneity. . . . The notion that a nation could be defined above all by blood ties (*Blutverbundenheit*) belongs to the tragic errors of our past. (Baumann, Dietl, and Wippermann 1999, 49)

Studying Generations in Theory

In this book, I use the term *generation* to refer to groups of people born roughly at the same time who have experienced similar social and historical events during childhood and adolescence in ways that affect their interpretation of and interaction with cultural, social, or political phenomena later in life (Mannheim 1952; Pilcher 1994). This usage of *generation* is different from the notion of generations bound by kinship (Pilcher 1994), in which generations are defined by the child-parent-grandparent relationship within individual families (see, e.g., Welzer, Moller, and Tschuggnall 2002). Instead, generations here are bound by formative experiences in childhood. Thus, they "situate the life history in a group context" (Borneman 1992, 48), connecting individuals' daily interpretations of their experiences with others in their cohort.

Despite widespread interest in generations (or cohorts) among sociologists who study outcomes such as political and social attitudes, educational attainment, or memories of the past (Schuman and Rieger 1992; Schuman and Scott 1989; Griffin 2004), there has been surprisingly little attention paid to the role of generations in *creating* social change—that is, in how generations themselves help to transform society. This was Karl Mannheim's original interest in generations—namely, the ways in which new generations' reactions to cultural, social, or political phenomena and events produce social change—or what Harold Marcuse (2001, 290) calls the "natural process of history." Generations react differently to the same phenomena and events, Mannheim claimed, because their reactions are grounded in key socialization experiences in their youth—the key period of which he specifies as ages fifteen to twenty-five, the most important period of political socialization for generations (Levy 1999, 15). This age range corresponds nearly exactly with the group of vocational school students I interviewed and observed for this book. Late adolescence and early adulthood is such a key period, Pilcher (1994, 488–89) explains, because variations in the "socio-historical world that predominated in their youth" mean that each generation develops "a distinctive historical consciousness which leads them to experience and approach the same social and cultural phenomena differently."

The affinity that members of a generation have for each other does not imply that they act or react to events as a monolithic entity, however. Individuals vary in their actions and reactions to events based on variations in prior socialization, by other roles and identities in their life, such as gender, racial and ethnic identity, or parenthood, and by their peer groups, marriage partners, or other formative experiences in their lives. Indeed, such variation among members of a generation means that they can be further divided into generational *subgroups*, or what Mannheim (1952) terms generational *units*. In this book, I am studying two generational subgroups—namely, middle-class educated teachers, and their working-class students—which I discuss at greater length below.

The lack of attention to the role that generations may play in creating social change is not only a theoretical gap. Mannheim's key theoretical treatise on generations, as Pilcher (1994) points out, lacks empirical foundation. Other scholars have taken up the question of how generations might play a constitutive role in social change (Cherrington 1997) but without focusing on the nation directly, or have looked in depth at the differences in interpretations of national and state narratives across generations (Borneman 1992), but without delving into the potential impact of such differential interpretations on social change. The question of what the relationship between generations, nationhood, and social change might look like in practice remains unanswered.

Studying Generations in Practice

While theoretically it makes sense that membership in a particular generation may affect an individual's interpretation of events and experiences later in life, studying how these processes happen in practice is challenging. In part, this is because—like other social categories—it is difficult to draw firm boundaries around particular generations. By their very nature, generations are fluid and overlapping, with no clear lines of demarcation to indicate where one generation has stopped and another has begun. There is thus a degree of arbitrariness in categorizing someone born in 1955 in one generation, for example, while a sibling born in 1957 might belong to the next generation. As Rosow points out, generations are "clearest at their centers, but blurred and fuzzy at the edges" (Rosow in Pilcher 1994, 487).

Moreover, there is tremendous variation within generations. As Dirk Moses (1999, 114–15) details in his discussion of the 45er and 68er generations in Germany, great caution should be taken not to essentialize all members of a birth cohort. Thus, when discussing a particular generation's approach to a social or political phenomenon or event, it is likely that an active and vocal minority within that generation comes to represent the entire group, while the "disinterested masses" remain either silent or unheard (Moses 1999, 115). As Marcuse (2001, 290) explains, for the 68er generation in Germany, youth did react in a variety of ways to their parents' explanations of the Nazi atrocities, either embracing, ignoring, or rejecting the older generation's accounts; but those who rejected their parents' explanations "were the most outspoken."

Thus, the year in which an individual is born can have a tremendous impact on that individual's experience later in life—on whether a young man is drafted during wartime or, born just a year or two later, remains an observer from the safety of his parents' home, for example. This is what Bude (1992, 80–81) describes when he refers to the "coincidence of cohort" for Germans coming of age before and during World War II. And despite these difficulties of creating specific demarcations around birth cohorts, some form of boundaries needs to be drawn in order to study generational effects. In this book, I have done so in the following ways, in reference to three generations of Germans:

The oldest generation, many of whom have already passed away by the writing of this book, were teenagers and young adults during World War II. They were not interviewed for this study, but are relevant be-

cause it is in reaction to this generation that the current older generation of teachers formed their sense of national identity and belonging.
Previous scholars (see especially Moses 1999) have labeled this generation the *45ers*—Germans born during the 1920s, for whom 1945 marked
the turning point in their lives.

The middle generation, or what I call in this book the "older" generation, are Germans born between the late 1930s and the mid-1950s,
who came of age in the late 1960s and 1970s. Moses (1999) identifies
this generation (the 68ers) as Germans born between 1938 and 1948;
I extend the birthdates on both ends to include participants born between 1936 and 1955. Germans call this group the "Generation of 68," or
simply the 68ers, in reference to the social protests and student movement which were this generation's most formative youth experience
(see, e.g., Schneider 2001).

What I call the "younger" generation in this book are Germans who
were born in the late 1970s and early 1980s, whose formative youth experiences took place during the 1990s—a decade of phenomenal transformations in and challenges to German identity. Buttressed on one
end by unification in 1990 and on the other end by radical changes in
German citizenship law in 1999, the 1990s were marked by constant
political and public discussions about Germanness, including but not
limited to the status of asylum-seekers, the east-west relationship, the
role of Germany in the European Union, the permissibility of national
pride, the introduction of a "Green Card" for certain immigrants, the
increasing migration of "ethnic" German returnees from eastern Europe
and the former Soviet States, the expansion of citizenship rights to
"nonethnic" Germans, and the increasing participation of youth in
neo-Nazi and right-wing extremist groups. I interviewed members of
this generation who were born between 1975 and 1983 and were aged
seventeen to twenty-five at the time of my interviews. They fit into the
category of what Jeffrey Arnett (2000) refers to as "emerging" adults, as
well as into the age range (fifteen to twenty-five) that Karl Mannheim
states is key for the political socialization of generations.

The fact that there is wide variation in how members of each of these
generations relate to the nation is worth repeating. The small number of
Germans I interviewed from the younger and older generations cannot
be said to speak for all members of their respective generations, who of
course express opinions reflective of a broad political, economic, and
social spectrum. Rather, as I explain above, this book reports on an in-

stance of two generational subgroups interacting—namely, a working-class, largely conservative, younger generational subgroup and a college-educated, largely liberal, older generation. This particular interaction of generational subgroups is an especially significant one, however, because it is replicated repeatedly in vocational schools across the country each year. These two generational subgroups, in other words, come into frequent and regular contact with each other, and thus German youth in other parts of the country are likely to find themselves in a similar configuration of generational subgroup interaction when compared to the students in my study. The findings in this study ought, then, to be relevant to instances where similar kinds of generational subgroups interact across social class and political lines, whether in Germany or elsewhere.

Although each generation is composed, then, of multiple subgroups which represent a broad spectrum of political, social, and economic opinions, there are moments when a particular subgroup's opinions come to represent the broader generation's viewpoint, even as alternative and contradictory views coexist with this viewpoint. For example, the antinational approach that the older generational subgroup in this book holds is reflected within the older generation more broadly, in statements made by the president, in television talk show programming, and in textbooks, as I discuss later in this book. While it is not the only viewpoint within the 68er generation, it is certainly one of the most vocal. It is this broad reflection within a generation that I refer to when I say that each generation in this book has a particular relationship to the nation. Specifically, the 45ers *ignored* the nation in the wake of World War II and the Holocaust; the 68ers *rejected* the nation as part of their efforts to call their parents' generation to account for their participation in National Socialism; and the younger generation—or at least the particular generational subgroup that I studied—is *reclaiming* the nation in an effort to establish what they feel is a "normal" relationship to the nation. I take up these generational trends throughout the remainder of this book.

The Research Questions and the Data

As my formal data collection and fieldwork began in the fall of 2000, I had identified a few key questions to guide my investigation into conceptions of citizenship and national belonging. Some questions viewed the German case as an instance of a larger phenomenon: given a state of increasing diversity within countries, how are nations and communities coming to live with difference? Increased migration has been met with stricter immigration policies in some countries, at the same time as naturalization requirements have been eased and multicultural curricula introduced into public schools elsewhere. In other places, changes in patterns of diversity or in political leadership have led to deadly ethnic, ideological, or religious conflict, ethnic cleansing, and right-wing extremist violence against foreigners. A second and related question relates to the implications of these sweeping changes for national identity. How are the collective identities of national communities affected by increasing diversity and cultural change? Theorists have been divided on this point. While some have argued that national identities and meanings are eroding in favor of global or "postnational" citizenship (see, e.g., Falk 2000; Soysal 1994, 1996), others have pointed out that the proliferation of ethnic and nationalist conflict demonstrates the increasing importance of local identities (Sandel 1992, 5). As Hall (1996, 343) explains, "So at one and the same time people feel part of the world and part of their village. They have neighborhood identities and they are citizens of the world."

Other questions focused on the German case more specifically. I wanted to know how young Germans today conceive of citizenship and national identity. Do all young Germans see themselves as the "citizens of the world" that Hall expects, or does this depend on the role that the global economy plays in their lives? Because the existing literature on citizenship tends to focus heavily on structures and institutions — such as laws, policies, and regulations and how they determine membership — I deliberately set out to investigate the meaning of citizenship and national belonging as these young working-class Germans experience it in their everyday lives. I also aimed to understand how vocational school civics teachers address these concerns in their classrooms and to observe how these topics were discussed by students.

Some clarification of terms may be useful here. I use the terms "German youth," "German young people," and "young Germans" throughout this book. In fact, the subset of young Germans I interviewed are largely working-class young people, and the reader should bear this in mind, although for brevity's sake I do not always include the term "working class." I identify the young people who I interviewed as "working class," although there is quite a wide variation among them in terms of their expectations for future employment and income. Some are likely to earn as much or more than university-educated Germans—especially those training in the high-tech, information technology fields. Others, such as the construction apprentices I interviewed, have almost no chance of obtaining a job at all upon graduation, and know they are headed into unemployment and uncertain futures. Rather than defining this group as "working class" by their income levels or employment chances, they are defined negatively (Lamont 2000, 10) by the types of universities they did *not* attend (and are generally ineligible for) and the kinds of professions to which they will *not* have access. These apprentices are training for blue-collar occupations; by and large, they will be prep cooks rather than sous chefs; they will be telecommunications wiring technicians and repairmen rather than computer consultants; they will be masons and roofers and technical drafters, not architects.[8] Moreover, the structure of the vocational training system—and the reliance of the German economy upon it—means that without lengthy retraining, these students can expect to remain in these occupations throughout their lives (Hamilton 1990; Miller-Idriss 2002).

From May 1999 until June 2004, I traveled back and forth between Berlin and the United States to collect the data upon which this book is based. A preliminary trip to Germany in the summer of 1999 and a pilot study in January–February 2000 helped refine my questions, test instruments, and select the schools which would ultimately make up the case studies for this book. Primary data collection took place in Berlin between August 2000 and August 2001 and during two two-month follow-up trips in the springs of 2002 and 2004. During the 2000–2001 school year, I interviewed sixty German vocational school students, aged seventeen to twenty-five.[9] That same year I conducted over 170 hours of classroom observation, primarily in civics (*Sozialkunde*) and related courses. I triangulated classroom observations by conducting interviews with twenty-two teachers, scheduled as soon as possible after classroom observations.

A year after our first interview, I conducted fifteen follow-up interviews with eight of the original student participants, reviewing the transcripts of the original interview and teasing out the key influences that these young people identified as having had a significant role in developing their opinions—such as parents, siblings, school, peer groups, music, or others. During the same trip, I also conducted twelve focus group discussions with an additional fifty-nine youth from the three schools, asking a subset of the same questions I had posed in interviews. Finally, I returned in 2004 to reinterview an expanded group of twenty-five teachers. All interviews and focus groups were conducted in German by myself. A fuller explanation of my research methodology and data collection strategies is detailed in appendix B.

During the interviews with students and their teachers, my intent was to examine the meaning of citizenship and national belonging. This approach draws on previous work by cultural sociologists and anthropologists, such as Sewell (1980, 10), who reminds us that "the whole of social life, from such symbolically elaborate practices as religious festivals to such seemingly matter-of-fact activities as building houses or raising crops, is culturally shaped." My research approach was grounded in an attempt to draw out the culturally shaped meaning embedded in Germans' everyday lives, interpret it, and approach a level of understanding about it (Sewell 1980; also see Bourdieu and Wacquant 1992; Geertz 1973).

During the interviews, I asked participants how they would define the term "citizenship" to an alien who had just landed in a spaceship, and asked what it meant to them to be a citizen in Berlin, in Germany, and in Europe. During student interviews, we talked about the relative importance of these three areas of belonging when compared with the rest of their lives, including their families, friends and peer groups, school, extracurricular activities, and religious memberships. I asked participants how they felt about Germany and how they would define the German nation or Germans in general, and what makes a "good citizen" or a "bad citizen." We talked about their feelings about foreigners in Germany, and about the radical right. They told me their opinions about naturalization and immigration policy and talked about what they would do differently if they were in charge of defining policy. I talked with students about how they felt about school and their civics class in particular, and I asked teachers whether they thought their students viewed any of these issues in ways that were different from their own opinions. I was especially interested to find out how young working-class Germans incorporate, reject, or modify elements of public and state narratives in their definitions of citizenship and constructions of national belonging, and ultimately, whether there were differences between students' and teachers' conceptions.

By coding and organizing the elements that participants discussed when they defined citizenship, the criteria they named when they discussed "good" and "bad" citizens, and the conditions they believed should be required for naturalization, I was able to come to an understanding of how these individuals think about citizenship and national belonging.[10] As Lamont (2000, 4) explains, this method "has power because it lets us see into the theories that people use to make sense of their lives, into the taken-for-granted categories they mobilize when interpreting and organizing the differences that surround them, without predefining specific dimensions of identity as particularly salient."

As my data collection progressed, I found myself casting an increasingly wide net to answer questions that emerged from interviews and school observations. Conversations and documents gathered from policymakers, researchers, and representatives of government agencies, union offices, and think tanks helped flesh out my understanding of the German school system, the labor market projections for the occupations for which these students were training, and processes of teacher training, curriculum reform, and apprenticeship placement, among others.

All of this research took place in German, which is not my native tongue—although I am comfortably fluent in it. Nonetheless, it is important to note that any investigation of citizenship and nationality by an outsider in Germany faces some linguistic barriers. The German word for citizen, *Staatsbürger*, does not convey quite the same meaning within the German language as *citizen* in English or *citoyen* in French. In fact, at least three terms capture the concept of citizenship: *Staatsbürgerschaft*, *Staatsangehörigkeit*, and *Volksangehörigkeit* (Brubaker 1992, 50; Preuss 2003, 38). I used the term *Staatsbürgerschaft* in interviews, both on the advice of native German speakers and because the concept is the most general term for citizenship. As Ulrich Preuss (2003, 38) explains, "Despite this variety of terms the central term for what is called citizenship, *citoyenneté, cittadinanza*, and so on, in other languages is *Staatsbürgerschaft* in German." *Staatsbürgerschaft* is the term that refers to a national policy of membership.

The German language does have a word to denote a deeper sense of national belonging. The term *Volk* refers to a connection to others based on ethnic heritage, descent, and culture. I will argue throughout this book that understandings of citizenship are tightly interwoven with conceptions of national belonging. Despite the linguistic differentiation in German between the term for citizenship (*Staatsbürgerschaft*) and the term for a national people (*Volk*), as a concept and a policy, I argue here that citizenship is not merely a technicality or a piece of paper for most Germans; rather, it operates in much the same manner in Germany as it does most anywhere else. It regulates patterns of inclusion and exclusion, deciding who is allowed to reside within the borders of a given country, participate politically, and enjoy the benefits of political and civic membership, from social welfare to health care, visa-less or eased entry to other countries, and restricted employment in certain governmental sectors, among others. Determining who has access to such privileges is more than just a matter of policy—it is deeply intertwined with conceptions of who belongs to the national community.

Finally, the reader should note that I focus in this book on instances in which the nation is deliberately discussed and defined, whether through interviews where specific questions about the nation were posed to respondents or during classroom observations where I focused on instances in which the nation—or related topics such as national pride—were a specific topic of discussion. In so doing, I neglect the wide variety of more mundane ways in which the nation is evidenced in the everyday life of schools and classrooms (see, e.g., Fox and Miller-Idriss 2008)—in rituals, ceremonies, everyday interactions and announcements, or in the titles of textbooks, guest speakers' lectures, and class field trips or international exchanges with other schools in Europe. The importance of such types of the construction of nationhood has been well established by others (see, e.g., Billig 1995), and I urge future scholars to expand upon my work here by designing empirical studies to specify more quotidian and "banal" instances of the construction and transformation of nationhood across generations.

one

Who Belongs to the Nation?

At least since Benedict Anderson (1991) introduced the notion that nations are communities of individuals who imagine themselves to be connected to one another, much of the theoretical and empirical work on nations, nationalism, and national identity has begun from the premise that nations are constructed entities with emergent and contested boundaries (Göçek 2002; also see Fulbrook 1997; Grant 1997; Levy 1999; Spillman 1996, 1997). The view of nations as imagined and constructed entities posits nations and national identity as based on a sense of individuals' attachments to other people who share their customs, language, traditions, culture, or residence within a set of borders—even though they may be dispersed across space and time and will likely never meet each other. This understanding represents a shift from previous views of nationhood, which perceived nations to be determined by primordial attachments which were "given" through birth into a particular community (Geertz 1973).

Imagining and Re-imagining Nations

This theoretical shift in the study of nations has had consequences for empirical studies on nations and nationhood, as the idea that the nation is "constructed" has inspired a growing sociology of the everyday experiences and practices of nationhood among ordinary individuals. Work in this emergent tradition examines the everyday experiences of individuals in the construction and interpretation of their national and ethnic identities (Brubaker et al. 2006; Condor 2000; Fox 2003; Fox and Miller-Idriss 2008; Glaeser 2000; Rothenberg 2002). Such scholarship broadens a prior emphasis on the ways in which the nation is constructed and mediated through official narratives, state policies, formal curriculum, or legal policies (see, e.g., Fulbrook 1999; Olick 1998) to focus on the experiences of ordinary citizens in shaping and reshaping the imagined community. In part as a result of this focus on the experiences of ordinary individuals, scholars have come to recognize that even when there is a single hegemonic version of national identity in a given nation, there are also, typically, various alternative or marginalized expressions of national identity that exist parallel to the dominant version (Cooke 2002; Göçek 2002). Particularly prominent among field researchers working in Europe and eastern Europe since 1989, many scholars in this new vein of research have focused on the responses and resistance of ordinary citizens to the mediation of national narratives and myths in various spheres of their lives, such as schools, workplaces, and the media. Empirical examples include investigations of how nationality is reproduced through symbolic boundaries of national difference that are maintained and reproduced in everyday practices in Estonia;[1] how nationhood and ethnicity are produced and reproduced in everyday life in Transylvania (Brubaker et al. 2006); the reception of modernist architecture in Hungary as architects were confronted in their everyday work with issues of national identity under late socialism (Molnár 2004); and the impact of political apathy among sectors of national populations on the efficacy of nationalist politics in Romania (Fox 2003).

Of course, ordinary people do not create national identities in isolation. Nations are imagined and constructed (Anderson 1991; Göçek 2002; Kastoryano 2002) through processes ranging from the everyday kinds of practices evidenced in activities such as flag-waving (Billig 1995) or reciting the Pledge of Allegiance in public schools (Rippberger and Staudt 2003) to the selection by intellectuals of historical narratives and national heroes (Suny and Kennedy 1999a, 2) and the mediation of knowledge about citizenship through public institutions, the media, and popular culture (Bourdieu 1999, 62; Giroux 1987; Steinmetz 1999, 11). Various individuals, whether elites and intellectuals (Suny and Kennedy 1999a) or ordinary citizens (Fox 2003), are involved in these processes of the construction, reification, and negotiation of nations and national identities.

Yet while the literature has clearly emphasized the constructed, transient, and emergent nature of nations—whether through the efforts of elites or of ordinary people—the overall focus has been on the how and when of nation-*formation*. Nations are thus something that have already happened, whether in the very distant or the more recent past (see, e.g., Hroch 1996). Nation-formation is depicted as a linear, one-directional process or as a one-time event that has been or can be completed, such as is implied when Brubaker (1992) argues that either the nation creates the state or the state creates the nation (Behnke 1997, 245; also see Calhoun 1997; Gellner 1983; Hobsbawm 1990, 10). For too long, the nation has been thought of as something that is static (although constructed), unified (even when diverse), and formed at some point in the distant past. Scholars have paid less attention to the ways in which the meanings attached to nationhood shift and are part of a process of continual re-imagining, even within relatively short periods of time (for exceptions, see Suny and Kennedy 1999b; Kennedy 1999; Levy 1999). As Suny and Kennedy (1999b, 397) explain, the "language of invention and imagination" used in many analyses of the nation can be challenged "because it leaves little room for the variable degrees to which nations are transformable."

This inattention to the potential for collective national identities to be transformed is a departure from the literature on other forms of collective identities, which has increasingly acknowledged the complexity of collective identities and the inadequacy of essentialized categories of identity according to bounded notions of gender, ethnicity, race, or sexuality (Calhoun 1995). Instead, scholars in these fields recognize that singular categories of collective identities do little to capture the layers of subtlety involved in complex negotiations of identity. In the case of nations, one such layer consists of the variations in national identity across generations within the same nation, which is the primary focus of this book.

Even when scholars acknowledge that changes in the conception of nations and nationhood can take place (see, e.g., Hobsbawm 1990, 11; Lepsius 2004), such accounts typically lack an explanation of how these processes take place. There is scholarship which details the ways in which citizenship (Soysal 1994, 1996) and political communities (Archibugi, Held and Köhler 1998) can be transformed. This work, however, focuses on changes in structures, systems, and institutions—such as related to globalization, civil society, or legal policies—and their effect on political communities, either without attending to questions of transformations in collective identity or by assuming that transformations in identity are derived from institutional changes.

This isn't to say that there are no clues as to how the meaning of the nation might change over time. Zimmer (1998, 648), for example, points out that changes in national identity are causally linked to international factors such as wars or ideological clashes, but does not explain how these changes in national identity actually take place, or whether similar kinds of changes can occur in the absence of significant international events. Cultural accounts of the relationship between ideology and individual action (Swidler 1986) provide a partial theoretical explanation for how dominant national narratives can influence individuals' actions or beliefs, but with limited application to periods that are not characterized by significant international or national upheaval or trauma. Historical accounts that trace the formation and reformation of nations are an appealing source to consider in the search for mechanisms contributing to transformations in national meanings. But historical examinations—such as those relying on narrative or path dependency models (see, e.g., Haydu 1998)—are often forced to rely on written accounts and documentation that primarily depict elite and intellectual perspectives. This leaves us with little understanding as to the mechanisms through which ordinary individuals engage in or experience transformations in the meaning of nationhood.

Other scholars have examined the role that the state plays in shaping or resocializing citizens' conceptions of national identity, such as through public schooling (Apple 1990; Aronowitz and Giroux 1993; Bourdieu and Passeron 1990; Gumbert 1986; Hahn 1998; Popkewitz and Brennan 1998). But focusing on the reproduction of national meanings during socialization processes across generations (Bourdieu and Passeron 1990) runs the risk of overemphasizing the constancy of national identities, even as we acknowledge that national identities cannot be understood as essentialized, stable, or static (Calhoun 1993, 1997). Such work has also tended to emphasize structural and institutional attempts to transform identities and collective practices among citizens of a given nation, without examining how such efforts are received by the individuals who are the objects of the state's attention. Literature that traces the reception of national or international narratives and the reaction of ordinary individuals to the nationalist politics, official narratives or state-sponsored identities in which their lives are embedded on the other hand (e.g., Fox 2003; Molnár 2004), leaves open the question of how the reception of such narratives differs across generations or whether differences can be construed as mechanisms of transformations in national meanings.

In sum, empirical accounts of the shifting meaning of nationhood for ordinary individuals are rare, both because the literature has emphasized elite perspectives and because it has focused its attention on the constructed and contingent nature of identities in an already-imagined nation.

So how do processes of change in the conception and imagination of the nation take place? If national identities can be transformed, what are the processes through which the meaning attached to, and the identification with, a nation shift? How are national identities renegotiated and redefined? The remainder of this book explores these questions by investigating transformations in the meaning of the nation across generations. We already know that new generations react differently to national wars or military actions, create new perceptions of historical events and traumas—such as slavery, genocide, apartheid, or the Holocaust—and develop awarenesses that previous generations did not have of injustices toward various groups according to race, gender, ethnicity, sexuality, or physical or mental handicap (Griffin 2004; Schuman and Scott 1989; Schuman and Rieger 1992). In the remainder of this book, I extend our understanding of generational transformation to encompass the collective identities associated with nationhood. As social and historical circumstances change, I argue, new generations re-imagine the nation. This process further reveals how multiple meanings of nationhood can emerge and exist simultaneously.

It is important to bear in mind, of course, that power plays a role in which versions of national narratives prevail. Some meanings come to acquire more resonance than others, at least in part due to unequal power relationships in terms of who is in a position to promote (through the media, through the educational system, or elsewhere) a particular version of the past or of current events (see, e.g., Carnoy 1992, 148; Dirks, Eley, and Ortner 1994; Hall 1988; Gramsci 1971; Laclau and Mouffe 1985; Morrow and Torres 1995, 251). While we know that such meanings are subject to continual reinterpretation and redefinition, the processes through which they are reinterpreted and redefined differently by various groups in any given society are not well understood. It is this task that I take up in this book.

To ground the claims that I will make later in this book, and in order to fully understand the debates around national belonging in Germany and what the transformations discussed in this book can teach us about how nations are continually re-imagined, it is also important to interrogate the literature on citizenship. This is particularly true in the German case, where questions of citizenship and national belonging have been so deeply intertwined historically.

Citizenship as Identity

While the state typically refers to the ruling apparatus—the institutions and structures, policies and policymakers that regulate the lives of individuals within a given territory (Althusser 1971; Bourdieu 1999; Steinmetz 1999)—the nation, as discussed above, is most often used to refer to an "imagined community" of individuals who are viewed as belonging together for reasons of shared ethnicity, heritage, language, culture, race, or territory (Anderson 1991; Guibernau 1999; Salecl 1994). Citizenship status reflects membership in the former, while national identity reflects an attachment to the latter. Although there are significant overlaps between the state and the nation, and although they are often equated in popular understandings, the literature has tended to treat the two concepts as analytically distinct and has, moreover, generally assigned analyses of identity to the realm of studies of the nation, while studies of citizenship have remained focused on structures, institutions, and policies.

The meaningfulness of citizenship has been called into question in recent years, moreover, as scholars have proposed that globalization and regional integration processes are unsettling the nation-state, causing national citizenship to be replaced with postnational, cross-border membership not tied to particular nation-states (see, e.g., Eley 1999, 10; Held 1996; Soysal 1994; Urry 1999). As Stuart Hall (1996, 343) explains, "So at one and the same time people feel part of the world and part of their village. They have neighborhood identities and they are citizens of the world." National citizenship has been further complicated by increasing migration and immigration across borders. Particularly challenging for nation-states whose national populations have been historically homogenous, the increasing national, cultural, racial, or ethnic diversity within nations has forced a reframing of national membership and notions of "who belongs" to national communities in many places.

In analyzing the impact of local, regional, or global and migratory transformation on conceptions of citizenship, the scholarship on citizenship and national belonging has focused heavily on the study of institutions, policies, and structural reforms. In this approach, scholars examine policies, laws, and regulations that limit access to, and regulate the practice of, citizenship, often using these structural and institutional elements as a measure of conceptions of citizenship among national populations. One consequence of this emphasis is that we have come to think of citizenship, at least within the theoretical literature, as a unified, bounded, and static entity that is shared by all members of the same national or ethnic group and whose meaning, for individual citizens, can be extrapolated from national policies. Whether inherited through birthplace or ethnic heritage or achieved through naturalization, citizenship has not been conceived of as a notion whose meaning can necessarily shift for individuals or vary across national populations. I argue in this book, however, that a nation-state's legal policies for citizenship and naturalization cannot be automatically extrapolated to the understandings of citizenship and national belonging among ordinary citizens, and furthermore, that it is problematic to assume a uniform conception of citizenship and national belonging for all of the members of a single nation.

The shift to an understanding of nations as constructed entities that was detailed above has not been extended to the study of citizenship. Instead, with few exceptions (see the recent work of Brubaker 2004; Brubaker et al. 2006), the literature on citizenship has remained focused on structural and institutional analyses (see, e.g., Joppke 2004, 2005a), in some cases implying that individuals' social practices and constructions of meaning automatically derive from legal measures and institutions (for example, see Brubaker 1992, 187; Ignatieff 1993, 102; Soysal 1994).[2] This body of literature has examined structures and policies that regulate inclusion and exclusion through immigration and naturalization laws, the development and expansion of social, civil, and political rights, and patterns of individuals' rights in, and responsibilities to, various local, national, and global communities (Balibar 1988; Beiner 1995; Bendix 1996; Brubaker 1992; Diderot 1994; Hall 1989; Kant 1994; Marshall and Bottomore 1992; Pufendorf 1994; Somers 1993, 1994; Soysal 1996). Research on citizenship that has gone beyond institutional approaches, such as that which has focused on examinations of political or civic culture (Almond and Verba 1963; Putnam 1993; Somers 1995), the sets of common goals, values, and virtues attributed to citizenship (Bellah et al. 1985; Etzioni 1995; Galston 1995; Walzer 1995), or its spaces of communicative action (Fraser 1997; Habermas 1992a), by and large, has not focused on the experiences of ordinary citizens in constructing cultural meanings and practices. In fact, there are very few empirical studies of citizenship at all (Lister et al. 2003). As a result, we know very little about what it means to individuals to be citizens or how their identities as citizens influence their everyday lives.

This gap in the literature can be traced to several trends in social scientists' current thinking about citizenship. On the one hand, there is a prevailing tendency in the scholarship to speak of citizenship as a phenomenon of declining significance (Soysal 1994). According to this argument, the growing importance of postnational memberships in bodies such as the European Union, combined with the increasing extension of civil, social, and even political rights for nonnationals within individual countries, means that state membership has become less significant (see Ludvig 2004). Such arguments are persuasive but inadequate for understanding the continuing importance of state membership, particularly for nonnationals (Joppke 1999b; Koopmans and Statham 1999). Even in countries where foreigners enjoy significant and generous social welfare benefits, citizenship status continues to provide nationals with additional advantages and significant security (Hansen and Weil 2001). In this book, I assert the continuing significance of national citizenship and national attachments and discuss the ways in which they are meaningful for ordinary individuals.

The perspectives of ordinary people are also poorly understood because the crafting of citizenship and naturalization policies, as well as their reforms, have been efforts led by elites (Hansen and Weil 2001, 10). As a result, studies which focus on transformations in citizenship have tended to analyze political debates and legislative changes which take place in transcripts of parliamentary debates, presidential speeches, and newspaper articles that are often more a reflection of intellectual and elite perspectives than they are of the understandings of the average citizens and nonnationals who are most affected by such reforms. Finally, the gap in the literature could also be due to efforts on the part of some scholars to deliberately decouple studies of citizenship from identity, defining citizenship instead as state membership (Joppke 2004, 2005a, b). According to this line of reasoning, which has been convincingly argued by Christian Joppke (2004) and Dieter Gosewinkel (2002), among others, the origins of citizenship policies were grounded in political, diplomatic, and strategic decisions on the parts of various states, rather than efforts to shape national populations in particular ways (such as by maintaining ethnic or racial homogeneity).

Therefore, citizenship policies should not be understood as a reflection of collective identity, as others have argued (Brubaker 1992), but as a set of policies that regulate individual exclusion or inclusion in a given state.[3] While this is a compelling argument for the study of citizenship policies, I aim here to extend previous scholarship by examining how, and whether, citizenship is understood by ordinary people in their everyday lives.

Citizenship and Belonging in the German Case

Germany's unique conception of nationhood, writes Nora Rätzel, comparing the German model to neighboring France, "lies in the fact that it is constructed biologically. German nationals are defined by their origin: one can only be born a German" (Räthzel 1990: 41). This peculiar German conception of the nation has historical origins. Early citizenship law in Germany was federalist, meaning that citizenship was determined through state membership in one of the states that made up the German Reich, such as Prussia or Bavaria (Fahrmeir 1997; Gosewinkel 2001, 2002). When the German Empire established guiding national principles for citizenship and naturalization in its 1871 constitution, it drew on the model of the Prussian state's citizenship policies, which determined citizenship through *jus sanguinis* (based on blood) principles, rather than through *jus soli* (based on birthplace or territory) principles. Despite some debate about the merits of modifying naturalization law along jus soli principles, which would formalize the state's relationship with already-integrated foreigners and help to strengthen the military (Gosewinkel 2002, 64–72), when the German parliament established the first national citizenship law in 1913, it retained jus sanguinis principles as the primary means of obtaining citizenship. There is not complete agreement about the motivation behind Prussia's restrictive policy. Dieter Gosewinkel (2002, 64) has argued, for example, that Prussia's policies were grounded in both anti-Slavic and anti-Semitic attitudes, while Andreas Fahrmeir shows that the Prussian law was not an ethnic policy (Hansen and Weil 2001, 14), as it was possible for foreigners to naturalize. Naturalization policies in Prussia and other German states did, however, discriminate against Jews and members of Christian sects (Fahrmeir 1997, 742). What is clear, however, is that Prussia's preference for restrictive citizenship and naturalization laws ultimately came to be the basis for Germany's first universal citizenship and naturalization policy—the Reich Citizenship Law of 1913 (*Reichs- und Staatsangehörigkeitsgesetz*).

This first national citizenship law established citizenship as something obtained almost exclusively through *filiation*—direct descent from a parent who is a German citizen (Joppke 2003)—and formed the basis of German law for the remainder of the twentieth century (see, e.g., Green 2001). While the jus sanguinis principles of the law were advantageous for a government which wished to maintain deep connections with the large numbers of German émigrés abroad, the law was also rooted in xenophobic tendencies. At the time of the 1913 law's crafting, as Simon Green (2000, 108) has argued, "the maintenance of the purity of the *Volk* had become a widely accepted political goal of imperial Germany." Despite the Nazi regime's abuse of jus sanguinis principles to justify their racist ideologies (Green 2001, 25), the same 1913 citizenship law was retained as West German citizenship law after World War II. This happened for several reasons. On the one hand, the retention of jus sanguinis was an effort to recover from the massive territorial and human losses sustained during and after the war, as well as to protect "ethnic" Germans who found themselves on the other side of a new border (Fulbrook 1999, 183). As part of the agreements ending World War II, Germany had lost all of the territories seized by the Nazis as well as some of its own former territory (O'Brien 1992, 377). The new West German constitution, the Basic Law, "assigned the state the responsibility of looking after the welfare of its citizens residing outside the Federal Republic" (378), and gave these individuals the right to resettle in the Federal Republic of Germany (Borneman 1997, 104). In practice, the law granted citizenship to all individuals (and their spouses, children, and even grandchildren) who had been citizens in Germany in 1937, before the National Socialists' territorial expansions—or who had lost citizenship after 1933 for political, religious, or racial reasons (Fulbrook 1999, 183; also see Storz and Reisslandt 2002, 27). Of course, it is worth noting, as Fulbrook (1999, 183) points out, that individuals who were applying for citizenship under the principle of ethnic descent or reapplying for it (on the basis of it having been revoked by the National Socialists) had varying degrees of difficulty in proving their German "ethnic" heritage—a process made more difficult for individuals whose families had been killed and possessions and documents seized and destroyed by the Nazis.

What became especially significant for the timing of the eventual reforms is the fact that the jus sanguinis policy also allowed West Germany to define individuals who were born across the border of East Germany as Germans, keeping the door open for a smooth unification process at some future date (Green 2000, 2001; Joppke 1999b, 2003; also see Borneman 1997, 104; Fulbrook 1999, 183; Storz and Reisslandt 2002, 27). In other words, the motivation behind the retention of jus sanguinis in post-1945 law—like the motivation behind the original 1913 law—was based on political strategy rather than racial ideology (Gosewinkel 2002; Green 2001; Hogwood 2000; Joppke 2004).

Because naturalization was difficult and very rare until near the end of the century, however, issuing citizenship primarily by *filiation* meant that German citizenship policy came to be a largely de facto ethnic policy. Until reforms in the early 1990s relaxed the requirements for naturalization, the process through which foreigners could become German citizens in the Federal Republic of Germany was through a policy called "discretionary naturalization." According to this policy, each state had the ability to naturalize individuals under specific conditions where naturalization was determined to be in the public interest, such as in cases where foreign spouses of German citizens, athletes, or other public figures wished to naturalize (Green 2001). The numbers of foreigners naturalized under these policies remained very low; by 1990, less than half of 1 percent of the foreign population in Germany were citizens (Green 2001, 36; also see Senders 1996). Despite a rapidly growing foreign population through the 1960s, 1970s, and 1980s, German citizenship and naturalization policy thus ensured that "ethnic" Germans constituted the overwhelming majority of German citizens. As a result, German citizenship policy came to be discussed and depicted as an ethnic policy (see, e.g., Levy and Weiss 2002), even though technically speaking, the "blood" in Germany's jus sanguinis policy, as Dieter Gosewinkel (2002, 70) has argued, was "formal and instrumental, not substantial in intention" (also see Joppke 2004, 86).

In East Germany, the question of German citizenship was vague in the initial decades after World War II. The GDR's first constitution (in 1949) referred only broadly to a "German people," stating that "there is only one German citizenship" (Fulbrook 1999, 188), implying a unified German citizenship among all Germans in both states. It was not until 1967 that a new Law on Citizenship clarified the GDR's policies, establishing a separate, East German citizenship (Brubaker 1992, 170; Fulbrook 1999, 188-89; Straughn 2001, 281-84). According to the 1967

Table 1. Post-1945 reforms in West German and Unified German citizenship law

Year	Reform	Significance and requirements
1977	Guidelines on Naturalization (*Einbürgerungs-richtlinien*)	Created first criteria for naturalization; established discretionary natural-ization; naturalization if in "public interest"; stated that Germany is not a country of immigration; emphasized cultural, not ethnic criteria; left final decision up to states; ensured natural-ization would be rare *Naturalization applicants must*: have 10 years of legal residence; show natu-ralization is in "public" Interest;[a] show "lasting orientation toward Germany";[b] demonstrate language proficiency; renounce previous citizen-ship; pay fee of up to 3 months' salary (max DM 5,000)
1990/1993	Reform and Amendment in Foreigner Law (*Ausländergesetz*)	Eased naturalization for foreign residents and young foreigners *Adult naturalization applications must*: have 15 years legal residence; have no previous criminal history; demonstrate language proficiency; have means to support self and dependents; renounce previous citizenship;[c] pay reduced administrative fee[d] *Naturalization applicants aged 16–23 must*: have 8 years legal residence; 6 years schooling in Germany (minimum 4 in secondary schools); have no criminal history; renounce previous citizenship
1999	Reform in Citizenship Law (*Staats-angehörigkeitsrecht*)	Automatic naturalization upon birth; eased eligibility for newer immigrants; restricted automatic citizenship for émigré families after second genera-tion *Automatic naturalization applicants must*: have one parent legally resident for 8 years; renounce other citizenship before age 23

(*Table 1. Continued*)

Year	Reform	Significance and requirements
		Naturalization applicants must: have 8 years of legal residence;[e] have no criminal history; demonstrate language proficiency; demonstrate commitment to German Basic Law; have means to support self and dependents; renounce previous citizenship; pay fee of €255/person; children w/parents €51

Sources: Baumann 1999; Beauftragte der Bundesregierung für Migration, Flüchtlinge und Integration 2005b; Green 2001; Hogwood 2000

a. The law officially said Germany is not a country of immigration; naturalization was intended to be a rare event.
b. Original German: *Die freiwillige und daurende Hinwendung zu Deutschland* (Green 2001, 30 and 49).
c. Exceptions in certain circumstances, e.g., if immigrant's home country refuses to relinquish applicant from citizenship.
d. Discretionary naturalizations (*Ermessenseinbürgerungen*) DM 500, simplified naturalizations DM 100 (Green 2001, 33–34).
e. Can be reduced to 7 years by participating in an integration class (*Integrationskurs*), or to 6 years for asylum-seekers.

law, citizenship in the GDR was possible in four ways: because of German citizenship at the time of the GDR's founding; through descent; through birth in the GDR; or through naturalization (Fulbrook 1999, 189). At least by 1967, then, the GDR's policies clearly reflect a jus soli form of citizenship, allowing for the acquisition of citizenship through both birth and naturalization. Moreover, in naturalization cases, the GDR favored ideological issues over proof of ethnic descent as the determining criteria for citizenship. Prior citizenship in a socialist state was more important than the individual's race or place of birth in naturalization decisions (Borneman 1997, 104–5). Ethnicity was a secondary consideration. As Straughn (2001, 292) explains, "GDR citizenship did not require or entail membership in any particular ethnic or cultural group."[4]

Like other legal institutions and policies, the citizenship and naturalization policy of unified Germany was the West German policy that had been in place before 1989, which was still based on the Reich Citizenship Law of 1913. Noteworthy reforms in German citizenship and foreigner laws began soon after unification (Baumann 1999, 69; Räthzel 1990, 43), however, for several reasons. With East and West Germany unified, the most significant reason for the retention of jus sanguinis in West German citizenship and naturalization policy—namely, the assurance that all, including East Germans, were German citizens—had disappeared. But reforms also came about because, with the opening of the Iron Curtain, the peculiarities of the jus sanguinis policy created an unusual paradox inside newly unified Germany's borders.

In the decades after World War II, reeling from the loss of millions of men in the war and facing the need to rebuild the entire physical infrastructure of the country, West Germany had begun a massive recruiting campaign in southern Europe and Turkey to bring millions of manual laborers to Germany as part of a temporary plan to ease the labor shortage. Guest workers did not have a right to citizenship and were expected to return to their home countries after several years of labor. Although the majority of guest workers did return to their countries of origin, those who remained formed a substantial immigrant community in Germany. Of the fourteen million workers who came between the end of World War II and 1973, about eleven million returned to their countries of origin, leaving three million foreigners who stayed in Germany and who often brought their families over from their native countries (Bade 1999, 19).

As the second and third generation of foreign migrants began to grow up in Germany, the inherent inequity in a policy of extending citizenship rights to the grandchildren of Germans who had lived their entire lives in other countries and who might not even speak German, while denying the same rights to individuals who were born and raised in Germany and who may not have ever visited their so-called "home" countries, became increasingly clear. The situation came to a head after political and economic transformations east of Germany prompted an influx of hundreds of thousands of "ethnic" Germans from Eastern Europe and the former Soviet States in the early 1990s, who arrived at the German border to take advantage of their right to German citizenship and thus ensure a better economic future for themselves and their families (O'Brien 1992, 380; Rotte 2000). Meanwhile, however, millions of second- and third-generation Turks and other immigrants whose families had come to Germany as guest workers in the decades after World War II were living in Germany as noncitizens. The stage was set for reform.

The first set of reforms in 1990 brought about changes in Germany's foreigner law (*Ausländergesetz*), which attempted to address concerns about the security of long-time foreign residents in Germany and made it easier for long-term residents to apply for citizenship (Räthzel 1990, 43). Following the 1990 reform and a 1993 amendment, the residence requirement for young people between the ages of sixteen and twenty-three to become eligible for German citizenship was reduced from fifteen years to eight, provided that the applicant had renounced his or her previous citizenship, had attended a German school for at least six years (at least four of those at the secondary level), and had not been in trouble with the law (Baumann 1999, 69). Moreover, naturalization now became a right, no longer dependent on a case-by-case approval based on criteria related to cultural assimilation, economic qualifications, or criminal record (Joppke 1999a, 638). In this as-of-right naturalization regime, all immigrants were eligible for citizenship after fifteen years, provided they renounced their prior citizenship and were not receiving state welfare support (Baumann 1999, 69). The administrative fee for naturalizations was also reduced (Green 2001). At the same time, Germany began to invoke stricter standards in evaluating the evidence which most "ethnic" Germans had to provide in order to prove their German background (Linke 1997; Räthzel 1990).[5]

These changes came about during a time when Germany was experiencing tremendous controversy about the status of foreigners. In reaction to the disproportionately large (compared to other European countries) numbers of asylum seekers which Germany had accepted during the early 1990s, primarily from conflicts in southeastern Europe, the public debate about foreigners was becoming increasingly tense (Hogwood 2000, 131). Violent attacks and fire bombings in both east and west Germany in the early 1990s resulted in the deaths of several foreigners and led to broad public outrage, as hundreds of thousands of Germans led candlelight vigils to protest the violence. Issues of immigration, citizenship, naturalization, and asylum law became increasingly politicized during the rest of the decade, particularly during election periods. While conservative politicians argued that the "boat" is full and reminded Germans that Germany is not a country of immigration, as was officially maintained in the 1977 Naturalization Guidelines (Green 2000; Hogwood 2000, 133; Joppke 1999b, 201), the center and left began to shift to a position that favored naturalization for long-term foreign residents in Germany. By the end of the decade, this position had taken hold in the mainstream (Hogwood 2000).

The reform of citizenship and naturalization policy created heated political debates during the 1990s (for a detailed discussion, see Cooper 2002; Green 2001; Hansen and Weil 2001; Hogwood 2000), and not all of the initiatives were successful (see table 1). Attempts by the center-left to reform the policy failed once, in 1997, and the final reform did not include a controversial measure supported by promoters of the reform, which would have permitted dual citizenship (Hogwood 2000; also see Münz and Ulrich 1999). Ultimately, however, the reformers prevailed, and the most significant reform in German citizenship law to date passed in 1999 and took effect in 2000. Although the jus sanguinis component of the law had been retained, it was supplemented by a jus soli policy (Hogwood 2000).

According to the new law, children born in Germany after the first of January 2000 are automatically eligible for German citizenship even if their parents are foreigners, provided that one parent has legally resided in Germany for at least eight years and has a secure resident status. If the child has another citizenship, it must be renounced before the age of twenty-three or else German citizenship is revoked. If there has been no formal declaration by the end of the child's twenty-third year, then the child no longer has German citizenship. This condition has been especially controversial because of the restrictions imposed on the German state by post–World War II German law, in which it is explicitly forbidden for the state to revoke German citizenship from any individual. The new citizenship law's designers worked around this restriction by claiming that individuals who do not give up their secondary citizenships by the age of twenty-three are *voluntarily* renouncing German citizenship, as opposed to having it revoked.

Children who had not yet reached the end of their tenth year by January 1, 2000 are also eligible for automatic naturalization if the conditions were the same at the time of their birth (i.e., one parent had lived in Germany legally for at least eight years and had a secure resident status). The reforms also reduced the required legal residency for naturalization applications from other immigrants from fifteen years to eight, among other changes (Ausländerbeauftragte des Senats von Berlin 2000; Beauftragte der Bundesregierung für Migration, Flüchtlinge und Integration 2005b; also see Storz and Reisslandt 2002, 27). In order to qualify for citizenship, naturalization applicants cannot have a criminal history and must successfully pass a language exam, commit to the democratic principles of the German constitution (the Basic Law), demonstrate financial means to support themselves and their family without reliance on social welfare or unemployment benefits, and renounce their previous citizenship.

The reforms have not increased naturalization rates as much as anticipated, which may be partially attributable to the difficulty of language tests and to the relatively high cost of naturalization (Ludvig 2004, 508). Naturalization fees are currently €255 per person or €51 for minors applying with their parents (Beauftragte der Bundesregierung für Migration, Flüchtlinge und Integration 2005b, 19). The lack of a dual citizenship option—which would have enabled applicants to retain citizenship in their native country—may also have made some applicants reluctant to apply for German citizenship (Hansen and Weil 2001, 14). Naturalization increased about 30 percent in 2000, but this was a smaller increase than each of the previous two years (Ludvig 2004, 507–8). Naturalizations in 2001, 2002, and 2003 decreased by 4.6 percent, 13.2 percent, and 8.9 percent respectively (Beauftragte der Bundesregierung für Migration, Flüchtlinge und Integration 2005a). In 2004 and 2005 naturalizations continued to decline, at 9.6 percent and 7.8 percent respectively, but they increased in 2006 by 6.2 percent (Beauftragte der Bundesregierung für Migration, Flüchtlinge und Integration 2007). Nonetheless, although the reforms did not completely disregard jus sanguinis principles, the new law marked a clear, or even "seismic" (Green 2000, 114), shift away from a conception of the German nation as ethnically or racially homogenous (Baumann et al. 1999, 49).

The Persistence of a Blood-Based Narrative about Germanness

Even as these changes in German citizenship law were being debated, popular and scholarly accounts of German citizenship and national belonging continued to paint a picture of Germanness as something determined by "blood." Rogers Brubaker's (1992) seminal work comparing citizenship policies in France and Germany helped solidify this conception—despite the fact that Brubaker's analysis of the German situation was more subtle and complex—during a resurgence of interest in questions of citizenship and national identity in the social sciences (Anderson 1991, 1999; Behnke 1997; Bendix 1996; Eley and Suny 1996; Gellner 1996; Hobsbawm 1990; Ignatieff 1993; Kennedy 2002; Salecl 1994; Suny and Kennedy 1999a) and remained a central and frequently cited work well over a decade later. Uli Linke (1997, 560), for example, cites Brubaker's (1992) work as she explains that Germany has a "genealogical ordering of society, in which blood functioned as a verbal signifier of descent and citizenship." Such analyses of German citizenship and naturalization law have, in turn, been extrapolated to discussions of German national belonging, which is also often identified as an "ethnic" rather than a "civic" form of national identity (see, e.g., Ignatieff 1993). Indeed, a frequent subtext in analyses of German national belonging is the role that blood-based understandings of Germanness play, especially in terms of continuities that can be traced from National Socialism (see, e.g., Räthzel 1990). Will Kymlicka (1995, 23), for example, notes that "some national groups define themselves in terms of blood. The most obvious case is Germany."

The linkage between blood and citizenship in depictions of German national belonging is partly due to the relevance of the long legacy of German "ethnic" nationalism, the role that biological and ethnic elements played in the development of the Volk concept (Brubaker 1992; Bade 2001; Fulbrook 1996, 1999; Ignatieff 1993; Sephocle 1999, 50; Storz and Reisslandt 2002; Willms 2001) and the importance of the notion of *Heimat* or *Fatherland* to German national identity (Hermand and Steakley 1996). Contemporary discussions of citizenship and national belonging are also, of course, informed by the indelible mark that the racist National Socialist Nuremberg Laws, the Holocaust, and the entire legacy of World War II left on the world's (and Germans') perceptions of Germans and German identity. Historical issues notwithstanding, however, the most obvious arguments pointing to the blood-based nature of Germans' understandings of themselves today rely on reference to the fact that principles of jus sanguinis have been privileged in German citizenship and naturalization policies.

In fact, the persistence of the narrative linking blood and citizenship in Germany masks the extent to which cultural elements have always played a role in Germans' conceptions of themselves and of the German *Kulturnation* (Sammartino 2004). There is general agreement among most scholars who work on the German case that culture is significant in constructing German national identity—the term *Kulturnation*, after all, refers to the notion that the German nation can be defined culturally, to "nationality as a function of cultural identity" (Huyssen 1995, 78; also see Mandel 1989, 37; Räthzel 1990, 33). But culture and cultural issues are raised less frequently than blood-based ones in most discussions about the nature of German citizenship and national belonging.

While public narratives on Germanness, then, have been characterized by a relative consensus in depictions of Germans' understandings as blood based, popular understandings of German citizenship and national belonging are more poorly understood. Paralleling trends in the broader literature on citizenship, recent empirical work in Germany has addressed the question of how ordinary Germans understand citizenship only rarely. More explicit discussions of the relationship between citizenship and identity or national belonging tend to be embedded in analyses of citizenship and the European Union (Delanty 1997), or in works on the impact of globalization on national identities (Castles and Davidson 2000). Several scholars have examined questions of national identity, particularly relating to differences between east and west Germans or to east German identity more specifically (see, e.g., Berdahl 1999; Glaeser 2000; Schweigler 1975; Staab 1998), but have not explicitly addressed questions of citizenship. Several empirical studies in Germany—both qualitative and quantitative—include topics related to citizenship (see Achatz et al. 2001; Alba, Schmidt, and Wasmer 2003; Almond and Verba 1963; Amadeo et al. 2002; Borneman 1991, 1997; Deutsche Shell 2000a, b, 2002; European Commission 2001; Glaeser 2000; Händle, Oesterreich, and Trommer 1999a; Schweikert 1999; Straughn 2001). But very few of these studies directly ask questions about how citizenship is conceived, to whom it should be extended, or whether ordinary Germans' conceptions are grounded in racial, cultural, ethnic, or civic understandings. Instead, empirical research questions have focused on issues of east or west German identity, national pride, xenophobia, and right-wing extremism (Alba, Schmidt, and Wasmer 2003; Kastoryano 2002, 2).

One exception is the German General Social Survey (known as ALLBUS after the German abbreviation for *Allgemeine Bevölkerungsumfrage der Sozialwissenschaften*), which in 1996 had a special focus on attitudes toward ethnic groups and citizenship. Using the ALLBUS data, Rainer Münz and Ralf Ulrich report that German origin is an "important" criteria for naturalization to German citizenship for over half (56 percent) of the respondents of the 1996 survey (see table 2). Despite this high percentage, it is the second least important criteria, second only to membership in a Christian denomination (9 percent). The most important criteria for naturalization are lack of previous criminal history

(87 percent), ability to support self and dependents (79 percent), and lengthy residence in Germany (73 percent). Ability to speak German (66 percent), adaptation to German way of life (63 percent), and being born in Germany (61 percent) were the next most important criteria (Münz and Ulrich 1998).

There are regional and generational differences in how citizenship is understood, however. For example, while 30 percent of residents in the former East Germany and 25 percent of those in the former West Germany feel it is "very important" for naturalization applicants to be of German origin, only 18 percent of Germans aged eighteen to twenty-nine feel the same way. In nearly every category asked—cultural adaptation, criminal background, ability to support oneself financially, birthplace in Germany, and length of residence—younger Germans were less likely to deem criteria for naturalization as "very important." The sole category where this was not the case deals with language ability; while 25 percent of younger Germans feel it is "very important" for naturalization applicants to speak German, this number drops to 22 percent for residents of the former East Germany, although it is higher for residents of the former West Germany, at 36 percent.

Studying Citizenship and National Belonging as Cultural Practices

This book analyzes citizenship and national belonging as cultural practices. Studying how citizenship and national belonging are lived and practiced among ordinary citizens, I argue, forces us to rethink our assumptions about the meaning of citizenship and nation and how they can be understood. Elite perspectives, rights, legal policies, and structural institutions are, of course, a crucial part of the study of citizenship. Citizenship status is determined by federal states, which use legal regulations to set eligibility requirements for citizenship, and thereby determine who has access to the rights, benefits, and responsibilities that are associated with membership. But the meanings associated with being a part of a country or nation vary along at least two axes, based both on who has access to membership (or to whom it is denied), as well as on the understandings that individuals and groups have as to how that membership should be lived and practiced. The emphasis in this book is on the second kind of meaning. How citizenship and national belonging are understood and practiced, I argue, is determined as much

Table 2. Survey of Germans' views about the importance of various conditions for naturalization

Condition for naturalization	Age 18–29 Not[b] (%)	Age 18–29 Very (%)	New federal states[a] Not (%)	New federal states[a] Very (%)	Old federal states Not (%)	Old federal states Very (%)
Should be born in Germany	17	25	15	38	17	30
Should be of German origin	18	18	15	30	17	25
Should speak German	9	25	12	22	5	36
Has lived here a long time	7	28	7	32	4	35
Adapt to German way of life	13	21	9	27	7	30
Christian denomination	68	1	69	2	55	3
No crimes committed	4	52	3	69	3	59
Can support himself	8	33	4	48	5	46

Source: Allgemeine Bevölkerungsumfrage der Sozialwissenschaften (ALLBUS) — German General Social Survey 1996. See note a.

Note: Data from the Allgemeine Bevölkerungsumfrage der Sozialwissenschaften (ALLBUS)—German General Social Survey 1996. From 1980 to 1986 and in 1991, the ALLBUS program was funded by the DFG. For all other surveys, state and federal funding has been made available through GESIS (Gesellschaft sozialwissenschaftlicher Infrastruktureinrichtungen). ALLBUS/GGSS is accomplished by the Center for Survey Research and Methodology (ZUMA–Zentrum für Umfragen, Methoden und Analysen e.v., Mannheim) and the Central Archive for Empirical Social Research (ZA–Zentralarchiv für Empirische Sozialforschung, Cologne) in cooperation with the ALLBUS scientific council. Data and documentation are available from the Central Archive for Empirical Social Research (ZA, Cologne). The institutions and persons mentioned above bear no responsibility for the use or interpretations of the data in this book.

a. As determined by the region of interview.
b. Categories are "not at all important" or "very important," which were the two end categories on a seven-point scale.

by ordinary people themselves as by states and elites, based on their shared understandings of what it means to be a member of a particular state or nation. These meanings cannot be automatically extrapolated from the laws, policies, and structures that elites have put into place in any particular state or nation, but must, rather, include an analysis of what people actually say when they talk about the meaning of citizenship and national belonging.

In the German case, this means examining how a younger generation of working-class Germans' resistance to a prevailing antinationalist narrative may be contributing to change in the meaning of the German nation. By examining generational transformations in conceptions of citizenship and nationhood, I broaden our understanding of nations as "imagined communities" by accounting for processes of change.

Studying citizenship and national belonging as cultural practices takes constructivism a step further—in response to the lament from Brubaker et. al. (2006, 7), who note "*That* ethnicity and nationhood are constructed is a commonplace; *how* they are constructed is seldom specified in detail." The constructivist approach has dominated recent sociological work on nations and nationalism, as scholars over the past several decades have demonstrated that ordinary individuals as well as intellectuals and states are involved in the construction of the nation and narratives about nationhood. In this book, I take the constructivists' claims a step further, arguing that nations are not only imagined and constructed but are re-imagined and reconstituted over time. Generations, I argue, play an important role in this process. Generational shifts in views about who belongs within the national community or the kinds of expressions of national identity that are to be sanctioned as patriotic sentiments or forbidden as nationalistic xenophobia, I suggest, can help to transform the meaning of the nation over time. The study of everyday conceptions of nationhood in Germany reveals patterns of generational change that ought to make us rethink the ways in which citizenship and national belonging can be understood more generally.

This study, then, sits at the intersection of citizenship and nationhood. As such, it has dual aims: on the one hand, to extend the constructivist approach to nationalism to account for the question of how transformations in national identity occur across generations, and on the other hand, to add a cultural dimension to institutional and structural studies of citizenship. The term "culture," in this sense, refers not as much to distinct and stable systems of norms, beliefs, and attitudes, tangible objects and elements of recorded culture, art and entertainment (Alexander and Seidman 1990; Kane 1997; Swidler 1986; Wuthnow 1987) as it does to the ways in which such elements shape the very practices of everyday life (Eagleton 2000; Jenks 1993b; Williams 1985, 87–93; also see Hall 1994; Kennedy 2002, 42).

For analytical purposes, I use the term "cultural" in this book as a contrast to biological, genetic, racial, or ethnic factors referenced in the construction of understandings of citizenship and national belonging. Here, cultural characteristics are elements which can be learned or absorbed through socialization processes and which may be unique to particular societies. This becomes an important distinction in the discussion about whether it is possible to "become German" (Eagleton 2000; Gilroy 1991; Jenks 1993a, b). While culture and ethnicity are deeply intertwined, in this book I distinguish analytically between the two terms by relying on a strict definition of ethnicity as based on descent, as detailed below.

Although the concepts of race, ethnicity, and culture are fluid, relational, and deeply intertwined with one another (Brubaker 2004), for the purposes of coding, I make an analytical separation among the three terms. For analytical purposes, I have classified students' and teachers' responses as reflecting a racial understanding of citizenship when their definitions of citizenship rely on genetic criteria or phenotypical and physical features, such as skin tone. This is not meant to support an approach to race as an "actually existing" phenomenon. As Rogers Brubaker argues, racial categories and systems of classification are "real and consequential" (Brubaker 2004, 11) even as we acknowledge the socially constructed nature of race.

I classify students' and teachers' conceptions of citizenship as "ethnic" when they rely on the German notion of Volk or on the notion of German heritage (*Herkunft, Ursprung,* or *deutsche Vorfahren*) in their definitions of German citizenship but do not explicitly reference physical appearance, racial categories, or genetic differences. Here I follow the strictest definition of ethnicity, where as Anthony Smith explains, "ethnicity refers to common descent" (Smith 1983, 180, cited in Brubaker 2004, 136). This definition of "ethnic" can be contrasted with "civic" understandings of state membership or nationalism (Brubaker 2004; Ignatieff 1993). Because of the jus sanguinis nature of German citizenship, I employ a third category to classify responses which rely on *filiation,* or descent from a parent who has German citizenship, when students' and teachers' responses do not clearly associate filiation with ethnicity. It should be noted that many responses fall into several categories, and were coded accordingly.

two

Being and Becoming in Germany

The trouble with the Germans, Napoleon reportedly once remarked, is that they are always becoming, never being. Indeed, the German nation has been in an almost perpetual state of change. In the previous century alone, as others have pointed out, Germany has been led by six different governments and political systems—a monarchy (until 1918), a democracy (the Weimar Republic, until 1933), a dictatorship (the Third Reich, until 1945), a West German democracy (until 1989), an East German communist state (until 1989), and since 1990, a unified, democratic Germany (Gagel 1995; Händle 1999, 13; Kuhn, Massing, and Skuhr 1993). But even before the turn of the last century, Germany was an emergent nation, dominated by regional identities and structures until 1871, when the creation of the new German Reich brought several smaller states and regions into a unified nation-state.

Perhaps reflective of the regional affiliations that dominated the political realm, early nationalist sentiments in Germany were more deeply rooted in cultural heritage than in a quest for geographic unity or a sense of political belonging. Cultural and linguistic aspects of Germanness, in fact, appear to have preceded the blood-based dimensions that later came to define popular understandings of German identity (see, e.g., Dill 1970; Fulbrook 1999, 180; Gosewinkel 2001; James 2000; Verheyen 1999; Wildenthal 2002; Willms 2001). When the concept of *Volk*—which has since become nearly synonymous with the German conception of nationhood—emerged in Germany in the early 1800s, it was a counterexpression to the French concept of "nation." The term Volk, Johannes Willms (2001, 30–37) argues, enabled a discussion or conception of a national community without the democratic structures that were inherent in the notion of a *nation une et indivisible*, as had emerged with the French Revolution. Nation was "synonymous with

Volk" (Greenfeld 1992, 364) and embodied the inner spirit of the people. While the French definition of nation established a community independent of ethnic heritage and based instead on residence and a common commitment to democratic principles, the German response—a nation made up of a German Volk—was based on a cultural conception of Germanness (Fulbrook 1999, 181) and implicitly or explicitly required ethnic heritage for political membership and belonging (Brubaker 1992; Ignatieff 1993, 85–89; Storz and Reisslandt 2002, 25–28).

In the German version of national belonging, particular emphasis was placed on a common ethnic heritage, language, culture, religion, history, and a sense of Heimat, and national belonging was viewed as part of an individual's destiny. As many have pointed out, some of the basis for the extreme nationalism of the National Socialists can be found in this very understanding of Germanness as a community of descent and ethnic heritage. Since the German Volk was to be clearly differentiated from other national peoples, its "purity," therefore, was something to preserve and protect (Storz and Reisslandt 2002, 26). While the notion of Heimat connected regional belonging with the nation, linking the everyday experience of one's local life with a larger sense of belonging (Applegate 1990), the cultural homogeneity at the root of the German Volk concept kept a German sense of national belonging linked to the German Romantic notion that "each people has its own unique language and culture and therefore natural right to self-determination" (O'Brien 1992, 382).

This notion of national belonging—as based on an ethnic connection to others who share the same culture, Heimat, and language—was reflected in some of the citizenship and naturalization policies in Germany in the 1800s, although there were regional differences (Ignatieff 1993; Wippermann 1999). Social policies during this period, moreover, extended relief to the poor to all individuals within a given territory (under certain conditions such as length of residence, in some cases), regardless of citizenship or ethnic heritage (Steinmetz 1993, 120). Gradually, however, the "ethnic" part of "ethnic heritage" began to take on more of a biological and less of a cultural connotation. By the time the Reich Citizenship Law of 1913 was passed, there was no remaining confusion about who should be permitted to be German—Germanness was redefined as something based on biological heritage. According to the new law, citizenship was defined as a community of descent, not one of residence or birthplace (Brubaker 1992, 115).

The Reich Citizenship Law, which was discussed in chapter 1, was passed amid widespread debate in Germany about how best to stem the increasing flow of immigration from Eastern Europe, and these debates continued after World War I (Sammartino 2004), when, according to Fulbrook (1999, 182), the "concept of German citizenship became more homogenously ethnic in character." Culture continued to play a clear role in conceptions of Germanness, however, and it is debatable whether race and culture were even understood as separate concepts by ordinary Germans at the time (Sammartino 2004). By the time Germany's first democracy (the Weimar Republic) was established in 1918, however, it was clear that national identity and national pride, while perhaps not supplanting the regional identities that had been so central through the mid-1800s, had become increasingly important and played a greater role in everyday German politics and culture (see, e.g., Detwiler 1999, 183).

When the National Socialists gained control in Germany, citizenship and naturalization laws became intertwined with the cultural, ethnic, and racial aspects of the Volk concept, as new policies restricted the definition of Germanness to those who shared, not only the same ethnic heritage and culture, but who were also categorized as racially "pure," being of German blood (Brubaker 1992, 166–67; Gosewinkel 2001). The Nuremberg Laws of 1935 revoked citizenship from German Jews and led to the ultimate attempt to exterminate anyone who did not conform to the National Socialists' idea of a racially pure state (Brubaker 1992, 165–68; Fulbrook 1999, 183). Non-Christians, the physically and mentally handicapped, homosexuals, and others who were found to be "unacceptable" according to these laws fled the country or were systematically eliminated in the Holocaust. This version of ethnic nationalism and the accompanying horrors of the Holocaust permanently changed Germany's sense of national identity and Germans' relationships to the nation.

In addition to forever tainting German national identity, the end of World War II was a defining moment for German national identity in other ways as well, most notably because it marked a split in the official narrative or story about German national identity. The end of the war set in motion the policies that would eventually lead to the division of Germany into two separate states: the Federal Republic of Germany (FRG, or West Germany) and the German Democratic Republic (GDR, or East Germany). The impact on German national identity was critical. In addition to differences in citizenship and naturalization policies, East and West German narratives about national identity and national pride diverged during their forty years of differing political, economic, and social systems.

National Identity in Post-1945 Germany

During the early years after World War II, Borneman (1997, 96) observes, the FRG and the GDR "were involved in what Hegel (1953) called a 'struggle to the death': seeking recognition (*Anerkennung*) of self without having to recognize the other in turn." Each country strove to create a narrative about identity that differentiated itself from its inherent "Other." This was complicated, of course, by their shared history, language, culture, and heritage, not to mention the millions of citizens on each side of the division who had ties to relatives, birthplaces, or hometowns on the other side. At the same time, Germans in both states were struggling to confront and deal with their personal role in the Holocaust as well as their own identities as Germans in the wake of the atrocities. In the process, a clear pattern emerged in each country in terms of the prevailing public and social narratives about Germanness and Germans' relationships to the past.

These divergent approaches are evident in the public and social narratives that emerged in each country, as traceable in public policies, newspaper articles, and accounts of political debates (see, e.g., Olick 1998, 1999). By focusing on such public narratives—which are often, but not necessarily, linked to official or state versions of national identity and nationhood—I do not wish to imply that there exists only a singular narrative about nationhood in Germany or elsewhere. There is clearly a breadth of official and private views about the nation, who belongs to it, and how individuals should relate to it (see, e.g., Mommsen 1983). Public discourse as well as private opinions about the nation are complex and complicated, and there is no such thing as a unilateral consensus about the meaning of the nation. In some settings, alternative narratives are never publicly voiced but are nonetheless central to ordinary individuals' reception and interpretation of the nation. Such alternative narratives can be detected in literature, film, popular culture, and in the voices of public intellectuals, poets, musicians, and protesters, among others (see, e.g., Hell 1997), especially in places like East Germany, where public vocal opposition to the state's policies and narratives was more difficult than it was in the West. In Germany, individuals from different parts of the political spectrum will have divergent views on the nation, as might citizens and noncitizens, men and women, ethnic minorities, or, as this book details, members of different generations. Thus multiple narratives of nationhood coexist and potentially compete with one another for dominance at any given time.

The simultaneous existence of multiple national narratives does not mean that all narratives carry equal weight in the public domain, however. At any given moment in a nation's history, certain narratives come to acquire more resonance than others. They are integrated into school textbooks and teaching practice, political speeches, scholarly arguments, official state policy, newspaper articles, and other public discourse. They are reinforced (and sometimes challenged) in the media, in public discussions, in the family, and in schools, often through no direct action or intention on the part of the state. They become a part of the public's unselfconscious understanding of their collective self, as chapter 3 will detail in its discussion about the taboo on national pride in unified Germany. When I speak of "prevailing" notions of nationhood, then, I am referring to the versions of the nation that acquire a sort of commonsense meaning among both elites and a significant portion of the general public at any particular sociohistorical moment, even as alternative and competing narratives coexist.

By focusing on these kinds of prevailing messages about nationhood, however, I do not mean to imply that alternative narratives are any less important in shaping individuals' identities or in shaping the meaning of nationhood for ordinary individuals in their everyday lives. Rather, it is simply that the scope of this book focuses on prevailing public and social narratives, their mediation through public schools and public school teachers, and the reactions to these narratives from German young people, and does not allow for a fuller discussion of alternative narratives or of the historical reactions of individuals in the GDR, the FRG, or in unified Germany.

Ignoring and Rejecting the Nation: West Germany after 1945

Public debates about German national identity after 1945, as well as public confrontations with the actual events of the war and the Holocaust, first began to surface in West Germany during the 1960s (see, e.g., Fulbrook 1999). While some of this twenty-year gap can be explained by the overwhelming demands required by the postwar reconstruction effort, the delay had psychological reasons as well, as many Germans deliberately tried to forget the recent past or were psychologically unable to confront it. As Norman Birnbaum (1990, 237) explains, "preoccupation with the Holocaust is broader and deeper in the Germany of 1990 than in that of 1945." The generation of 1945, or 45ers (Moses 1999), in other words, largely avoided and ignored the nation, preferring to keep national categories and nationalism in general at a distance (Alter 1992).

By the 1960s, however, as young Germans became aware of the horrific actions of their parents' generation, the student protest movement forced the first beginnings of a public acknowledgment about the events of the Third Reich. Memorials were established at former concentration camps (see Fulbrook 1999) and a series of plays, such as Hochhuth's *Der Stellvertreter* (*The Deputy*), and exhibitions confronted the German public with the Nazi past.[1] The young generation of Germans pursuing these confrontations came to be known as the 68ers, in reference to the student protests of 1968 which served as the defining episode for their generation. Faced with the silence of their parents' generation about their actions during the war (Moses 1999; Marcuse 2001) and well aware of the Nazis' manipulation of national sentiments, the 68ers simultaneously called their parents' generation to account for their actions and rejected the nation and anything national. In so doing, they saw themselves as correcting the "political and moral deficiencies of German public and private life" (Moses 1999, 95) and thus as Germany's "saviour from its National Socialist past" (Bude in Moses 1999, 95). The 68ers, in other words, sought collective salvation in a wholesale rejection of the nation.

Germany's political leadership had disavowed the notion of a national community in the immediate postwar period in order to present Germany as legitimate after 1945 (Phillips 2000b, 2–5), but thus it was really the 1960s that marked the emergence of a taboo on nationhood and an antinationalist consensus that became "central to the self-understanding of the Federal Republic of Germany" (Huyssen 1995, 77) in the 1960s.

The taboo on German national pride that developed in post–World War II West Germany was not just a result of internalized shame because of the Holocaust, however. It was also directly tied to a particular West German understanding of pride as something indicating superiority over other nations or peoples, especially in ethnic or racial terms. Nationalism and national pride were directly linked during the Third

Reich to biological racism and eventually, to the extermination of all who were deemed to be "inferior." After the war, West Germany was unable to redefine national pride in alternative terms, and national pride remained linked, at least psychologically, to a sense of superiority over other nations or peoples.

The difficulty West Germans had with the concept of national pride is illustrated in the calls by many West German intellectuals, led by Jürgen Habermas (1992b, 91), for an alternative "constitutional patriotism" grounded in the West German constitution and the democratic institutions it helped establish, which these intellectuals claimed could be differentiated from the patriotism of Germany's nationalist past (see selections from Habermas in Maier 1988, 45). Any other form of national pride, Habermas argued, would alienate and isolate Germany from the West, and there could be, therefore, no return to a "conventional form of their national identity" (Maier 1988, 45).

Verfassungspatriotismus (constitutional patriotism) became a "politically correct" way to be a patriot since it removed one from the actual nation and its history of ethnic nationalism (see Huyssen 1995). But Habermas's suggestion was motivated by more than a desire to be politically correct—he insinuated that there could be no return to a national identity based on an imagined connection to others through anything other than a commitment to a common set of democratic principles because any other form of national identity posed too much of a danger. As Charles Maier (1988, 58) explains, Habermas suggests "that the proclivities for Nazism from 1933 to 1945 lay embedded in a culture that might still transmit them in 1986. . . . Habermas apparently felt that the potential for Auschwitz was still inherent in every German's cultural inheritance." His proposed alternative concept of "constitutional patriotism" was "the most sublime variation of the tabooization of the nation" (Bohrer 1992, 69).

This constitutional patriotism, as M. R. Lepsuis explained in 1989, was "the central result of the delegitimization of German nationalism" and was seen as wholly separate "from the idea of an ethnic, cultural, collective 'community of fate.'" (in Habermas 1992b, 90). Pride took on a dangerous connotation, becoming linked with the conscious or subconscious fear among Germans that National Socialism emerged because of something specific to the German character and that there was, therefore, always a potential threat of its resurgence.

Habermas was not alone among German scholars in his antinationalist approach. Günter Grass, who at one point promoted an alternative form of attachment to the nation by suggesting that Germans use the term *Kulturnation* instead of nation (Huyssen 1995, 78), was also one of the most vocal opponents of German unification from the 1960s onward. Grass (1990, 13) argued that the Germans essentially could not be trusted to unify because "nothing would be gained but a troubling abundance of power and the lust for more power. In spite of all our assurances, even the sincere ones, we Germans would become, once again, something to be feared. Our neighbors would draw away from us with distrust, and the feeling of being isolated would rear its head, giving rise to the dangerous self-pity that sees itself as 'surrounded by enemies.'"

The only other alternative sense of national pride offered to the West Germans by way of a formal or official narrative about Germanness was rooted in consumerism and economic progress, especially in the 1950s and 1960s. Economic achievement became the only potential basis for a national identity and for what Levy (1999, 85) calls "a non-ethnic representation of German pride." A good German was a good consumer and a good worker, and the nation was defined by its economic success. As Maier (1988, 8) comments, "West German nationhood meant production." Jürgen Habermas (1992b, 88), discussing Wolfgang Mommsen's 1983 study of West German national identity, agreed with Mommsen that the "self-confidence of a successful economic nation, forms the core of the political self-understanding of the population of the Federal Republic — and a substitute for a national pride that is widely lacking."[2]

Whether the reasons were based in the past (shame, a conception of national pride as forever tainted, or a conviction that national pride itself was rooted in biological racism and a sense of superiority over others) or in the present and future (legitimacy in international relations or fear of a resurgence of National Socialism), the prevailing view in the FRG from the 1960s onward was one that invalidated and delegitimized national identity, national pride, and the nation in general. By the mid-1980s, this view was increasingly tied to the notion of collective responsibility for the Nazi past, so that national identity and national pride were associated with pro-Nazi tendencies. Fulbrook (1999, 36) explains that the West German approach to the past developed "into an almost ritualized incorporation of national guilt in the official re-presentation of the past." National pride and national guilt, apparently, could not coexist.

By the mid-1980s, however, there is also evidence that the prevailing antinationalism and complete rejection of the nation had begun to fragment. For the first time, debates began to emerge about how exactly the Third Reich and the Holocaust should be remembered. The earliest and most compelling evidence for this fragmentation is the *Historkerstreit* (historian's debate) in the 1980s, which took up the question of whether the Third Reich was so atrocious as to be completely historically unique, or if it could be relativized and categorized with the genocides, ethnic cleansing efforts, and abuses of other totalitarian regimes throughout history, such as Stalinism (Brinks 2000; Huyssen 1995). This period also witnessed the emergence of a new level of public debate about the Holocaust itself and how it should be remembered, especially during debates about the establishment of memorial sites and as a result of a television miniseries called *Holocaust*, which aired in the United States in 1979.[3] Such debates began to pave the way for Germans to address the past and opened up discussion about whether it was possible to achieve a sense of reconciliation (*Wiedergutmachung*) with the nation. By the time unification came about, the leftist "antinationalist consensus," Huyssen (1995, 77) claims, had already begun to splinter, and the 1990s saw increasing openness in discussions of the Nazi past. As Jeffrey Olick (1998, 553) argues, "events since 1989 have involved a more successful 'normalization' of the Nazi past than efforts since at least 1982, and arguably since the late 1970s."[4]

To broadly generalize the prevailing tendencies across the first two post–World War II generations—and bearing in mind that in both cases there were less vocal alternative narratives present—the initial years after World War II in West Germany were characterized by an absence of nationhood. The generation of 1945, in other words, generally ignored the nation, focusing instead on the tasks of reconstruction. Their children—who would become known as the 68ers—on the other hand, largely rejected the nation. From the 1960s at least until the 1990s, an antinationalist narrative prohibiting pride in the nation prevailed, and pride itself became inextricably linked to the extreme right-wing. Highly politicized debates about memory, interpretation, and collective responsibility—including, for example, the continuing process of reparations for former victims of slave labor (Verheyen 1999, 59)—further contributed to a sense of institutionalized and collective shame.[5] The prevailing view of collective memory, national identity, and national pride in East Germany during the same period, however, was strikingly different.

Liberation and the Nation: East Germany after 1945

From the beginning, East Germany's view of the Third Reich and of World War II differed significantly from that of the FRG, even as— like in West Germany—its public narrative about national identity was formed very much in reaction to its "Other" across the border (Fulbrook 1990, 216; Verheyen 1999, 85–87; James 2000, 171–73). The GDR regime identified itself first and foremost as the victims of, resistors to, and victors vis-à-vis National Socialist fascism. Sheehan (1992, 165) argues that national identity in the GDR was based in large part on a moral claim of "antifascism, which served to distance the regime from the German past and to empower its attacks on those allies and heirs of fascism who continued to flourish in the West" (also see Wegner 1996). Thus the GDR did not officially assume the kind of collective guilt the FRG took on for the Holocaust or the war itself (although individuals in the GDR certainly suffered with their own personal histories and consciences). According to Fulbrook (1999, 58), the GDR "externalized the enemy and internalized the victim as heroic opposition." East Germany was depicted as a "liberation" state that had freed East Germans from the evils of fascism, while the FRG was depicted as the successor to the fascist Nazi regime (Straughn 2001, 296).

Although based in part on the reality of communist persecution under the Nazi regime, the GDR's efforts to divorce the GDR from the Nazi past also aimed to increase loyalty to the antifascist state. As Dirk Verheyen (1999, 80) explains, "In contrast to a West Germany allegedly controlled by ex-Nazis, nationalist revanchists, and capitalist reactionaries, the GDR was defined as the vanguard of a future socialist and democratic Germany." GDR leaders constantly pointed out the fact that many former Nazi leaders continued to be in leadership positions in the FRG, and in propaganda efforts, linked the FRG's government to fascism (Fulbrook 1999, 58). In fact, the GDR used the term fascism to apply not only to the former Nazi regime but also to current critics of the "self-professedly anti-fascist state of the GDR" (Fulbrook 1999, 56). German fascism, according to the GDR, was a product of capitalism (Olick 1998, 559), not of uniquely German conditions or history. This approach presented fascism as an abstract development that was not specific to Germany and thus distanced the GDR from responsibility or blame for the Holocaust (Borneman 1997, 102–5).

Moreover, the GDR was supposed to be a state of citizen-workers bound together by ideology, not by a connection to a *national* identity, which was viewed as a "bourgeois" model of belonging (Straughn 2001, 269). In addition to its antifascist emphasis, in the early years, the GDR explicitly tried to deconstruct and devalue any sense of national identity at all, promoting instead loyalty to an ideological state made up of workers and peasants who had been oppressed under capitalism (see Vastano 1992). As Straughn (2001, 269) observes, as a "post-fascist state," the GDR "had to renounce, as far as possible, its connection to any merely national history."

In reality, however, ordinary East Germans struggled with the legacy of fascism and were haunted by their own experiences with it (Hell 1997). The propaganda-laden nature of the GDR's version of antifascism was arguably clear to the vast majority of GDR citizens, and so it seems unlikely that the narrative offered a complete release from the kind of collective guilt imposed on their counterparts in the West. But the narrative undoubtedly had some impact on East Germans' national or collective identities. Even if the GDR's official narrative about national identity "may never have been a living reality among the bulk of the East German population," Verheyen (1999, 80) notes, citing the work of Rudolph (1983), "it left identifiable sociocultural and psychological traces because it influenced the contours of everyday life in East Germany for four decades." Fulbrook (1999, 35) argues that although the official story was not internalized, the moral of the tale was accepted: in East Germany, there was "no need to be 'ashamed of being German.'" By the 1980s the GDR even began to reintroduce cultural nationalism and national pride as part of an effort to compete with what many East Germans viewed as a more attractive alternative in the West (Straughn 2001, 297). These efforts ultimately failed, as the rapid changes in 1989 made abundantly clear.

In sum, the prevailing public and social narratives in East and West Germany about national identity and national pride were distinctly different, even as they were influenced by the same history and culture. The institutionalized shame and collective guilt in the FRG, together with a definition of national pride as linked to biological racism and a sense of superiority over others, led to a taboo on national pride and a rejection of the nation, while the GDR's narrative about resistance, liberation, and heroism at least offered the possibility to East German citizens of a release from the same fate. While both East and West Germans certainly were deeply affected and traumatized by the past, the West Germans, to a much greater extent, translated this experience into a taboo of nationhood more generally (Schröder 1999). At least by the time of the debates leading up to German unification, the existence of both narratives was openly acknowledged by scholars. Ulrich Greiner (1992) describes an argument made by the sociologist Ulrich Overmann, for example, that only a unified Germany could adequately address responsibility for the Holocaust. As Greiner (1992, 81) writes: "The division of the 'national people [*Nationalvolkes*]' (Overmann) into a morally impeccable anti-fascist part (the GDR) and a morally contestable part that relied on economic efficiency (the FRG) had missed the political dimensions of responsibility for Auschwitz."

It is also worth noting that in general—especially around the time of unification—West German scholars and intellectuals, if not the general public, were somewhat more public about their concern—or obsession—with "the German question" compared with their East German counterparts. In one collected volume of speeches and newspaper articles about German unification (James and Stone 1992), for example, nearly every West German author discusses issues of the nation, nationalism, or national identity, while hardly any of the East German scholars so much as mention it, except when asked directly in interview questions. It may be that East Germans were simply consumed with the collapse of the GDR's system and everything the massive transformations entailed; as a vice president (*Erster Vizepräsident*) of Humboldt University explained in a 1997 speech, the difficulty in defining "belonging" in terms of a Volk or a nation is for west Germans an issue of fundamental nature, while east Germans simply have had "more burning questions" to deal with (Schröder 1999, 32). But it could also be the case that for east Germans, the national question had never been as pressing as it was for west Germans as a result of the divergent public and social narratives about national identity and national pride that developed in each country.

As I pointed out above, there were indications that the prevailing narrative about national identity in West Germany had begun to fragment by the 1980s. In East Germany, the fact that the GDR's prevailing narrative about national identity and national pride had also begun to fragment by the 1980s is also abundantly clear, both from the state's own attempt to introduce cultural nationalism and national pride and from the increasing resistance put forth by its own citizens to the system. By the time German unification took place, of course, the East

German narrative had completely crumbled since the idea of building national loyalty to an antifascist state, in the wake of that very state's deterioration, was no longer possible. Rather, it was the West German narrative that continued to prevail in discussions of German national identity in the post-unification period.

Public and Social Narratives on National Belonging in Unified Germany

The taboo on national identity and national pride that had consolidated in the FRG carried over into a broad public discourse about national identity in the post-unification era. This was especially clear in my observations of teacher practice in civics classrooms and in the public and political debates about the contentious issue of German national pride discussed later in this book. For example, expressions of national pride in contemporary Germany remain directly linked in Germany to the extreme right-wing. Perhaps the clearest evidence of this is that the phrase "I am proud to be German" is still used in German social science surveys as a measure of right-wing attitudes (e.g., Schweikert 1999). The taboo is also the predominant national sentiment to which young people reacted in interviews when I asked them how they felt about being German.

The transition of the taboo on pride and nationhood into unified Germany took place against a backdrop in which issues of German guilt, xenophobia, and right-wing violence were front and center in public and political discourse. First, a series of events in the mid-1990s resurrected the debates that had raged in West Germany about German responsibility and guilt for the Holocaust. The media covered a series of legal trials which would force German firms to pay reparations of billions of dollars to the survivors of forced labor camps during World War II, and several prominent German companies began to investigate their own histories in such matters (Eley 2000). Meanwhile, a sharp increase took place in outbreaks of violence against foreigners in both eastern and western Germany, including a series of particularly violent attacks in 1991 and 1992 and a rise in violent crime again in 1999 and 2000. By the time Goldhagen's *Hitler's Willing Executioners* was published in the mid-1990s, detailing the "enthusiasm of the German perpetrators" for genocidal death marches and the murder of Jews, "controversy was raging in Germany" (Eley 2000, 4). The nature of these debates demonstrated clearly that a sense of collective guilt and institutionalized shame that had solidified in West Germany in the post–World War II era continued to characterize much of the (unified) German narrative about national identity and the German past. And finally, broad public debate about potential reforms in Germany's citizenship and naturalization law began to challenge the continued depiction of Germany as a biologically or genetically grounded nation in which jus sanguinis (based on blood) principles prevailed (Brubaker 1992; Cesarani and Fulbrook 1996; Fulbrook 1996; Joppke 1999b; Kastoryano 2002; Preuss 2003; Sassen 1999; Weil 1996).

As these debates about potential reforms in Germany's citizenship and naturalization policies got underway in the mid-1990s, they became the focal point of a discussion about Germanness and who really belongs in Germany. This discussion was intensified by the rapid influx of east Germans and "ethnic" Germans from Eastern Europe and the former Soviet States, which set up a dichotomy in immigration between those who were "really German" and those who were not. Scholars are not in complete agreement about the impact that "ethnic" German returnees and east German migrants have had on German national identity, however (see, e.g., Levy 1999, Räthzel 1990). Daniel Levy (1999), for example, traces a shift in official government rhetoric about "ethnic" German returnees in the post–Cold War period, as the CDU-led government's strategy to increase public support for the returnees changed from an emphasis on ethnic ties to a highlighting of returnees' potential economic contributions. Other scholars, however, contend that the biological relationship between east and west Germans became increasingly important in emphasizing the connectedness of "Germans" after unification—despite their cultural and social differences. To increase support for unification and encourage Germans to welcome their German "brothers and sisters," for example, Räthzel (1990, 40) notes that the German government deviated from its general taboo on national pride and instead invoked patriotism, emphasizing that east and west Germans were connected by their common heritage and history, even if forty years of different cultural and political socialization had caused a temporary rift. Even some on the political left justified Germany's policies of immigration and automatic citizenship for "ethnic" Germans based on their "blood ties (*Blutsbande*) to the nation" (Linke 1997, 560).

In the meantime, "non-ethnic" Germans remained largely confined to "Otherness," even when they had been in Germany for multiple generations (see Mandel 2008). Jenny White (1997, 760) contends that even in discussions about right-wing violence, Turks remain foreigners, "at best cocitizens, an essentialized ethnic Other" who are not regarded as German residents. Bade (1996) characterizes the situation as grotesque, describing a hypothetical situation in which a Turk born in Germany, who is not a citizen, might be called upon to assist a non-German-speaking "ethnic" German returnee, who is a citizen, with a language problem. In such a situation, the seemingly foreign German returnee was legally considered a native, while the native Ausländer was legally foreign (Bade 1996, 243).

"A" German Identity? East and West German Identity

One of the most significant issues affecting German identity after 1989 has been the persistence of two seemingly distinct identities in eastern and western Germany. This topic has been one of the richest areas in both quantitative and qualitative or ethnographic work over the past decade, as scholars have examined the distinct identities present between east and west in the police force (Glaeser 2000), differences in east and west German cultural identities (Probst 1999), the individual experiences of East Germans during the time of the *Wende* and the fall of the Berlin Wall (Borneman 1991), differences among school students in east and west Berlin (Merkens 1999) and among apprentices in east and west Germany more broadly (Schweikert 1999), to name just a few. What these and other studies have made clear is that a persistent disconnect between east and west Germans remains evident, even in Berlin.

The notion of a shared nationality between east and west Germans was a vital part of the initial euphoria surrounding reunification (Breuilly 1992), as Germans on both sides of the wall rallied around the notion of a common Volk. Newspaper photos from around the globe showed east and west Germans dismantling the wall and reaching out to embrace one another. But before long, tensions became evident. One of the jokes that circulated in the post-1989 period, for example, describes an east German enthusiastically calling out in unity to all Germans, "We are one people" (*Wir sind ein Volk*), while a west German answers, "We are too" (Schröder 1999, 29). The "wall inside Germans' heads" has proven much harder to dismantle than the physical wall that divided the two countries.

Much of the tension between east and west Germans is exacerbated by continued disparities in economic and social conditions. Unemployment in the east is much higher than in the west. Of the 80 percent of east German teachers retained after unification (Händle, Oesterreich, and Trommer 1999b, 261), for example, the majority are still paid significantly lower than their west German counterparts. After unification, federally employed east German teachers' salaries were set at 70 percent of west German teachers' salaries. The discrepancy was justified with an argument about the lower cost of living in the east, and by the fact that the federal government could not afford to pay 100 percent for everyone immediately. The gap has been shrinking, but during the year in which I conducted ethnographic research in Berlin, east German federally employed teachers were still earning only 88.5 percent of what their west German counterparts earned, even when they were colleagues in the same school, doing the same work.[6]

Many west Germans have taken exception to the high costs of unification and complain about the financial strain of reconstruction in the east. Many east Germans, on the other hand, have resented the obliteration of all east German institutions and structures, especially due to the often accompanying sweeping rejection and devaluing of all east German culture, heritage, and way of life (Cohen 1999). These parallel resentments have helped to create additional distance between east and west Germans, further contributing to a sense that east and west German identity remain largely entrenched and separate in the post-unification era (see Glaeser 2000).

Tensions and differences exist even among German youth who have spent the majority of their lives in unified Germany. For example, 12 percent of east German youth, compared with 23 percent of west German youth, reported an interest in politics in 1996 (Gaiser et al. 1998, 148). Among the young Germans I interviewed, the vast majority did not raise issues of east or west German identity on their own, even as we discussed what it meant to them to be German, to live in Berlin, or where they felt they belonged. But when I asked them directly about differences among east and west Germans in their peer groups, they often spoke about cultural differences that remained evident between east and west Berliners. Their immediate friendships and peer groups tended not to be integrated, even though their schools and classrooms were.

Conclusion

In post-unification Germany, several intertwined national narratives that had dominated the post–World War II era have been challenged, dismantled, or otherwise transformed. Contested notions of east and west German identity, Germany's changing role in Europe, the continuing legacy and shame of the Holocaust, changing patterns of immigration, and the reform of citizenship and naturalization laws, among others, have coalesced in public debates, calling into question the very notion of what it means to be German. Throughout these transformations, however, a prevailing narrative about German national identity and, in particular, about national pride has persisted. According to this narrative, national pride is an illegitimate expression of national belonging and is linked to the rampant nationalism and racism of the Third Reich. While alternative expressions of nationhood—such as constitutional patriotism or Kulturnation—have been proposed by intellectuals, the prevailing narrative generally asserts that it is not possible to be proud of collective accomplishments. In the following chapters, I examine the ways in which these transformations are evidenced in generational differences among Germans, focusing on working-class youth and their teachers.

three

Germany's Forbidden Fruit

National Pride and National Taboos

In the midst of a public controversy about national pride in 2001, president Johannes Rau announced that one cannot be proud of something that one has not achieved oneself. It is acceptable to be glad or thankful that one is German, he claimed, "but one can't be proud of it" (Hops 2001; also see Oschlies 2001; Tagesspiegel 2001c). Rau's statement reflects a standard public narrative on German nationhood which renders unacceptable a feeling of pride in a collective, as opposed to an individual, accomplishment (Rothenberg 2002, 124). As a German civics textbook used in a classroom I observed explains:

> One can only be proud of something if there is an element of one's own accomplishment in it—if one has personally earned it. To be German means, first and foremost, to be a descendent of German parents. Only very few German citizens became citizens via naturalization. There is no cause to be proud of things that one can't do anything about. (*Leitfragen Politik* 1998, 344)

Although the prohibition on national pride is usually justified on these grounds—namely, that one can be proud only of individual, not collective, accomplishments—reactions to national pride are also inextricably linked to the virulent nationalism of the Third Reich and to the extreme right-wing in general. This was most clearly evidenced, in recent years, in a public controversy about national pride that President Rau was responding to with his comment (above) in the spring of 2001. The debate began on a radio show on the *Westdeutscher Rundfunk*, a German radio station, when Jürgen Trittin (Greens) accused Laurenz Meyer, general secretary of the Christian Democratic Union (CDU), of having the "mentality of a skinhead" and being on the level of "violent racists" for having said, during an interview for *Focus* magazine, that he was proud to be German. Trittin later apologized to Meyer for the remark, but maintained his critique of the statement, "I am proud to be German" (Hops 2001).

The remark—and the ensuing debate—made front-page headlines around the country and made the news elsewhere in the world as well (see Cohen 2001; Fried 2001; Dietrich 2001; Rudolph 2001). Within a day, politicians were scrambling to make statements about how exactly they felt about the German nation. The controversy continued for weeks, as Germany continued to be swept up in "pride" fury. Well-known politicians, academics, writers, and public figures made public statements about where they stood on the question of national pride; letters to the editor espoused multiple viewpoints from citizens, and political talk shows advertised roundtable discussions on the topic: "Are you proud to be a German?" (see, e.g., Hops 2001; Krupa 2001; Schwennicke 2001).[1]

As time passed, the semantics of the debate turned out to be extremely important; the word "patriot" was acceptable; "pride" was not. Rau argued that it is necessary to differentiate between a *patriot* and a *nationalist*; a patriot is someone who loves his fatherland, whereas a nationalist looks down on the fatherlands of others. "We need to protect ourselves from nationalistic tones," he warned. And Federal Chancellor Schröder told the *Süddeutsche Zeitung*, in a carefully worded statement, that "I am proud of the people's achievements and of the democratic culture. And in this sense, I am a German patriot who is proud of his country" (*Tagesspiegel* 2001b). Although the SPD made an effort to distance itself from Trittin—most notably when Chancellor Schröder called Trittin a "risk factor," President Rau defended him, as did the leadership of the Greens. (For a fuller account, see Fried 2001.)

The semantic difficulty around the word "pride" in the 2001 debate is one reflection of the extent to which the word for "national pride" (*Nationalstolz*) became a signifier, in the post–World War II era, for right-wing extremism, racism, and rampant nationalism. As discussed in chapter 2, the first generation to come of age in West Germany after the war—the so-called "1968 generation"—had thoroughly rejected national identity and in particular national pride, arguing that national pride is a racist and exclusionary sentiment which ultimately degenerates into rampant nationalism and the most dangerous forms of racism. Because this view of national pride survived unification more or less intact in unified Germany, the concept of national pride remained psychologically linked to racism. The phrase "I am proud to be a German," for many people, still denotes an implied superiority or racism (see also Hedetoft 1993, 288).

Although the taboo on pride is usually justified by the impossibility of feeling pride in a collective accomplishment, the taboo on national pride was born and solidified in an explicit rejection of National Socialism and the perceived dangers of national identity and national pride. It became simply unacceptable to be proud of being German or to talk about a German nation or national identity (Griffin 2004; Huyssen 1995) more generally.[2] This hegemonic moral discourse about pride forces Germans to express their relationship to the nation only in certain ways—or rather, prohibits them from expressing pride in particular terms.[3] As Andreas Glaeser observes, one cannot "say 'I am proud to be a German'" and cannot "wear the emblem of the federal armed forces, the iron cross, on [their] t-shirt," and shall not "fly black, red and gold in your front lawn."[4] In fact, prominent German scholars have even come forth, over the years, with alternative vocabulary that Germans could use instead of the term nation or national pride, such as Habermas's (1992b) notion of "constitutional patriotism" (see also Bohrer 1992; Huyssen 1995; Maier 1988) and Günter Grass's suggestion that Germans use the term *Kulturnation* instead of *nation* (Huyssen 1995, 78).

There are clearly contested views of the narrative prohibiting pride, but even some of the contested views strengthen the linkages between the word "pride" and racist or nationalistic sentiments. Organized right-wing extremist groups use national pride as part of their marketing and recruitment strategy, as I detail elsewhere (Miller-Idriss 2005). For a generation who came of age in the decades after World War II and who had intentionally rejected national pride, the use of pride by the radical right only helps to strengthen the taboo and their belief that national pride signifies racism, xenophobia, and a dangerous form of rampant nationalism. The use of the phrase "I am proud to be a German" as a measure of right-wing extremist attitudes on German social science surveys, as discussed in chapter 2, is one clear illustration of this.

Indeed, as the creation of such alternative vocabulary terms illustrates quite clearly, the sentiment of pride is perhaps less problematic than its verbal articulation. Many Germans find it acceptable to feel some measure of pride in German goods or production capabilities, in Germany's economic strengths, or in German composers, poets, novelists, or philosophers. However, there is wide variation within the population, and what appears to be unacceptable, particularly for the 1968 generation, is the verbal articulation of such pride, particularly if it is done so by the use of the phrase, "I am proud to be German." In other words, it is what pride *signifies* (Saussure 1966) that makes it taboo, not merely the sentiment. As a result, national pride remains a difficult topic for most Germans, who stammer around the topic in interviews, revising their phrasing, replacing "proud" with "happy" in talking about their relationship to the nation. Despite this difficulty, a clear trend emerged in my interviews in how members of the older and the younger generation discuss the troubled terrain of national pride.

In interviews with German teachers, both aspects of the pride taboo emerged, as many teachers noted that it is not possible to be proud of a collective, rather than an individual, accomplishment, and simultaneously talked about their inability to feel pride because of the linkages between pride, the Nazi era, and the right wing today. Older teachers in particular talked about their generation's deliberate rejection of national pride and the nation. Interviews with students show that young people are aware of and resent these pride taboos, even if they do not understand why pride is taboo. As more and more of the students I interviewed raised the issue of national pride while we were discussing what it means to be German, it became clear that a generational shift may be occurring in how Germans relate to the nation and, in particular, whether they feel proud of—or want to feel proud of—being German. These findings, therefore, illustrate both the extent to which multiple understandings of nationhood can exist simultaneously, as well as the ways in which generational shifts act as a mechanism through which national meanings can be transformed. New generations, in other words, actively re-imagine the nation.[5]

Older and Younger Generational Views on National Pride

Germans' feelings about the nation are complicated. Teachers' responses in interviews, which reveal the complexity inherent in discussions about pride, are not always consistent with their efforts in the classroom. They expressed a wide range of feelings about the nation: some categorically reject the nation and any sense of pride; some express a sense of guilt and shame for Germany's actions in World War II; some feel pride in specific aspects of German history or culture (such as the Middle Ages or the German Constitution); and some feel no particular sense of pride, but wish that they did, noting that there is a need for more German pride. Despite this wide range of responses, there was a clear trend in the patterns of teacher responses, by generation.[6] Specifically, while an older generation of teachers continues to feel significant discomfort with, and, in some cases, a strong distaste for, national pride, younger teachers are expressing more resistance to the taboo, revealing beliefs that are more consistent with their students' views about the nation than with the older generation of teachers' views.

For the generation of Germans who came of age in the 1960s, the nation was not only taboo, but something which they explicitly rejected. In the West, after two decades of near silence about the crimes committed by Germans during World War II, the student protest movement in the late 1960s was at the forefront of calling the perpetrators of the Holocaust and other war crimes to account for their participation. Herr Mais, a teacher in his early fifties, reports that when he was young, the crimes of the older generation were never talked about in schools.[7] It was the younger generation of teachers who came into schools in the 1960s, he notes, who began to introduce these topics in classrooms.

In their efforts to push for accountability, what Germans call the "Generation of 68" also consciously rejected identification with a collective national community and any sense of national pride, even as they absorbed the guilt and shame associated with World War II. National pride was thus viewed as an absurdly illegitimate expression of national belonging and one which could only lead the national community down a dangerous path of virulent nationalism and racist exclusion. Germanness, in turn, was deeply connected to emotions of guilt and shame. "In my generation, 'German' always has first to do with guilt," Frau Dann, a civics teacher in her mid-fifties, reports. Herr Martin, a teacher in his late forties, argues:

> To be a German citizen . . . one must always see it in the historical context, eh? A great, great amount of harm and misery was brought into the world, that's something . . . with which we are constantly confronted . . . therefore, in my generation one would never say that one is proud of [being a German] or anything like that. That is forbidden.

While many teachers talked about their generation's deliberate rejection of the nation, they also frequently referenced the more standard public rationale for invalidating pride—namely, that one cannot be proud of collective accomplishments. Herr Weiss, a civics teacher in his mid-fifties, observes:

For Germans it's of course more difficult than it is for the French or the English because we have to carry our history around with us . . . and German— . . . in my generation we very consciously broke away from that. And it goes so far that many people say they feel uncomfortable or something; for me it is relatively arbitrary—that I happen to have been born in Germany, that's nothing I earned, but it's also not my fault, I can't do anything about it. . . . I think in my generation it was very important that one very strongly distanced oneself from an exaggerated nationalism.

The older generation of Germans, according to Herr Weiss, thus made a deliberate break with what he simply calls "German." His quote not only notes the conscious rejection of the nation by his generation, but also reinforces the public narrative invalidating pride in a collective (rather than individual) accomplishment when he notes that being German is "nothing I earned." Other teachers agreed with the public narrative, arguing that it is not possible to be proud of collective accomplishments. Herr Weiss said that "one can only use 'pride' for something that one has accomplished oneself," while Herr Martin, a teacher in his late forties, notes that "it is hard to say that someone can be at all proud of being born in some country, that's just luck. Simply. (Laughs.) Or bad luck. One has to work hard at something in order to be proud of it." Upon further questioning, Herr Martin reiterates his point, noting that "we are here, we were born here, and that's just a lucky coincidence still . . . but there's nothing that I can be proud of in that."

Teachers' feelings about the nation are complex, however, and their responses reveal the extent to which they struggle with their own relationship to their national identity. Herr Mais explained that his generation actively confronted their parents and others who were participants in World War II: "A great displeasure developed in the younger generation, especially among the intellectual population, where one was really angry at the fact that [the older generation] didn't want to look at it." But he also acknowledges that being German has been difficult for his generation:

To be a German citizen is a difficult thing for people of my generation. Unlike in other countries, to feel German, at least in the perception of residents of neighboring countries, but also from many Germans, is very often immediately associated with, not with national pride, but with a national chauvinism.

In fact, Herr Mais wishes things were different:

I find it a little bit too bad, but on the other hand because of the historical events, it's understandable. That we have such an . . . uncertain national feeling. It has its reasons, but of course it is a bad thing because in the end people need something, to define themselves as part of something, and I think in the end such a definition also has to be positive; one can't have a definition like "I belong to the people who were the most perfectly organized industrial mass murderers," or something, that actually can't be as a national identity. So it's a very difficult thing . . . I would wish (laugh) . . . that one perhaps didn't have such a broken relationship to [the nation], but I notice that even with myself, I can't bang on my chest with a really full heart and say, "I am proud to be a German." I also think that is an unlucky statement because this statement was first used by neo-Nazis, back then . . . , so one would have to be politically blind not to see in what corner you place yourself [with that phrase], and in the end it's also nonsense . . . in the end no one can take credit for the nationality he belongs to, eh?

Thus Herr Mais expresses regret that he is unable to have a positive sense of national identity, citing the relationship of pride to Nazism and simultaneously invoking the public narrative invalidating pride in a collective identity when he ends his remarks by explaining that national pride is actually nonsense because one cannot take credit for a nationality. Herr Franz, a teacher in his mid-fifties who was born in the West, agrees:

For some people—for me it's relatively neutral—but there are people who say they are proud to be German. I can't say that. . . . If someone wants to say it, I can accept it. Although it's no achievement, whether someone can be proud, rather, one is it, simply, because one comes from there or because one lives there.

Here, although Herr Franz indicates that he is tolerant of individuals who wish to express pride, he also rejects it as a legitimate expression of national belonging. One can't be proud of merely "coming from" or "living in" a place, he contends. Other teachers explain that they are unable to feel pride because of their association of pride with the Nazi era. Frau Stein, who was born in the East and is now in her early fifties, reports that she carries too much guilt about World War II to ever be able to say she is proud to be German: "'Yeah, I'm proud to be

German.' I can't say that. . . . Because, perhaps there is too much of a guilty consciousness with it, although I myself can't claim any personal responsibility for . . . things from the Second World War; I was born after the war."

Other teachers in the older generation agree that pride in the nation is simply not possible, although some were more explicit than others in expressing their beliefs about the illegitimacy of national pride, as we will see in chapter 4. Herr Meyer, a civics teacher in his mid-thirties, believes that pride is always linked to the radical right: "The problem is that as soon as there is a certain national pride, the media shoves it into the National Socialistic corner."

Younger teachers in particular emphasized that the taboo on pride should be relaxed. Herr Metzer, a teacher born in the West who is now in his early forties, does not personally identify very strongly with Germany, but feels nonetheless that it is now time to relax some of the prohibitions on German national identity:

Being a German citizen, for me . . . is a particular responsibility in the sense of ensuring that Germanness is not conceived of in a narrowly ethnic way, rather, to call upon Herr Habermas, rather it should be a form of constitutional patriotism, beyond that though, Germanness is actually not especially important to me. . . . And I think, I don't really know if one needs a positive national feeling in order to be happy in this country. I still consider this difficult, in the context of the Second World War that I was discussing earlier, but I also think that in some ways we could now see it in a more relaxed way.

Other teachers—particularly younger ones—expressed an even stronger desire to break down the taboo on national pride. Frau Schmidt, a teacher in her early thirties, argued that Germans "probably need much more of a normal relationship to our country" and that "we lack a normality with our patriotism, still. Unfortunately." Herr Preuss, who was born in the East and is now in his early thirties, was one of the youngest teachers I interviewed and argues that his generation should be allowed to be proud:

In the end we must indeed preserve it, this . . . thing that concerns National Socialism and . . . and also always warn, always show that what happened took place because of errors, from obedience, from subordination, [but] on the other side . . . I don't carry, our generation [carries] no guilt . . . and therefore one can, in my eyes, be proud to be German, right?

Herr Preuss also expresses frustration at how national pride is tagged as a right-wing extremist statement: "No one trusts themselves to say it publicly, at social, public events . . . or in sport. . . . [Pride] is immediately saddled with radicalism, nationalism." And Herr Meyer talked at length about his relationship to Germanness:

> Earlier I was taught, as a German, to carry guilt for the history. In school [I was taught that]. In the media and so on and so forth . . . and then at some point there was a change. I would say, toward the end of [my] twenties, as I began to work, my image shifted, that I didn't see guilt in the history, and that I, that I simply find it sick in Germany that we have no healthy national pride.

Not all of the younger teachers I interviewed desired a healthy national pride. Frau Main, a civics teacher in her late twenties, says that she is "not exactly proud of the word 'Germany'" because of Germany's history and said that she doesn't like the word 'nation' "because for me it is always connected to National Soc-, nationalism . . . with Hitler's time." But Frau Schmidt, Herr Preuss, and Herr Meyer, civics teachers in their early-to-mid-thirties who bridge the older and the younger generations whose attitudes form the basis of this book, all believe that a younger generation should be permitted to express national pride. Their views are consistent with the perspectives of the students I interviewed, as the following sections detail.

Internalizing the Taboo on National Pride

Some of the younger generation has internalized the very taboo on national pride expressed by their teachers, textbooks, the media, and other adults in their lives. Although the dominant trend in our conversations about national pride reflected students' resistance to the taboo on national pride, many of these young people simultaneously explained either that it is impossible to be proud of being German because of Germany's role in World War II, or that pride is not a concept that can be expressed for collective accomplishments. Twenty-one of the young people I interviewed referred to national pride as a taboo or stated simply that it is not possible to be proud. Henning, an eighteen-year-old future scaffold-builder, reports:

> Hmm . . . to be German . . . well I don't want to say that I'm proud to be a German, because the Germans have made a whole lot of mistakes,

I'd say, in the last fifty years or . . . hundred years, regarding the war and everything, that was shitty.

Here, Henning says that he doesn't want to express pride because of the fact that Germans have made mistakes. For him, it appears that expressing pride in being German would imply he was also proud of Germany's past in World War II. Other young people explained that they were not proud of being German simply because a sense of pride in a collective identity is not possible and suggested that pride is a sentiment which can only be felt for one's own accomplishments. This is a clear reflection of the public narrative on national pride, as reflected in the statement by President Rau above as well as in the excerpt from a civics textbook. Detlef, a twenty-three-year-old cook apprentice reports:

> One can't simply say this sentence: "I am proud to be a German" . . . that comes across as if one wants to place oneself over everyone else, I'd say. . . . Well, what I personally think, there is no "proud to be German" for me. . . . There is no way in which I am proud—only of myself or what comes from my family.

In addition to explaining—in a reflection of the explicit aspects of the taboo on pride—that he can be proud only of accomplishments that come from his family or from himself (and not from the nation), Detlef also indicates that expressing pride in being German necessarily implies a sense of superiority over others. Another clear reflection of the taboo on national pride came from Sarah, a twenty-year-old technical-drafting student at the construction school, who described a debate that her civics class had just had about the issue of national pride. In her discussion, she reveals not only that the class felt national pride was not possible—but also links feelings of national pride to xenophobia and racism. The debate, she observes,

> [was] about the word "pride" and that many (people) think in a negative . . . no . . . that they associate negatives with "pride." And it was about this (phrase) "I am proud to be a German" and German citizens . . . and the large part of the class said that it's total crap, one can't be proud of something that one didn't do anything for, one was just born here, one is a German citizen and that's it.
> CMI: And is that your opinion too?
> Sarah: Yes. Well I would never judge someone because of their color or their citizenship or something else—

CMI: Was there an actual debate then, or was the whole class . . .

Sarah: Yes, there was a discussion, I mean in that class not everyone participates, but a lot do, and we were really all in agreement that one can't be proud of something like that. Because that's exactly as if one said, "I am proud that I was born."

Sarah's description of the class debate is intriguing for several reasons. When she described the majority of the class as being of the opinion that pride can be felt only for individual, not collective, accomplishments, I followed up by asking whether she also had the same opinion. Although my question referred directly to her previous comment about national pride, her response—that she would never judge someone by the color of their skin or because of their citizenship—reveals how clearly the notion of national pride is linked in her mind to racism and xenophobia. As she returns to a direct discussion of national pride, however, she reverts to the public narrative about pride: namely, that one cannot be proud of things one has not achieved oneself.

For some of the students I interviewed, national pride has been internalized as a right-wing concept, supporting a broader public narrative in which national pride is automatically or implicitly linked to the right wing. Eleven of the sixty young people I interviewed identified national pride as a right-wing concept or linked pride to the right wing in their discussions of the topic. Heike, an eighteen-year-old technical-drafting student suggests:

What it means to be German, that is simply . . . well there are again two things, on the one hand right (wing), there a right-winger says he is proud to be a German, and other citizens say it means nothing to them to be German.

For Heike, clearly, only someone who identifies as a member of the extreme or radical right would say he or she is proud to be German. Moreover, anyone who is not right wing has no identification with being German at all. Peter, a twenty-five-year-old information-technology apprentice, also clearly identifies the concept of national pride with the extreme right, noting that there is a difference between two expressions of German identity: "The sentence, 'I am happy to be a German' is totally different from 'I am proud to be a German' because that's a right-wing extremist sentence."

Although, as these examples reveal, there were a few students whose comments indicate that they believe national pride is simply a right-wing concept, the right wing came up much more frequently during discussions of national pride in cases where students talked about how unfair it is that pride is automatically linked to right-wing extremism. Joerg, a twenty-two-year-old Turkish-German male, born in West Berlin and training for a career in information technology, remarked:

> The only problem in Germany is that, that one can't say "I am proud to be a German." That can't be said because "I am proud to be a German" is always negatively associated with Germany's history. . . . You can't say it because of the Nazi-, Nazi, here, because of Hitler back then.

Here, Joerg does explain that the phrase "I am proud to be a German" is linked to Germany's National Socialist past, but he describes this as a "problem" rather than a simple statement of fact. And Jochen, a twenty-one-year-old cook apprentice, reports:

> I find it somehow really nice to be German because I like the whole social system. I think it is still one of the best in the world, one is so well insured here. But somehow it's not in fashion to be proud of being German, and. It's, I have a little problem with that because it's simply, then right away you are perceived as a right-wing radical, or a Nazi. And I don't like that.

Similarly to Joerg, Jochen senses that national pride automatically links one to the extreme right-wing, but unlike Joerg, he does not ground this in Germany's history in World War II. Instead, he explains it is not "in fashion" to be proud of being German, implying that there is something arbitrary about the taboo on national pride. Without a fuller understanding of the rationale for the taboo, young people like Jochen may feel even more resentment of it. Even students who did not automatically link the notion of national pride to the right wing clearly recognize that national pride is delegitimized by society, and many of them feel directly affronted by the taboo on national pride. Alexander, a twenty-four-year-old hotel worker trainee explains, in response to a follow-up question about a comment he made regarding identifying with a state:

> Well, there are a lot of Germans now in my age group . . . who really have a lot of problems with this expression because . . . one doesn't just say, "Yes, I'm proud to be a German," those are all expressions, they are a little bit taboo, yeah?

Alexander explicitly references his generation in talking about the constraints on expressing national pride, which he identifies as a taboo. This taboo is not simply something that exists passively, moreover. Rather, these young people perceive that if they attempt to express national pride, they will be shunned by others—both Germans and non-Germans. Anja, an eighteen-year-old hotel worker trainee, born in East Berlin, remarked simply: "If I ran around here saying, 'I am proud to be a German,' then it would immediately be, 'You racist, you.'"

Anja's perception is that pride in being German is directly linked with racism and that expressions of national pride are interpreted by others as racist remarks or as indicative of racist beliefs. According to these young people's perceptions, the prevailing narrative about national pride in Germany today continues to be anti-pride. This is also consistent with the classroom observations that I discuss in chapter 4. These young people's discussions about national pride also reveal, however, that in many ways, they simply conceive and understand pride differently than their parents and teachers. With the exception of the students quoted above whose comments indicate that they conceive of pride in ways that are in concert with the taboo on national pride, most of these young people's views on pride reveal that they think about national pride in importantly different ways.

This means that the signification of national pride is splintering in Germany along generational lines. For an older generation, as discussed above, pride cannot be expressed in anything other than individual accomplishments. When national pride is expressed, it signifies racism and rampant nationalism. For a generation of Germans in their late teens and early twenties, however, being proud of being German does not prevent one from acknowledging the horrors of the Holocaust and does not mean that one thinks one's own nation is superior to others. Pride, for many members of the younger generation, reflects a normal relationship to the nation and a sense of pride in Germany's economic, social, and cultural accomplishments, or aspects of Germanness that either predate World War II or have been achieved in the postwar era. Finally, for a select group of young people who spent the first half of their lives in East Germany and remember vibrant displays of (East) German pride, I discovered that the taboo on national pride is confusing. Pride, for these young people, is something which has been taken away from them. In various ways—whether due to generational claims, definitional differences, or patterns of (n)ostalgia (see Berdahl

1999)—the relationship between the term "national pride" and what it signifies is shifting in Germany, helping to further splinter the national narrative that has placed a taboo on expressions of national pride for decades and thus illustrating the processes through which understandings of the nation can be transformed and re-imagined. The following sections discuss the shifting signification of national pride in greater detail.

The Shifting Signification of National Pride

These young people's discussions of national pride reveal that even when they recognize the signification of national pride as linked to the right wing, they often define national pride differently than it is defined by an older generation. Most of the young people I interviewed view national pride as something normal and desirable: pride is something which they feel is denied to them and which they would like to be able to express. They feel that national pride is something important—a necessary and natural emotion. Enrico, a twenty-four-year-old, training in information technology and born in East Germany, observes:

> Clearly, I'd say that everyone somewhere is a little bit proud of his country and . . . if a Frenchman says, "I am proud to be a Frenchman," then he's not accused of having an exaggerated sense of national pride; it's simply the case that, well, somewhere one has achieved something in this country, or the country has achieved something that it's worth living for and I'm totally simply proud of that.

Enrico's perception is that national pride is a normal part of belonging to a country. "Everyone somewhere" is proud of his or her nationality, but only Germans are taken to task for it, he complains. Moreover, he argues that having achieved something as a country or having achieved something in a country should allow one to be proud of that country. This is a direct—albeit perhaps subconscious—response to the public narrative about pride in Germany, as expressed through President Rau's claim that it is acceptable to be proud only of one's own achievement and that being German does not count as an achievement, as discussed earlier in this chapter.

There are other reasons why young people felt that it should be acceptable to be proud of being German. Stefan, a twenty-one-year-old mason apprentice at the construction school, born in East Germany, reports:

Yes, I think you should know where you come from and what you [stand] for . . . I mean somewhere you have ideals for your country or a little bit of pride and you should be allowed to represent that, everyone has that.

Again, Stefan argues that "everyone" has the feeling of national pride, but it is not permissible to express or "represent" it. Here, pride is connected to wanting something more for a country, to having "ideals," and to a sense of national identity and principles that are broader than individual needs. Like Enrico, Stefan clearly feels that national pride is currently not permissible and would like it to be allowed.

Sometimes students extended the taboo beyond the issue of national pride, claiming that Germans are not permitted to have a sense of national identity at all. Kai, a nineteen-year-old communications-electrician trainee at the IT school, born in East Germany, explains:

Kai: Well, the French and so on have a "we-feeling" and Germans should also have that, even if I didn't know how I should express it, but you should have the permission to maintain a certain "we-feeling."
CMI: And you think that you don't have this permission now?
Kai: I don't have it, no.
CMI: And why do you think it's important to have this "we-feeling"?
Kai: Well, because a person can't exist without a "we-feeling," clearly. A person has to know what he . . . why he is there and who is there for him, that's important for a person.

Using the phrase "we-feeling," Kai's explanation begins with the same argument about national pride as evidenced in the previous two quotes: namely, that national identity is a normal expression, that other countries are allowed to express it, and that Germans also should be allowed to do so. He believes it is so important, moreover, that people "can't exist" without it. National identity, Kai believes, is even an explanation for why one exists ("why he is there") and helps identify who ought to offer support when support is needed ("who is there for him"). As it became clear that Kai believes that having a "we-feeling" is critical to the actual existence of a collectivity, but also feels that Germans aren't permitted to have this feeling, I asked him to explain this contradiction. What is it that the Germans do to exist, according to Kai, if they don't exist through a "we-feeling"? Kai's response further clarifies his understanding of the boundaries of the taboo on national pride:

Well, he defines himself then through work (laughs). Through such things. That actually don't have much to do with life, that is more like, a matter that they managed to force somehow and the language, the language, yeah. Because they are still allowed to identify through the language, well no one takes offense at that, I'd say . . . well one says "I speak German, I am proud to speak German," one is still allowed to say that, through that the people still find (themselves) together, but one is not allowed to say, "I am proud to be a German," or something, that's not possible.

In fact, these young people's discussions about the naturalness of national pride reveal just how differently they conceive of and define national pride, compared with the understanding of national pride reflected in the prevailing public narrative about national pride in Germany. As I explained in further detail earlier in this chapter, part of the taboo about German national pride results from the fact that during the Third Reich, national pride was directly linked to racism and eventually to the attempted extermination of those who were considered inferior to the Germans. But the young people I interviewed do not define national belonging in ethnic terms—instead, as chapter 6 details, I found that they draw primarily on cultural characteristics to determine who is a German and draw on cultural elements to explain their understanding of the German nation. Culture is, furthermore, the most common factor in students' definitions of the German nation, which according to these young people, is not made up of a Volk based on ethnic or racial elements, but rather of people living within the borders of a geographic space who feel connected to that place. As Frank, a future scaffold-builder, explained, "I think the nation is pieced together out of the people who feel bound to Germany."

If the taboo on national pride is in part a result of an understanding of national pride that refers to ethnic or racial superiority over other groups, but young people's own definitions of Germanness or desire for national pride does not rely on or reflect ethnic or racial elements, then their resistance to the taboo—and their desire to rearticulate national pride—might be understood in *definitional* terms. These young people define Germanness and pride in ways that are different from the understandings inherent to the taboo on national pride, so they therefore see the taboo as unfair. Moreover, these young people also clearly feel—in opposition to the typical signification of pride—that pride can refer to collective accomplishments (such as those of a nation) and not only to individual accomplishments.

This "definitional resistance" occurs because students are resisting the taboo on national pride based on a different understanding—or definition—of pride. As Enrico, an information-technology apprentice, reports, "and um, I think that national pride doesn't have anything to do with whether you're a fascist or a National Socialist, you are simply conscious of your nationality."

Young Germans' resistance to the taboo on national pride, in other words, can be understood in part because they define Germanness and national pride in terms that are very different from the way it is typically perceived. While the taboo is premised in part on an understanding of national pride as directly linked to feelings of ethnic or racial superiority vis-à-vis other groups and to the extreme right-wing, most of these students define Germanness in cultural terms and see national pride as a normal expression related to the accomplishments of a given nation, and they are therefore resentful and angry about a taboo that they perceive to be unfair. As I discovered, their desire to be proud of being German reflects a wish to be proud of the same kinds of elements they use in defining the German nation—Germany's accomplishments, the progress it has made in rebuilding after unification, and its political decisions, among others. They are proud of Germany's social, educational, and legal systems, especially the social welfare system and safety net, the high-quality products, and of Germany's role in helping other nations in need, particularly by providing international humanitarian assistance. They also draw on pre–World War II German history and culture, especially famous German authors and writers, geographic elements, and contemporary sports heroes.

Students' explanations of what they are proud of often began with a disclaimer about Germany's past in the Third Reich, before turning to the precise elements that they are proud of about Germany—or what they would like to be proud of, if they were permitted to express pride. The following excerpt, expressed by Daniel, a nineteen-year-old concrete-worker apprentice who was born in East Germany, is typical:

Daniel: I'm a German, OK . . . I can't do anything about that, in that sense, well, I am proud to be a German, but . . . I wouldn't be weeping if I . . . was English or something.

CMI: And what are you proud of?

Daniel: How the whole social system is here, that in that sense you're not neglected, that you'll not be left on the street, in the sense that there are offices that do something for you, and that's typical of Germany,

I'd say. In that sense it's nice, that we probably, or that we never, if the system stays like this, that we actually never would have problems . . . that we always have food to eat.

According to Daniel, Germanness is not an essential part of his identity. It would be acceptable to be another nationality (at least one like English), but he happens to be German and is proud of the safety net built into the German system and the fact that one is not abandoned to the street, to hunger, or to extreme poverty. This was a frequent explanation of why students were proud to be German. Marcel, a nineteen-year-old communications-electrician trainee who was born in East Germany, explains:

Hmmm . . . somehow I am also proud, not that I'm proud of the things that Germany did [back then], but rather of the education system, the social system, I could say that everything is well organized. I'm also proud to live here, of the human rights, the politics . . . I'm also personally proud of it.

Marcel makes a clear differentiation between things that it is acceptable to be proud of (the social system, the education system, human rights and politics) and things it is not acceptable to be proud of (World War II) and implies that it is possible to be proud of Germany despite Germany's role in World War II. Marcel's claim contradicts the prevailing public narrative about national pride, namely, that it is unacceptable to be proud of collective accomplishments. It also challenges the implicit link between national pride and exclusionary or racist sentiments.

Even as students discussed what it is they are proud of, the taboo on expressing national pride was never far from their minds, as Matthias, a twenty-year-old information-technology apprentice illustrates:

In and of itself it's not a mistake to say that I'm proud of it because . . . that I live in Germany, because if things are going bad for me . . . then I know I have health insurance, that means I don't have to worry how I will get the money for an operation and so forth, and that makes one proud somehow, and it also makes one proud to work here and that through that other citizens who don't have work—with the money that one earns, one gives a small part of it up as unemployment insurance, and that they can live a little from that, and everything like that makes me proud, the only thing that bothers me is that really this sentence, "I am proud to be a German," that that is really pushed into the negative because the wrong people often use it.

Matthias argues that it is not wrong to be proud of being German or to express pride and references elements similar to those from other students in explaining what he is proud of. But he also acknowledges that "the wrong people" (i.e., the extreme right-wing) use national pride and believes that the taboo is perpetuated by the explicit use of pride by the right wing.

Throughout our conversations, these young people's rearticulation of national pride continues to reveal the ways in which the signification of national pride has shifted and is shifting, from signifying racism and rampant nationalism to signifying a "normal" relationship to the nation and pride in the social welfare system, economy, and quality of life in Germany. The following section discusses the ways in which these young people drew on generational claims as a justification for this resignification of national pride and a changed relationship to the nation.

Generational Claims: Changing Meaning in a New Germany

The young people I interviewed argue that their generation should have a different relationship to the nation. Born into the third generation after World War II, they feel increasingly distanced from the war and the crimes carried out by their grandparents' generation. They feel angry at being made to feel responsible for the actions of older Germans and frequently referenced their own generation when voicing resistance to the taboo on national pride, arguing in particular that the taboo on national identity was unfair because their generation had nothing to do with the Third Reich. Enrico, an information-technology apprentice, observed:

> Here in Germany, if you say that you're proud of your country, then you'll be immediately written off as a fascist or a Nazi but . . . that's the problem, you're judged so superficially. . . . We're always being remonstrated about something from our past . . . but really, no one knows what my past is and . . . what happened fifty years ago, that isn't my past, I can't identify with that, and as long as . . . these remonstrative guilt feelings don't stop, until then you won't be able to say that you're proud of your country.

This was a typical response of these young people to the question "What does it mean to be German?" Born in the late 1970s, Enrico says he "can't identify" with what happened in National Socialism and feels unjustly judged. Claims like this one, about a general sense of unfairness in the attribution of blame and guilt for World War II, were frequent among these respondents.

Students' discussions of the taboo on pride often dovetailed with complaints that Germany is held to a different standard than other countries, which they argued is unfair to their generation (Stierstorfer 2003). As Dirk, a future concrete-worker, remarked, "In France they've closed their borders, but if Germany did that, then it would be, 'yeah, you crappy Nazis, you don't want the foreigners.'" Many of the young people I interviewed had traveled outside of Germany on school trips, usually within the European Union, and based their perceptions of foreign countries' views of Germany on their experiences while traveling. Others referenced the depiction of Germans in Hollywood films, foreign newspapers and television programs, and comments made in internet chat rooms. Kai, training in information technology, explained:

> Because for example you can't say "I am proud to be a German." Because then you are immediately . . . you hear, "well, then you identify also with Germany's past" . . . that makes it hard, Frenchmen, the English, the Spaniards are all allowed to [be proud], and we are not allowed. . . . People take offense at it . . . it's as if you think that German history around 1940 was great and that you have an immediate aversion to foreigners and to everything that's not German . . . that's how you're depicted.

International comparisons about national pride also play a role in these young people's justification for the desire for national pride. Jochen, a cook apprentice, reports:

> For example, what I always find so great is, in America, well maybe it's also a little exaggerated, maybe I just see that in films. There almost anyone can run around with an American flag on his jacket. If I put a German flag on my jacket, I've already lost, well. And that is, those are the little things. Well, it doesn't work here, it's not possible. I think, as an American one can be proud of his country, and there one isn't right (wing) then, there one is simply only a proud American, and that doesn't work here and that's not good.

Whether referring to the internal taboo on national pride or the perceived constraints on expressions of national pride imposed by foreign countries and outsiders, students referenced the fact that Germany has changed as a country since World War II and that it is not fair to assume that Germans' views have not changed along with other changes in the country. Alexander, a twenty-four-year-old skilled hotel worker trainee born in West Germany, who had traveled extensively in foreign countries and talked a great deal in the interview about the prejudices he had encountered against Germans overseas, simply stated, "There is still this old image of Germany. And we . . . there is a new Germany, somehow. Everyone is not the way [they were back then]. I think a lot has changed." And Markus, a twenty-one-year-old scaffold-builder apprentice born in East Germany, observed that "as a German you take a lot of crap, although it's not like that at all anymore, and that's the thing. We haven't all been right wing for a long time now, the way it's depicted on the outside."

The apparent shift in a younger generation's view about pride was also illustrated in one classroom observation with a young teacher, who was only a few years older than some of her students. In a deviation from educational practice which supports the taboo on national pride, this teacher raised the issue of national pride in a more positive sense. During a reflection session after a class field trip, she told the class that she thought it was time for Germans to be allowed to express national pride. Since this teacher was only a few years older than most of her students, this observation appears to support patterns of generational resistance as well.

Young people not only referenced the unfairness of the pride taboo when talking about their German identity, some students also claimed that their generation has a particular obligation and responsibility to address the Third Reich, especially in the sense that they should learn from the mistakes of their forefathers. Yet they also feel that this responsibility should not prevent them from expressing pride in being German and that they should not be made to feel guilty for what happened during the Holocaust. A balance is necessary, as Benjamin, a twenty-two-year-old IT system electrician trainee born in East Germany, reports:

> What it means to be German? First of all, it means a lot of responsibility . . . because of the Third Reich and the suffering, the suffering that happened to them, that that can't be so easily forgotten and certainly should

not be so easily forgotten . . . but because of that for me, as the third generation after, so many stones so to say are laid in the way. . . . People should remain conscious of what happened then, but . . . the chance should also be given to show, "Hey look, I am a German. I have this history, but I don't belong to that. I didn't live it then and didn't experience it and give me a chance to show what it means now to be German." Well, to show that one can also be open to the world.

As Benjamin explains, Germans in the third generation should never forget what happened in World War II, but neither should they be held directly responsible for it. Germans of his generation have earned the right to show "what it means now to be German," he argues. In fact, patriotism was directly linked to the responsibility to remember Germany's role in World War II, at least for some students. Klaus, a twenty-two-year-old construction worker trainee born in West Germany, believes that in Germany, national pride comes with a particular responsibility:

Because . . . you can also be proud to be a German, despite what happened historically . . . because, well, precisely because of that, if you are proud to be a German for example . . . well, "proud" is the wrong word . . . if you are a patriot . . . have a patriotic feeling . . . , then you also have the duty to understand what happened in the second World War and you also have the duty . . . as a citizen of this country, . . . to always remind the ones who came after, and the next generation, of it.

This short excerpt also reveals some of the semantic difficulties that students encounter when discussing national pride. Because the very word "pride" is so taboo, students sometimes stopped themselves from using the word, or interrupted themselves to explain what they meant by pride. Here, Klaus caught himself using the word "proud" and then interrupted his comment to explain that "'proud' is the wrong word." After replacing the phrase "proud to be a German" with "if you are a patriot, have a patriotic feeling," he could continue on with his point.

To sum up, a clear trend in young people's responses during discussions of national pride was to resist the taboo on national pride based on generational claims and an appeal to fairness for the third generation after World War II. Although some of these students feel that there is a responsibility attached to being German as a result of World War II and the Holocaust, they also believe that they should not be held directly accountable for the actions of their grandparents' generation and feel that the taboo on national pride is a direct result of just such an imposed accountability. They also perceive the reactions of other nations to Germany as negative and believe that Germany is held to a different standard because of its role in World War II, which they feel is unfair to their generation.

A final intriguing element related to issues of national pride that emerged during the analysis of these interviews relates to young people's experience in the former German Democratic Republic (GDR). For young Germans born in the former East Germany, pride in the GDR was strongly encouraged and easily expressed, and some of them feel that the ability to express pride has been taken away from them.

Forty-one of the students I interviewed were born in East Germany, and because they were aged seventeen to twenty-five, most were old enough at the time of unification to have had some significant experiences as young people in the system, although they were not old enough, generally speaking, to have reached an age of critical political consciousness. Their early experiences in the GDR were still formative, however, and several of these young people made specific reference to their memories of national pride in the former GDR in the context of discussing the taboo on national pride.

I label the pattern of these responses "(n)ostalgia," a term used to refer to the specific nostalgia that East Germans have expressed since 1989 for aspects of culture or daily life in the former GDR (see Berdahl 1999). Although east Germans did not necessarily discuss pride more often or in qualitatively different terms during the interviews when compared with their west German peers, they did sometimes add a justification for their resistance to the taboo on national pride and for their desire to be proud—namely, that they were allowed to be (and encouraged to be) proud in the former East Germany. While we were discussing his earlier comment that it's not in fashion to be proud of being German, I asked Jochen, a cook apprentice, whether this had always been the case. As he explains, national pride was a part of the experience of being East German because

> with us, well, in the East it was, one was raised with a certain national pride. We were all in these Pioneer groups and I was allowed to wear my blue neck scarf, and my red one. And we were, yeah, proud *Ossis* [East Germans], I would say, proud citizens of the GDR. And yeah, now it's like, the people who are still proud of their country now, they mostly cover it up, and then, yeah. You have the choice. Either you say, you

turn your back on Germany, or you are proud of it, but then you have to accept that you'll be labeled as a Nazi.

According to Jochen, expressions of national pride are not only taboo but are interpreted as expressions of right-wing and antiforeigner attitudes. Moreover, in using the phrase, "the people who are *still* proud of their country now" (emphasis added), Jochen reveals that he thinks of the experience of Germanness as continuous—that is, the East Germans he talks about were not proud of a different country—rather, they were proud of being German, and the option to be proud has been taken away from them. Those who are *still* proud "mostly cover it up."

Jochen's perception that national pride was encouraged in the GDR is supported by evidence from the East German educational system. Peggy Piesche (2002, 55), for example, documents the importance of national pride in the socialization processes of the former East Germany, explaining how schooling emphasized identification with the nation and quoting the GDR's Education Law of 1965, which identified the task of schools as, among others, to raise young people so "that they feel, think, and act as patriots of their socialist fatherland and as proletarian internationalists."

As Piesche illustrates, there is some support for these young people's perception that the "national feeling" was stronger in the GDR. But it is also important to bear in mind that some of these sentiments may be directly related to the particular age that these young people were at the time of the GDR's collapse. They were old enough to have experienced some of the political socialization that took place in the former GDR, but they had likely not reached an age of critical political consciousness and were most likely passive participants in the events leading up to the Wende in 1989. If this is the case, their memories of pride in East Germany may have largely remained untainted by the cynicism that their older peers or family members developed as they increasingly began to demand political changes in the GDR. Similarly, they may be less bitter about what many eastern Germans perceive as a failure of the GDR to implement reforms rather than "capitulate" to a West German "takeover" through unification. Whatever the underlying reason, however, it does appear that young eastern Germans have an additional and unique expression of resistance to the taboo on national pride, directly related to what they perceive as a loss of pride compared to their memories of national pride in the GDR.

The previous sections have demonstrated that some German young people today are, by and large, resisting what they perceive to be a continuing taboo on national pride and are reconstructing a view of the nation that permits a pride in collective accomplishments of the nation. Because this conception of nationhood differs so clearly from the public narrative which prohibits pride in the nation or in collective accomplishments, this finding demonstrates that multiple conceptions of nationhood can exist simultaneously. It also reveals how the changing signification of a concept like "pride" can act as a mechanism that splinters a public national meaning. The views of this younger generation of working-class youth, however, are not acknowledged or valued as legitimate alternative conceptions of nationhood; instead, they are relegated to the realm of taboo expressions of national identification and tagged as right-wing extremist sentiments.[8] In the media, in presidential speeches, in classroom discussions, and even in school textbooks, these young people are bombarded with messages that present national pride as an illegitimate expression of national belonging, that indicate that national pride implies a sense of racist superiority, and that tell young people, quite clearly, that it is morally wrong to feel pride.

Understanding Generational Differences

Teachers are not unaware of their students' desire to express pride. Indeed, many of the teachers I interviewed clearly indicated that they realize that young people want to express pride or that they understand the difficulty that the taboo on pride poses for their students, who are a further generation removed from the atrocities of World War II. Even when teachers do not themselves feel any sense of national pride, they nevertheless may understand their students' desire for pride. Although Herr Weiss thinks that the phrase "I am proud to be a German" is "moronic," for example, he acknowledges that "they [students] apparently need it, they must be allowed to react to their nationality somehow emotionally . . . and for them that's pride, then." Herr Martin observes:

> I do have the feeling that the students go more in the direction of saying, well what's up with that . . . why can't we, can we identify more and say, it's actually great to be here, to live in Germany or it's actually great to be a German or something like that. Why is it always dictated to us, that "yeah, psst, just don't say you are proud to be German" and so, "racism, racism," or something like that.

Teachers remain wary of national pride, however, and of its potential connections to right-wing extremism, as I discuss more in chapter 5. Herr Metzer, the forty-one-year-old teacher quoted earlier, told me that Germany's history in World War II makes it difficult to have a positive national feeling. But he also says, "I can understand it, when young people say that they would like to—in certain respects—be allowed to behave [toward the nation] positively." He then issues a warning, though, with an oblique reference to the radical right: "Whereby I would always want to note that there was no- . . . yes, that there the question is, what the content of the whole thing is. . . . 'Nation' is after all just a hollow expression."

Some teachers also understand that the taboo on pride contributes to their students' anger. Herr Mais, a teacher in his early fifties, suggests that "this broken relationship that my generation has to Germanness and so on, that's not there for them, y'know? They do get it, that a lot of people have this [broken relationship] in Germany, but for them that creates a lack of understanding and, in part, also anger."

While many teachers appear to be aware of the interest in pride among their students, the students do not seem to understand the reasons behind an older generation's concerns about the nation and their prohibition on national pride. Only one student referenced generational differences. In some detail, Benjamin, a twenty-two-year-old information-technology apprentice, described differences in conceptions of the nation between an older, a middle, and a younger generation. He sees "large, serious differences" between the different age groups in Germany in terms of how they relate to the German nation. The connection between the nation and the Third Reich is "still ringing in the ears" for the oldest generation, he notes. But what he calls the "make love not war and so on generation of 68" stands in opposition to the oldest generation and are "against everything totalitarian in principle." He sees a split in the youngest generation, to which he belongs and who "have to live with the history that we had absolutely no influence over." Most of Benjamin's peers, he observes, are defined by consumption and consumerism rather than by their relationship to the nation, noting that for the majority of his generation

the German nation is no longer something important or something tangible or something life-sustaining [*Lebensbestimmendes*] as it was for the previous generations, who were either totally for it or who defined themselves in opposition to it (*der ihren Sinn darin bestand dagegen zu sein*) as with the generation of 68.

But for others in his generation who are not doing well financially or who are having other problems with school or girlfriends, he describes a risk of potentially "falling back" like the oldest generation. These "losers of the consumer society" reach to fascism or neo-Nazism as the nation becomes a place where they can "try to compensate."

Benjamin's understanding of generational differences in Germans' relationships with the nation is unique among his peers, however, at least according to the findings from my interviews. It is also worth noting that Benjamin, like a few of the teachers interviewed, additionally noted that age doesn't account for all of the differences in conceptions of the nation—social differences as well as one's background and environment are also important, he argues.

A Broader Shift in the National Pride Taboo

With the exception of right-wing extremists (who loudly express national pride), a public narrative prohibiting pride—the roots of which can be traced primarily to the former West Germany—has remained strongly present in Germany since unification. This narrative renders national pride an unacceptable and illegitimate expression of national belonging and allows the word "pride" to be used to refer only to individual, not collective or national, accomplishments. It remains difficult for Germans to say the words, "I am proud to be German," without being automatically linked to the extreme right-wing.

As this chapter has detailed, however, a generational shift is taking place in Germany around the troubled terrain of national pride. An older generation of teachers—particularly those who came of age as part of the generation of 1968—largely have significant difficulty with the concept of national pride, whether it is because they reject the nation more generally, because they feel guilt or shame for Germany's actions during World War II, or because they feel that pride is something to be felt only for individual, not collective, accomplishments. Their students, however, more generally resist the taboo on national pride in several ways that help to illustrate how generational shifts can help transform the meaning of the nation.

The younger generation expresses *definitional resistance* when their justifications for national.pride reveal the extent to which pride simply signifies something different for them than it did for their parents' generation. For an older generation of Germans, particularly in the west, national pride signifies rampant nationalism and racism. Moreover, it is deemed to be impossible to take pride in a collective accomplishment. For a younger generation of Germans, national pride signifies a normal relationship to the nation, and pride is desired or expressed for the social welfare, education, and political systems and Germany's economic and technological accomplishments since World War II. These young people also expressed a second form of resistance, which I have labeled *generational resistance*, based on a claim to bearing a different generational relationship to the Holocaust. According to this argument, Germans today can acknowledge the horrors of the Holocaust and accept responsibility for teaching future generations so that nothing like it occurs again, but this should not prohibit pride in the country's collective accomplishments, culture, and history before and after World War II. Finally, for a specific group of young Germans who spent significant time in the former East Germany, a unique category of responses to the pride taboo is categorized as *(n)ostalgia*. For young Germans born in the former East Germany, pride in the nation was strongly encouraged and easily expressed. Their perception is that the ability to express pride has been taken away from them.

Whatever form young people's resistance takes, it seems clear that a shift is taking place in Germany around the question of national pride, as a younger generation actively re-imagines the German nation. Younger Germans perceive a taboo on national pride as unfair and outdated and argue for the permissibility of expressions of national pride based on Germany's achievements since World War II. Some gradual shifts in broader society seem evident as well. During the summer of 2002, in the wake of Germany's loss in the final round of the World Cup, Germans greeted the returning team like heroes, one teacher reported to me, describing never having seen so many flags in the street. The flags appeared to indicate a shift in Germans' feelings about the nation and the emergence of a "normal" expression of national pride. And some willingness to accept pride as a sentiment has been forthcoming from national leaders, even if the word "pride" itself remains problematic. In December 2001, for example, Wolfgang Schäuble (2001), a former and current minister of the interior (CDU), published an article in a leading national newspaper, the *Süddeutsche Zeitung*, entitled "It Doesn't Have to Be Pride, Exactly." Schäuble argues that even if the word "pride" is too complicated because it admittedly "doesn't pass over everyone's lips easily," the sentiment is necessary: "Love of fatherland and patriotism remain necessary—with or without pride."

Three years after the "pride debate," in his first speech subsequent to the vote nominating him as Germany's new president in May 2004, Horst Köhler told the nation, "I love our country," setting off the latest round of debates about Germans' relationships to the nation. Just as they had three years earlier, journalists and talk show hosts, chat room users and public figures took up the question of whether it is acceptable to be proud of being German—but this time, there was a noticeable difference. Instead of automatically condemning the notion of national pride, Germans increasingly began to suggest that it might be possible, and even desirable, to develop a closer relationship with the nation. As the television station Phoenix stated, in advertising a talk show about national patriotism, "patriotic tones are being heard again in the political debates in recent times much more clearly, apparently more as a matter of course" (Phoenix TV 2004). A well-known actress, Nadja Auermann, told the *Stern* magazine that it is unhealthy not to have a national feeling: "Actually all countries are patriotic. Except Germany" (*Stern* 2004). But a clear affinity with the notion of pride was still not present—rather, Germans' relationship with the nation continues to be complex. A journalist for the Berlin daily paper *Tagesspiegel* argued that Köhler's sentence represented progress in the ongoing debate about national pride and that "love" was a preferable term to use when talking about one's feelings about the nation. "May one say: 'I am proud to be a German?' One may, but one doesn't like to. . . . Rather: love" (Ulrich 2004). And in a discussion with the *Frankfurter Allgemeine Zeitung*, Köhler explained that Germany "can't just simply copy other countries' patriotism. But that doesn't mean that it is taboo. We need to discuss this question openly because we have a certain deficiency here" (*Frankfurter Allgemeine Zeitung Weekly* 2004).

By the fall of 2005, a consortium of media and advertising groups in Germany had kicked off a television advertising campaign to improve German pride, in the hopes that improving Germany's self-image would speed an economic recovery. The television spots featured famous Germans—from skater Katharina Witt to Albert Einstein—as well as ordinary Germans—with the motto "You are Germany" (Bernstein 2005). Even more striking were the massive public displays of patriotism that took place throughout Germany when the country hosted the 2006 World Cup. Ingeborg Majer-O'Sickey (2006, 83) describes her arrival in Freiburg in June 2006 amidst a sea of flags: "black-red-gold mini flags flew from car windows, balconies, baby carriages, people, and even dog collars. Transcending generations, class, and ethnicity, everyone seemed to have one." Hardly anyone questioned the patriotic displays, she notes, except members of the press and "some grouchy '68er" (87), referring to the generation of 1968.

Patriotism, it seems, has come into the mainstream in Germany. These broader societal shifts need to be studied in greater depth, but if it is true that a broader, cross-generational German public is beginning to embrace the nation, then this indicates that one of the prevailing post–World War II narratives about German nationhood is being dismantled. The shift in the meaning of national pride, particularly for a younger generation, appears to be helping the continual re-imagining of the German nation. In this manner, emergent identities and expressions of national identity among parts of a national population may potentially help to transform public versions of the nation or of national belonging. This, in turn, reveals one way in which nations are constantly reshaped and continually re-imagined.

four

Raising the Right Wing

Educators' Struggle to Confront the Radical Right

Generational shifts are also detectable on the fringes of the German political scene, and this is particularly true among the radical right-wing.
In the decades after World War II, right-wing extremism was rooted in
the remnants of National Socialism, largely supported by former Nazis
from the middle and upper classes and consisting, at least in the west,
of formal political parties, publications, and cultural organizations (see
Kreutzberger 1983, 18–19; Steinmetz 1997). But by the 1980s and 1990s,
right-wing extremism had become a phenomenon of young working-
class men. The percentage of right-wing violent crimes committed by
youth under age twenty was 35 percent in 1986, for example, but had
climbed to 70 percent in 1991 (Paul 1995, 40). Suddenly, young people
born well after the end of National Socialism began to embrace right-
wing subcultures through attendance at extremist music concerts or
adherence to the skinhead and neo-Nazi "style" of heavy black boots,
shaved heads, and bomber jackets. One late spring afternoon, I met
Herr Weiss, a civics teacher in his mid-fifties, at his home in west Berlin. Over coffee and cake, he explained how he has observed a generational shift in the base of right-wing extremism in his own lifetime:

> Well, [my generation] directly confronted the generation who were active
> participants, who participated in the World War, in the dictator system
> of the National Socialists, or were themselves in the party or the ss or
> the army, those were the fathers and grandfathers . . . and that provoked
> opposition . . . protest, and that was then, that was the 60s, the protest
> movement. Today, it's totally different of course . . . well . . . perhaps [the
> teenagers today] are compensating for a sort of underdog consciousness
> with "Oh, we are a big state again." Well, immediately after unification

there was a swell like that . . . "Germany is something again, is stronger and bigger again," and through such a feeling then, the nationalism is newly revived. That's already something different than in my generation. In the younger generation then there were hardly any right-wing radical tendencies. Those were really old Nazis, who founded the NPD and . . .

These shifting patterns of right-wing extremist participation began to receive serious national and international attention in the wake of German unification in 1990 due to a sharp increase in outbreaks of violence against foreigners in both eastern and western Germany, including a series of particularly violent attacks in the early 1990s. In 1991, a man from Mozambique died after he was thrown from a moving train by several skinheads, and several months later, a large group of people attacked two buildings housing asylum-seekers in eastern Germany. The asylum-seekers were evacuated after several days of rioting. In 1992, a Turkish woman and two Turkish children died after their west German home was fire-bombed. As right-wing violence declined in the mid-1990s, however, political debates shifted to other issues, such as the status of third-generation guest workers and the reform of German citizenship laws. When right-wing crime rose again sharply in 2000, the topic was forced back onto the national agenda (see, e.g., Krupa 2001; Schwennicke 2001; *Tagesspiegel* 2001a, c). The German government estimated in 1996, for example, that there were 6,400 violent right-wing extremists in Germany—by 1999, the number had climbed to 9,000 and climbed again to 9,700 in 2000. The total number of right-wing extremists is estimated at about 51,000 people in Germany. Violent acts with right-wing extremist motivation also rose, from 630 in 1999 to 874 in 2000 (as reported by the Verfassungsschutzbericht in *Erziehung und Wissenschaft* 2000, 10; Krupa 2001).[1] In addition to the statistical increase in violence during the early part of the new century, there are reports that levels of xenophobia and support for the right wing are growing among German young people—in particular, for youth in eastern Germany. One recent study of ninth-grade students in Rostock, a city in northeast Germany, for example, showed that every third student sympathizes with right-wing opinions and every sixth student is prepared to use violence against foreigners, the homeless, or those with alternative lifestyles or opinions (*Erziehung und Wissenschaft* 2000, 4).

Schools have an explicit mandate to counteract the radical right-wing and in recent years have received increasing attention as a site where right-wing extremism needs to be dealt with more seriously. By the time I began my fieldwork in the fall of 2000, the radical right had emerged as a concern for many of the teachers, administrators, and other educators with whom I came into contact. As I discovered, however, educators' efforts to affect the right wing may inadvertently increase the appeal of the radical right, both as an oppositional subculture and as a space to express national pride, which is otherwise taboo.

Defining the Radical Right

The population of students that I studied — primarily male, blue-collar apprentices mostly from the east — is the group of young people deemed most at risk for recruitment into, or participation in, right-wing radical or extremist activities and groups. Despite wide debate about the most significant causes of right-wing extremism, there is some consensus among most German researchers about patterns of xenophobia and the characteristics of typical right-wing radical individuals more generally (see, e.g., Backes and Jesse 1996; Hopf, Silzer, and Wernich 1999; McLaren 1999). Specifically, right-wing radical individuals in Germany are more likely to be employed males in vocational programs or vocational occupations and from families with lower levels of parental education, and levels of xenophobia tend to be higher in the east (Poutrus, Behrends, and Kuck 2000; Rippl and Seipel 1999; Schnabel 1993; Schnabel and Goldschmidt 1997).[2]

The right-wing students I interviewed were the exception, not the rule, among the students I interviewed and interacted with, and the actual number of right-wing radical students in the schools I observed is difficult to estimate. Teachers' estimates about the percentage of right-wing radical students in their classrooms ranged broadly, with some teachers feeling that right-wing radicalism was not a problem at all among their students, while others estimated that the majority of their students sympathized or were involved with the radical right. More important, however, is the fact that the population that teachers feel they need to reach is not limited to students who are active members of right-wing radical or extremist groups. For the purposes of this chapter, I include among the "radical right" both students who are active members of right-wing radical or extremist groups as well as students who express right-wing, nationalistic, or xenophobic views in classroom discussions or interviews but may not be active members of groups.

This population of students posed a significant and vocal concern for many teachers I interviewed. Students at all three schools identified themselves to me as current or former participants in right-wing radical scenes, if not active members of organized groups. In one of the schools, students with radical right views or memberships are a presence in most classrooms, and in some classrooms in that school they represent the majority view among their classmates.

Teachers face significant difficulties in trying to identify which of their students are a part of the radical right since many of the usual assumptions about right-wing radicals—that they are young, male, east German, working-class vocational school students—apply to many of their students. Most of the students who identified themselves as right-wing told me that they are not very open about their political views in the classroom (or they complained that if they are open about their opinions, they are silenced). Other students said that they didn't think right-wing students would "show themselves" at school. Moreover, the variety and rapid change of symbols that young people use to identify themselves as right-wing radicals, combined with the popularity of some of the symbols as part of a youth subculture, makes it difficult for parents, teachers, and educators to know and identify who among youth are in fact a part of the radical right. Students may also dress differently in the school setting than in their private lives.

These challenges are not limited to schools—in fact, defining the radical right in the German context more generally is not a simple matter. Contemporary right-wing radicalism in Germany can be understood as a cluster of six elements: 1) biological racism, 2) a social Darwinist belief in the struggle for existence, 3) demands for the exclusion or elimination of "inferior" groups, 4) authoritarianism, 5) acceptance of private vigilante violence against enemies, and 6) hatred of the "left" (Steinmetz 1997, 340).[3] German authorities make a legal distinction between right-wing extremism and right-wing radicalism. Although both categories contain similar elements of nationalism, xenophobia, racism, and authoritarianism, right-wing extremist movements are those considered to be in violation of the German constitution, the Basic Law. Right-wing radicalism, while offensive and troubling, is not illegal (Jaschke 2001, 24–30). The students discussed in this chapter primarily fall into the category of right-wing radicals since it is not always clear whether students' beliefs are directly linked to illegal behavior or not, except in cases where they indicated they had participated in violent or illegal activities.

Finally, it is worth pointing out that part of the difficulty in understanding the right wing and in identifying who is a part of it is the variety of groups that are considered a part of the right wing. While the elements of right-wing extremism identified by Steinmetz (1997) clarify what characterizes a right-wing radical or extremist, the extremists and radicals only represent one aspect of the broader group of young people engaged in the right wing. During my interviews with young Germans, I learned that, not only are there many types of right-wing radicals, but also that these different groups reflect distinct subcultures within right-wing extremism and radicalism. These distinctions become especially important during students' own descriptions of their political opinions since they use the terms to place themselves within or outside of the right-wing radical scene. Each of these groups has multiple further divisions and groupings, but the youth I interviewed described four main groups.

Fascists and *neo-Nazis* comprise two similar groups consisting of politically active right-wing radicals—those who are involved in right-wing parties, plan demonstrations and marches, and organize the right-wing radical movement. They are "fanatically committed to resurrecting national socialism as a political and social order" (Weaver 1995, 145) and are typically involved in formal political parties and fascist organizations. Rene, an information-technology apprentice who identified himself as a skinhead, said that "Nazis want to have the whole country be pure German or only want to have whites and then maybe eventually have control of the world." *Neo-Nazis*, he explained, are the "new Nazis," and *fascists* are more or less the same as Nazis.

Skinheads were described to me as the most likely to be violent and tend to be, as a group, fixated on partying, music, and alcohol. Meredith Watts (2001, 611) describes the skinhead culture as revolving around "music, fanzines (fan magazines), concerts, and other more or less organized symbolic and cultural events." Rene, the IT-apprentice quoted above, said that skinheads "actually just want to have parties and drink on the weekends." They are described as relatively apolitical, fixating on simplistic complaints about foreigners like "they take our jobs away" and are the groups most likely to be responsible for attacking and beating up foreigners on the street at night.[4] They are also sometimes described as followers or "'groupies' of the fascist political groups who search for acceptance from these groups but are not politically motivated" (Weaver 1995, 144). They may attend fascist organizational and political party meetings but are more likely to "serve as security guards at political meetings" and are "usually poorly informed about the tenets of national socialism" (145).

Hooligans are soccer fans and soccer gangs, known for causing riots and damage before, during, and after soccer matches. They are usually characterized as part of the radical right because many of their political views tend to be nationalistic, racist, and xenophobic, but they also tend to be less focused on political issues and more likely to engage in antiforeigner violence as part of pre- and post-soccer-game drunken brawls. In a characterization of violent rightist youths, Weaver (1995, 144) places *hooligans* into the category of youth who are either "non-ideological and apolitical," using "violence to gain attention," or "youths from dysfunctional homes who learned violence as a means of communication."

It is important to note that there is overlap among these groups and that some groups actively recruit from other groups. There are significant distinctions within the groups as well. Claudio, a student I interviewed who identified himself as a former *hooligan*, told me that different-colored shoelaces signify what type of group you belong to and where you stand on certain issues, but said that the colors meant different things in different parts or districts of the city. In his neighborhood, he said, "white shoelaces means for example that you're ready to fight, you're immediately ready to start hitting." Black or red shoelaces conveyed different messages. All of these distinctions, and the students' explanations of the groups, illustrate the extent to which the right wing has emerged as a set of distinct and complex subcultures among German youth in ways that are often not clearly linked to political opinions or goals. Right-wing extremist groups market products such as CDs, clothing, lighters, jewelry, and perfume and cologne, often using national pride slogans. One right-wing group advertises a perfume called *Walküre*, describing it as "the flowery scent for today's national woman," and promises female customers that "with this perfume you are guaranteed to be attractive to every patriot."[5] Right-wing groups sponsor rock concerts and fund bands that produce right-wing music, with lyrics that are filled with hate and that promote violence against foreigners, Jews, left-wingers, and women who commit "crimes against the German *Volk*" by having relationships with foreigners, among others (see, e.g., Farin and Flad 2001).

The effectiveness of organized radical right-wing groups' efforts to create a youth subculture around music, clothing, and other products should not be underestimated. A year after the original interviews I conducted with young working-class Germans, I returned to Berlin to re-interview several young men who had self-identified as current or former right-wing radicals or had expressed views sympathetic to the right wing during our first interview. The role of youth subcultures in recruiting these young men into the right-wing scene became clear in these interviews. Martin, an information-technology apprentice, reported how he became involved in the right-wing subculture and how he managed to distance himself from it.

"I've Learned You Can't Generalize"

Born in 1980 in a small town in East Germany, Martin moved to East Berlin with his family when he was seven. He lives in a rented house in northwest Berlin with his parents and his younger sister. His mother works in a hotel cafeteria, and his father, who used to be a crane-driver, now works in the stock and ordering department of a gourmet food company. His brother, twenty-three, is a professional athlete and now lives in another state with his fiancé, who is of Turkish-German ethnic heritage. After graduating from the middle-level school (*Realschule*), Martin completed an apprenticeship as a sales assistant before he realized that he really wanted to do something technical. He is in the final two months of an apprenticeship to be an information-technology systems electrician, one of four new certified occupations in information technology in Germany.

In his early-to-mid teens Martin became involved with a neighborhood group of right-wing radical young men, whom he describes as a mix of violent skinheads, skinheads, and neo-Nazis with a political perspective. He became involved with the scene through his best friend and doesn't seem to have made a conscious political choice to be a right-wing radical. He listened to the music, cut his hair short, and wore a bomber jacket because he thought it was cool, remarking that "I didn't even know that I was in the scene." All of Martin's other friends also became involved in the scene. As he explains, they had all been friends since kindergarten, and they developed as a group:

> It was two or three of them, who lived that life, who listened to the music, who had this perspective, and since we all knew each other from elementary school, you just hung around with them and then somehow hardly even noticed that you'd gotten involved in the group.

Although he says he heard about violent confrontations between the group and foreigners, he was never involved in any himself. The group would get drunk at night and get into fights and violent confrontations with gangs of Turkish youth in Berlin. "I saw my friend afterward and he was all swollen . . . that's nothing for me." As they got older, he gradually drifted away from the group, and his involvement lasted three to four years total. His brother's new Turkish girlfriend, whom he found very nice and who ultimately became an important confidant and advisor in his life, was one of the main motivations for his departure from the scene. Martin also notes that he came to know a number of foreigners at school who were all very nice. The contradictions between his experiences with foreigners and his participation in a right-wing radical social scene eventually became too much for him.

Although a few of his friends became more involved in the scene, Martin says that it was not difficult to get away from the group—partly because he was younger than the friends who became more involved—and partly because he is a big, strong person. "They couldn't do anything actually," he says. He still sees some of the former friends on the street and greets them, but he said he always finds an excuse why he can't spend time with them. In particular, he distanced himself from his former best friend, who has continued to be involved in the scene, began drinking very heavily, and has been in and out of jail. "As it got more and more extreme," he reports, "you started to think it over . . . no, I didn't really want to do that or he's always starting something with people . . . even if we're just going to the movies, and that's no fun."

According to Martin, his family was not even aware of his involvement in the radical-right scene. Although he listened to right-wing rock music, he did not own any of the music himself and says he always listened to it at a friend's house. His clothes and haircut were simply the style at the time. His parents are not very politically engaged, and while his parents and especially his mother initially had problems with his brother dating a Turkish girl, Martin reports that the girlfriend is now fully accepted by the family. Martin says that his brother's fiancé had the most significant influence on his political opinions and on his life. He believes that friends and the surrounding neighborhood and culture have the biggest influence on young people's involvement in the radical right.

Martin describes himself as someone who likes music, is a loyal and good friend, and is fairly intelligent. He says that was probably part of the problem he had with the right wing: "they were all idiots." Although Martin claims to have distanced himself from the right wing, some of his comments during his first interview illustrated that his views on foreigners were mixed. He said that there are good and bad aspects to immigration—while it brings new ideas, many foreigners engage in criminal activity in Germany. Foreigners should be required to learn to speak German very well, he said, and argued that it should be a condition of German citizenship "that they become German citizens, and not . . . German-Turkish or Turkish." When we discussed his transcript a year later, however, he noted those comments as an area where his opinion had changed significantly. One of his teachers is Turkish, and during a class discussion about foreigners and especially about Turks, "the teacher actually explained it all really well . . . and I somehow just got it. Actually, that they are all also just humans and that there are . . . different cultures and that's it. And there are always a couple of black sheep, but you have them everywhere. And you can't generalize."

While Martin ultimately distanced himself from the right wing as he entered into richer relationships with "non-ethnic" Germans and foreigners, not all young men in the right-wing scene experience such political transformations. Paul, a self-identified right-wing radical who I interviewed three times, is a good example.

"Too Lazy to Be a Neo-Nazi"

Paul was born in 1982 in East Berlin and grew up near the Berlin Wall. In 1989, when the wall fell, his family moved to a district of Berlin that would become renowned for the highly visible right-wing extremist youth who live and hang out among the housing complexes in the neighborhood. He attended a comprehensive school (*Gesamtschule*) in a neighboring district and graduated with an expanded lower school degree (*erweiterte Hauptschulabschluss*). He lives at home with his mother and an older brother, who at the time of our interview was serving in the German army. His father left when Paul was two, and Paul does not know much about him. His mother works for a social service agency in Berlin.

Paul wanted to be an auto mechanic but was not accepted for any apprenticeships in that field. He was fired from a previous apprenticeship (also in construction) because he was late too often. He is now training to be a concrete worker, but wishes he had chosen another occupation because "if you do this job for a long time, you get stupid." Paul leaves home by 5:30 a.m. in order to catch public transportation to his apprenticeship site, arriving by 7 a.m. When he returns home around 5:30 p.m., he usually heads directly to the soccer field, where he spends his evenings with friends. On weekends he goes to professional soccer games and discos, or visits family in northeastern Germany, where they have "good parties." Paul expects to be unemployed after he completes his apprenticeship in a few months. He plans to enroll in the army and hopes to extend his mandatory service to at least four years, and says he would consider being a professional soldier.

Paul is a right-wing radical but is, he observes, "too lazy" to be a neo-Nazi, whom he characterizes as more active, organizing and marching in demonstrations, which he finds boring. He says that if it's about "We want all the foreigners out completely, then I'm for that of course too . . . but I'm also too lazy to really do anything big about it, to join in with that." He says there are two kinds of right-wing youth: those who talk and those who act (or those who are "partly right" or "completely right"). He describes himself as in the middle, but more on the side of those who talk. Most of his friends are in the partly right-wing group, which means that they don't really show that they are right-wing radicals: "we have the opinion, but we wouldn't act on it. . . . Mostly I don't act on it, but if it, if it really comes to [that], then I do it too." He has been involved in violent fights with foreigners, which he says came about because they attacked his friends. In general, though, Paul supports violence, even if he's not always actively engaged in it, and speaks critically of those who express right-wing views but do not engage in violence, like his brother. His brother, he explains, "would belong to the group who doesn't do anything at all. That thinks that all the foreigners need to get out and so on, for example, but he would never do anything. He's too quiet for that, too lazy." His mother is also antiforeigner, but similarly to his brother, would not engage in violence herself.

Paul believes that one should really have German ancestors in order to be a German. But he does not support the view that Germany should be a space for an "Aryan race," in large part because although he used to think he was Aryan because of his blue eyes and blond hair, he discovered rather recently that his grandfather was Czech, which, he notes, means he (Paul) can't be Aryan. He is lukewarm on the topic, however, remarking that if the Aryan Reich should return again, he "wouldn't have anything against it."

Paul describes himself as stubborn, demanding, headstrong, and helpful. He says (with some pride) that he is "ready to be violent" (*gewaltbereit*). When he was younger, he said, he held back from everything because he was young and weak. Now that he is older and stronger, he does not hold back. He would mostly be violent for personal reasons—such as if a friend was beaten unfairly. "But not if somebody said, for example politicians, 'We have to . . . attack someone,' because . . . then I would say, 'why now?' then I always look for the logic behind it." Paul voted for the PDS in the last election—the former East German communist party. He says that he voted for them because they are "for the east" (*sich für den Osten einsetzt*).

Soccer, family, his health, and friends are the most important things in his life. In general, he thinks that friends and family are equally important in influencing a child's political opinions, but he does not believe that his own family influenced his. Although he describes his mother as being antiforeigner and his brother as having similar opinions, he says that his family is "not at all right-wing." He thinks that his political opinions "just developed," partly through watching the media.

Being German, Paul says, is not important to him. German is not a "philosophy" or a "life approach" (*Lebenseinstellung*) for Paul. He happens to have been born in Germany and "has to live with it." But he is upset by foreigners who come to Germany and take Germans' jobs or create terror. Foreigners who are born in Germany are partly German, he says—but not completely. It depends on how the family raises the child: "If they teach the child German things, then it's normal that the child would at some point become German. . . . For example a Turk, he comes here and instead of German he's taught Turkish. That's, then they should not live in Germany, they should go back to Turkey." If they live in Germany, "they should know German, they should know the German constitution and they should live by German rules, not their rules. Like for example, women have to be all wrapped up and shit like that."

Martin's and Paul's experiences, while only snapshots, are in many ways typical of the experiences of many young men, especially in east Germany. Their peer groups as adolescents—and the pervasive right-wing subculture in their neighborhoods—were particularly important elements in their engagement with the right-wing scene.

Engaging the Right Wing

How are teachers engaging with youth like Martin and Paul? As I discovered, they spend much of their time focused on learning how to more accurately identify the right-wing students in their classrooms and crafting argumentation skills to better confront statements that right-wing students make in class (Miller-Idriss 2005). Learning to better identify radical right-wing students, however, is not as easy as it sounds. The symbols that right-wing radical youth use to identify themselves to each other and others—especially the ones that go beyond the more standard and recognizable bomber jackets, high black leather boots, and shaved heads—change, often rapidly, as new symbols are banned by schools or even the government. The German government bans, for example, the display of swastikas and modified swastikas—so young people have come up with new symbols, such as the number "88," which stands for the eighth letter of the alphabet ("HH"), which stands for "Heil Hitler." When schools began banning the number "88," some young people starting wearing T-shirts that had "100–12" (one-hundred minus twelve) on them. Elsewhere, the number "18" is used for "Adolf Hitler" (*Politische Zeitschrift* 2000, 4).[6]

Some of the symbols are subtle and might be easily overlooked by teachers and other adults. Neo-Nazi groups and other right-wing radicals, for example, have taken to wearing T-shirts with the British brand Lonsdale displayed across their chests. The sporty brand was designed for boxers and became popular with a wide range of youth subcultures in Germany (Flad 2001, 106). But neo-Nazi groups find the brand appealing for another reason: when their bomber jackets are zipped halfway up, the shirts show the letters "nsda" within the word "Lo*nsda*le," evoking NSDAP, the initials of the National Socialist Party. More recently, right-wing groups have marketed their own brand, Co*nsdap*le, which when worn with a half-zipped jacket, displays the full initials of the National Socialist party—NSDAP.[7] Neo-Nazi groups have also marketed other brands that are only available in shops that are part of the right-wing extremist scene. In an examination of right-wing clothing and styles, Flad (2001, 108) observes: "Whoever wears such clothing demonstrates that s/he is a part of the scene or at the very least makes use of contacts in the scene."

The formal state and school curriculum does not provide much assistance to teachers who wish to address the topic of the radical right in their classrooms. The state curricular framework leaves schools with a great deal of flexibility on how they address topics such as the radical right or xenophobia. Teachers "are still often left alone with the growing problem of right-wing extremist attitudes among students," a local newspaper in Berlin reported in December 2000 (Miller 2000). The curriculum framework for social studies for vocational school students recommends that school curriculum include twenty hours (over a three- to four-year period) of instruction on Nazi-Germany and its consequences, part of which includes a discussion of neo-Nazism and the radical right. Xenophobia is also mentioned as a topic that might be included in discussions of human rights or immigration (Senatsverwaltung für Schule, Jugend und Sport 1999). Each school revises its own curriculum plan based on the state's recommendations, and teachers design classroom practice with the school curriculum plan as a guideline. In other words, although both the state curriculum and the school curricula in the schools I studied recommend that teachers spend some time dealing with the issue of neo-Nazism and the radical right, neither provided guidelines for how teachers ought to go about this task.

Many of the teachers with whom I spoke expressed a sense of helplessness about right-wing radicalism among their students. Although they want to address the problem, teachers do not know what to do and feel they need training and help from outside. For some, facing right-wing extremists in their classrooms is something they have dreaded. Frau Cordner, a teacher in her early forties, reports:

> When I was at university, that was actually a huge fear that I had. I always thought, "What will happen if one day I find myself sitting across from a Nazi," y'know? And how would I react?

Teachers reported that there were very limited resources available for them when they wanted to confront the issue of the radical right in their classrooms. There is not much support coming from central authorities yet, either. One teacher I interviewed reported that she called the Berlin School Senate (the highest school authority in Berlin) to ask for help dealing with radical-right students in her classroom. Although she called several times, and although there is supposed to be someone at the Senate specifically responsible for such concerns, no one ever returned her phone call. (She eventually went to the teachers' union for help, and they put her in touch with a private organization that deals with the radical right.)

Not all teachers attempt to directly confront right-wing extremism in their classrooms, of course, even when they are aware of it. Teachers may be uncomfortable with the subject in general, may have concerns about tarnishing the school's image, may experience immediate fear of potentially violent students, or simply feel uncertainty about how best to address the situation. But even in the absence of significant resources or training, many of the teachers I observed were making obvious efforts to try to influence students' political views, especially about the radical right and about foreigners, even as they often avoided dealing with the subject of the radical right directly. I found, first of all, that many teachers approach right-wing students with compassion. Frau Cordner, the teacher quoted earlier who said that before she began teaching she was afraid of confronting right-wing students in her classroom, thought she would be angry:

> [I thought that] I would certainly be terribly upset and would feel hatred toward that person. That's not the case . . . There is often frustration, but I always still see the students as students, as people with their limitations too, y'know? And I see that for . . . many of them it is not a, um, well-grounded opinion, rather for many it's a form of provocation, they know that . . . if they say something like that, then it will lead first of all to a half-hour's [class] discussion (laughs) . . . or they repeat it because they've heard it.

In the classroom, the picture that emerges of individual teachers is one of improvisation. Not only are teachers largely unprepared in any formal sense to deal with right-wing extremism in their classrooms, but given the diversity within the right-wing scene and the widespread use of symbols to signify various group memberships and degrees of involvement, teachers often struggle to understand who exactly is a part of the right wing among their students. As a result, teachers often find themselves making split-second interpretations of students' comments and having to decide on the spot how to respond to them in the classroom. Herr Hahn, a teacher in his early fifties, reports: "I personally have the difficulty of having to determine whether . . . [the things that youth say in class] should be categorized, that they have a strong national consciousness, or if the sentence is rather categorized as something that is against foreigners."

In addition to trying to determine the difference between statements that might be patriotic expressions of national identity versus those that indicate exclusionary, xenophobic, or virulently nationalistic sentiments, teachers also sense that some students make right-wing comments to get attention or as part of an oppositional subculture. Herr Hanson, a teacher in his early forties, expressed frustration with the rapid response of schools to what he feels may (merely) be oppositional comments:

> Once in a class here, I had some [students] who noticed, they can provoke a teacher, and they always gave responses that had dual meanings [*zweideutige Antworten*]. And they [school authorities] called a class conference because of National Socialistic incidents. That is, but that was a joke. It was simply . . . there wasn't anything serious behind it, but then there had to be a meeting with the department chair, two people from the department, the class leader, three teachers from the *Träger* [apprenticeship training body], they came from all directions of the sky. It is something totally dramatic.

Teachers can send students home from school if they display symbols that are legally forbidden, such as a swastika, but in order to do this, they need to understand which symbols are forbidden and which are not, and whether additional restrictions ought to be imposed at the school level. At the construction school, local police conducted a workshop in the spring of 2001 in order to help teachers learn how better to identify right-wing students in their school and classrooms, and earlier that year, the civics department head distributed a handout to civics teachers with a list of banned symbols. At an April 2001 civics faculty meeting, teachers engaged in a lengthy debate about whether to recommend that the school ban bomber jackets and heavy black boots, both of which symbolize right-wing membership among youth but are not legally banned. Identification was also a significant part of the training provided to future vocational school civics teachers at a weekend training seminar offered by the Technical University of Berlin.[8] At the workshop, a representative from the Anti-fascist Press Archive and Educational Center in Berlin[9] led a three-hour presentation reviewing the dress, organization, symbols, music, culture, and subcultures of the right-wing scene.

Argumentation is also a central focus of the resource materials and training offered for teachers by central school authorities and the police (see, e.g., Goether et al. 1999). The intent is to help teachers develop effective responses to xenophobic, racist, or historically false statements made by students, such as "foreigners are taking our jobs away," "the

Neger come here,[10] seek asylum, and we set a Mercedes in front of their door," or "Hitler himself wasn't so bad, it was really his rear-rank men" (see Hufer 2001, 30–31). Teachers report that learning how to respond to these kinds of comments is an especially important aspect of classroom work, so that they can correct misinformation or misrepresentations put forth by right-wing students. Many of the counterarguments provided for teachers offer facts and data that can be used to challenge misinformation about immigrants, asylum-seekers, the European Union, or unemployment.

Argumentation is also the second stage of training in a local Berlin teacher-training project targeting the radical right. This phase of teacher training is explicitly aimed at helping teachers learn to position themselves against the right, to know the main arguments of the right wing, to learn how to respond effectively, and to be able to create distance. Because many of these teenagers are breaking taboos, such as on issues of national identity, teachers are often unprepared to discuss these issues because the issues have been social taboos for so long, and they need training and help with how to engage these issues in the classroom.[11]

Teachers at the construction school in which I observed classrooms and interviewed students and teachers have not yet reached a consensus on how best to address the problem of the radical right in their classrooms. Among teachers, opinions were divided on the efficacy of focusing on identification and argumentation. Some felt strongly that a ban of right-wing symbols and clothing would be an important symbolic step for the school. Others argued, however, that teachers need to focus less on the symbols and arguments and more on the psychological background of these students. "Otherwise, I'm just a cosmetician, not a doctor," one teacher remarked at a faculty meeting, saying, "We need to talk *with* the students." A workshop for teachers run by the local police (which focused on identification and argumentation) spurred mixed reactions: while some teachers felt supported and were happy to have more information about how to identify and respond to right-wing students, others bemoaned the lack of a pedagogical approach. "It wasn't really a workshop for educators," one teacher told me, pointing out that it didn't help him figure out what to do in the classroom with these students.

Moreover, it is clear that right-wing attitudes are not limited to the students who openly display right-wing symbols. Frau Dann, a civics teacher in the construction school, reported that xenophobic attitudes are a problem among most of her students,

> I mean, OK, we saw it during the last class, the xenophobia and so forth. In that respect the other [students] aren't any better, you know? . . . I mean, [the right-wing student] wears that special outfit, but the others aren't all especially [different] in their opinions, you know?

In sum, I found that teachers' efforts to address directly the radical right focused on improving identification of right-wing radical students and learning how to react to them in the classroom through effective argumentation. I also found, however, that teachers were trying to address the radical right indirectly by attempting to address students' xenophobic tendencies and to influence how young people view the presence of foreigners in Germany. Although many of these efforts were not overtly linked to teachers' efforts to address the radical right, there was a relationship between efforts to address xenophobia and teachers' concerns about the radical right. This is evidenced, at least in part, by the fact that teachers made a more consistent and frequent effort to shape how students view foreigners at the construction school, where teachers also expressed the greatest concern about the presence of right-wing radical students in their classrooms. Some of the teachers also directly referenced the radical right in their arguments about why students should view foreigners or violence against foreigners differently, as the examples below detail.

Efforts to Transform Views on Foreigners

Several teachers made direct efforts to change how students think about foreigners and who belongs in Germany, often during lessons about other topics. Perhaps taking their cues from workshops that have focused on argumentation and argumentative approaches, the teachers I observed favored the use of rational arguments (as opposed, for example, to appeals to emotion or morality) to try to shift students' political opinions about topics related to foreigners or right-wing violence. Some of these efforts were directly linked to arguments about the radical right. For example, Herr Krug tried to shift students' opinions about black market labor by redirecting blame for the problem to Germans, pointing out that German capitalists are at fault for creating the situation: "Those [people] with very short hair say that it [the problem of black market labor] is the fault of the foreigners, but it's not their fault, it's the fault of the employers, who have set up the system." The reference to people with "very short hair" is a direct criticism of the radical right, and his comment was clearly intended to counter right-wing political arguments with factual information, namely, that German employers have set up an employment system which allows foreign laborers to be paid less than German laborers. Prejudice against foreigners, in other words, is often based on problems that originate with Germans and blame should be placed accordingly.

Another teacher, Herr Jaeger, urged students to think through to a logical conclusion what would happen if a radical right-wing party came to power in Germany, using the recent spate of violence against foreigners to illustrate. He pointed out potential repercussions for German firms and the German economy because foreign countries and individuals would boycott German goods, and he referenced the current situation in the state of Brandenburg, where foreign investments had dropped significantly as a result of increased right-wing violence and attacks against foreigners. Tourism had also suffered in the region as a result:

> If the NPD came to power . . . Germany would become poorer and poorer . . . Through the activities of these people [the radical right-wing], millions of Deutschmarks have been lost in the state of Brandenburg, for example. No one wants to invest there. What would happen in Germany? Daimler-Benz would go bankrupt.

In focusing on the potential consequences for Germany if a radical right-wing party came to power, Herr Jaeger emphasized that such a situation would be an economic disaster for the country. Like his fellow instructor who mentioned people with "very short hair," Herr Jaeger argues that "these people" are causing financial loss to Germany, referencing the radical right without directly mentioning them.

Teachers also made a concerted effort to shape students' political opinions about foreigners even when the radical right was not part of the discussion. They frequently pointed out the legal and constitutional support for foreigners in Germany, reminding students that in Germany, the rights present in the "Basic Law" are "for everyone living within Germany's borders, not just for Germans." They also tried to encourage students to see foreigners as a more natural part of Germany's history. For example, teachers referenced the influx of guest workers from Turkey, Italy, and other southern European countries after World War II, pointing out that workers were actively recruited by the Germans because there was a shortage of German laborers. Herr Jaeger pointed out to one class that the influx of guest workers during this period was actually part of a pattern of immigration from other countries that had always taken place in periods when Germany needed working men. The need for foreigners in the German economy, in other words, has historically been an issue; waves of immigration over the past several centuries—such as the immigration of Huguenots and Swedes—have coincided with time periods when there were not enough German laborers. In discussing these waves of immigration, Herr Jaeger told students, "So we are all foreigners ourselves, really."

Other teachers tried to place the German experience with foreigners in the European context. One teacher in the information technology school put up an overhead showing that the percentage of asylum-seekers Germany had absorbed since the early 1990s, relative to its total population, was actually quite small compared to other European countries. This information appears to have been relatively effective in shaping students' opinions about foreigners, as I learned a few days later, when I interviewed a student from the same class. In a discussion about the number of foreigners in Germany, the student told me that he thought there should be more foreigners, and cited the statistics from the same overhead, explaining that he hadn't been aware that Germany had accepted proportionally fewer asylum-seekers compared to the rest of Europe, and that he now thought Germany should take in more foreigners. This was the only time I heard this argument during a student interview.

One argument I heard frequently—both in and out of schools—concerned the continued population decline in Germany. As a result, Germany needs foreigners as laborers and to support future retirees, by paying into the social welfare system. "Germans are not reproducing enough," Herr Jaeger stated simply during a class in the fall of 2000. He linked the current discussion about retirement in Germany to the issue of immigration, pointing out that Germans are not reproducing at fast enough rates and that in order to keep the population high enough to support future retirees, millions of non-Germans will continue to be needed as part of the German workforce.[12]

There were other efforts to address xenophobia more directly. One teacher, Frau Schwartz, engaged students in a discussion about a demonstration against xenophobia that was to take place in Berlin later that week. The students overwhelmingly thought that demonstrating was meaningless. One student said that politicians only participate in order to gain popularity; another expressed cynicism about ordinary people who participate, saying, "they demonstrate and then by the time they're back in their cars they're acting like [jerks] . . . angry at the people in traffic." Another asked, rhetorically, "What good would this demonstration do against people who are right-wing?" Frau Schwartz told students that such a demonstration can show the strength of the opposing side: "It shows that there is another opinion, that there are a lot of people who disagree."

There were times when teachers' efforts to address the right wing seemed rather unfocused. One teacher, Herr Ring, read aloud segments of two autobiographical essays students from another class had written for an assignment. (The students' identities were kept confidential.) He had asked the students to write a story about themselves basing the topic on an important experience from their own development. Both essays that Herr Ring shared in class were written by right-wing radical students. Reading from one student's text, he quoted: "Honestly I am happy if a foreigner dies . . . today I am right-wing, I will stay right-wing, I will defend my fatherland." Herr Ring seemed to be expressing exasperation at the essays, telling the class "and I have to grade these." When the students asked what kind of a grade he gave the essays, however, Herr Ring sidestepped the question, not answering it. He pointed out to the students that although his class could have chosen any topic to write about, several students chose political topics. He then transitioned back to the topic at hand, without engaging students in a lengthier discussion about the content of the other students' essays or why he had deemed it important to bring them up in class. This illustrates some of the teachers' struggle with the challenge of right-wing extremism. Clearly, Herr Ring was disturbed and unsettled by the essays and struggled with how to react to them. By sharing them with another class, he may have wanted to begin a discussion about the issue of the radical right, of the concept of "fatherland," or of violence against foreigners. But he never engaged in this discussion, leaving his intentions unclear.

Like his colleague Herr Ring, Herr Jaeger engaged in a strategy to address issues of xenophobia that may have been somewhat lost on the class. As he began a discussion about how many children Germans need to have in order to keep the population stable, Herr Jaeger commented (in a *very* sarcastic tone), "and by *Germans*, we don't mean everyone that was born here, not the colored people, only the Germans." In response, Dietrich, a right-wing radical student in the back of the room called out emphatically, "Exactly!" Although Herr Jaeger clearly meant the comment sarcastically, the way in which it might have been received by students—especially with no further discussion or explanation—seems very unclear. Instead of directly confronting Dietrich's response or developing his own comment, moreover, Herr Jaeger engaged in another intriguing interaction. He turned toward the entire class and said, "You know, sometimes you can recognize foreigners by their last names, because their names aren't German." Then he turned to Dietrich, the right-wing radical student, who has a "foreign-sounding" last name, and the following dialogue ensued:

Herr Jaeger: Dietrich, are you married?
Dietrich: No, it's my father's name, a Swedish name. Yeah, it's terrible.
Herr Jaeger: (in a friendly and logical tone) Well, why don't you send your father back to where he came from?
Dietrich: He can't.
Herr Jaeger: (in a meaningful way, to Dietrich and the rest of the class) Well then . . .

Again, Herr Jaeger immediately moved on from this discussion back to the topic at hand, without pursuing it further. Despite what were very good intentions on Herr Jaeger's part, if students did not catch the sarcasm in his comments about what "kinds" of Germans need to have children, they could walk away from class having heard an authority figure say that "colored" people are not German.

It is particularly intriguing that most of these discussions of foreigners, immigration, xenophobia, and the radical right stayed within the realm of rational argument or reason. Teachers did not appeal to a sense of morality or to Germany's past when advocating for an inclusive policy toward foreigners or when trying to combat the rise of the radical right, for example. It is also worth pointing out that although teachers as a rule emphasized rational and argumentative approaches in an apparent effort to convince or teach students about the radical right, there were a few notable exceptions in teaching strategy and pedagogy. The two exceptions I observed involved teachers using hypothetical situations to encourage class discussions about the radical right. In both cases, the teachers appeared to avoid overt attempts to directly influence the kinds of things that students said. In one of these cases, a teacher asked the class to discuss what they would do if they witnessed neo-Nazis attacking a foreigner in a subway station. In the other case, the teacher called on three students with shaved heads and asked them to describe how people would react to them if they walked down the street together wearing bomber jackets and heavy black boots. Both hypothetical situations led to lengthy and engaged discussions about the issue of the radical right and xenophobia in Germany and in Berlin.

National Pride and the Radical Right

Expressions of national pride, especially the phrase "I am proud to be a German," are typically tagged as right-wing extremist expressions in Germany. In part, the linkage of national pride to the right wing results from the increasing appropriation of national pride by right-wing extremist groups, whose vocal proclamations that they are "proud to be German" do carry tones of ethnic or racial superiority. Badges with the slogan "I am proud to be a German" are for sale on right-wing party websites (Cohen 2001), and the NPD has handed out stickers with the slogan at information stands (Parade 2001). A 1993 song by Frank Rennicke, one of the best-known right-wing extremist musicians, is titled "Ich bin stolz, ein Deutscher zu sein" (I am proud to be a German).[13] While the lyrics to this song are in and of themselves fairly neutral, the fact that the song was written and performed by a right-wing extremist musician, whose other songs are openly racist and xenophobic, links the concept of national pride more clearly to the right wing. Another right-wing extremist group, Kraftschlag, sings a song "Trotz Verbot nicht Tot" (Not dead despite the ban), which also links the concept of pride to racism and the extreme right: "For the purity of our race we are ready/ To take to our weapons/ Our time is coming. For Germany and Europe/ This time it should be/ For the rebirth of the good/ Proud, white, and pure!"[14]

There are also attempts by other groups to reclaim German national pride from the right wing, however. For example, the initiative "Germans against rightist violence" launched a campaign in the fall of 2000 with posters and advertisements throughout the country, displaying photographs of multicultural, mostly dark-skinned individuals wearing white T-shirts bearing the phrase, "I am proud to be a German" (Hops 2001; Putz 2000; Schwennicke 2001).

Some of the young people and teachers I observed and interviewed indicated that the attraction of national pride for the right wing results at least in part from the taboo on expressions of national pride. During a civics class discussion about the parliamentary debate on national pride in March 2001, one student argued that if everyone would say that they were proud of being German, then the phrase "wouldn't have any power anymore" for the right-wing extremists. Herr Meyer, a civics teacher in his mid-thirties, observes:

> The problem is that as soon as there is a certain national pride, the media, in part, simply shoves it into the National Socialistic corner . . . which, in my opinion, leads again to extremism. Well, I think, simply, it has to be said that we have to learn from history, and that, we should all also know what happened then and should be conscious of the fact that something like that can happen and also certainly could happen again, but in Germany in the entire educational system, in any case as I see it, from my history, from my development, there is always a guilt conveyed along with it.

Politicians and academics have also suggested that the attractiveness of national pride — and of the right wing — lies in the nature of the taboo itself. In a March 2001 speech at a conference in Leipzig against violence, xenophobia, and right-wing extremism, for example, President Rau argued that young people become involved with right-wing extremism, not based on their convictions, but rather in order "to break taboos" (Oschlies 2001). Others have also pointed out that the radical right-wing has become a site at which to break social taboos and engage in political and social protest. As Weaver (1995, 152) argues, these German youth "know that Nazi symbols are effective in gaining society's attention. Painting a swastika on a school wall or raising a 'Sieg Heil' salute brings the immediate attention of parents and teachers, the press, the government, and the world."

Some of the students I interviewed suggested that there is a link between the development of right-wing extremism and the desire to be proud. Kai, an information-technology apprentice, reported:

> I also think that . . . the hatred of foreigners results from this knowledge, that you know you're not allowed to say it, [that you are proud to be a German] because then you're immediately depicted as evil, but you want to say it somewhere, because you have to feel like you belong somewhere . . . and you also know that if you say it then . . . it [will be] seen nega-

tively and for that you immediately hate the other nations again, I'd say, because you can't be a German with abandon [*nicht so preisgeben darf Deutscher zu sein*].

According to Kai, xenophobia results in part from a reaction to the internal taboo on national pride as well as from resentment toward other countries for their unwillingness to let Germans express national pride.

Jochen, a cook trainee born in the east, explained why he thinks participation in the radical right is highest among younger east Germans and how it is related to the problem of national pride and national belonging:

> And there was no one who was stronger or richer or anything, it was just a group. And that's simply disappeared and all of the people who lived in that time, who were a part of that, I think there are a lot of people who simply need a group. To have something again that they can be proud of. And back then we could be proud of our . . . that you were a *Thälman-pionier* or a *Jungpionier*, you could be proud of that.[15] I think it's a little bit about the search for something to be proud of and they want to be proud of Germany, but can't be, because, yeah, because they think too many foreigners are there.

According to Jochen, higher participation in the radical right among east Germans is directly linked to their desire to be proud of something. As younger children, they were able to express pride in their *Pionier* groups, but as adults, they are prohibited from expressing a sense of national pride *except* within right-wing radical political circles and groups. Teachers also sensed that participation in the radical right is sometimes linked to a desire for identification with a group. During a discussion about the social disadvantages that many east Germans face today, Herr Metzer, a civics teacher in his early forties, believes that young east Germans who get engaged in the radical right are often seeking to construct a sense of identity. As he noted, "A retro-expression of 'nation' and perhaps also a particularly right-wing extremist expression of 'nation' is an additional point [*Haltepunkt*] with which something like an identity can be constructed, during these overwhelmingly confusing times." Frau Dann, a civics teacher in her mid-fifties, explains:

> National pride, for many students, is the lifeline [*Rettungsanker*]. These right wing radical groups, well especially here at the construction school,

where I also see, that they are so . . . this big bald-headed guy [*dicke Glatzkopf*] is sitting there, you know? Radiant, and he has somehow, imaginarily, his right-wing radical group behind him. You know? He is not sitting here alone. And here, sitting next to him, is the little pipsqueak [*kleine Würstchen*], who simply admires this man, what kind of self-confidence he has. You know? (long pause) . . . [Teenagers] want actually to belong somewhere, and over the years their youth centers have been taken from them and there have been lots of cuts in the youth [policy] area, and in the DDR the youth were still looked after, the children and youth were looked after, and that's not the case with us [in unified Germany], and I can understand really well, that they seek something like that and need it. Many of them want to define themselves with national pride, and really like to use "I am a German" as a way of keeping everyone else at a distance, even if they don't mean it badly at all. But they want to identify positively, and our society gives [them] too few possibilities to do that.

Other politicians have also argued that the continued insistence of political, educational, and social leaders on an antinationalist discourse may be pushing young people further to the right. This was certainly the case for some of the students I interviewed, who suggested that teachers' continuing efforts to delegitimize students' sense of national pride drives students toward the radical right, which becomes the only space for positive expressions of national identity.

In sum, I found that teachers were struggling with the issue of how best to address the problems of xenophobia and the radical right in their classrooms. When they did address it, their efforts were focused on using rational arguments, such as trying to convince students that foreigners were needed or that the consequences of the radical right could be devastating for Germany. As I talked with more and more students, however, I began to suspect that teachers' efforts might be ineffective.

What Should Be Done? Young Germans' Suggestions

I asked students whether they thought the radical right was a problem (as opposed, as some have argued, to something that was merely exaggerated by the press), and if so, what they thought should be done about it. Most students saw the right wing as a significant problem, but felt that many of the approaches to confront the radical right were misdirected. Most of them believed that the participation of youth in right-wing radicalism or extremism is caused by a lack of perspective, general dissatisfaction, and a desire to be a part of a group among young men who do not have much of a sense of a positive future for themselves. Some students blamed parents, the media, and schools for falsely socializing young people, and many thought that punishments for right-wing crimes should be more severe. But by and large, the students overwhelmingly favored social approaches to reaching out to radical right young people.

The most frequent suggestion from students was to improve educational interventions for right-wing youth or those at risk of becoming right-wing. Martin, for example, a former radical right-wing young man, thinks that the government should sponsor more social programs and discussion sessions with young people. It would help if adults talked with these youth, he said, instead of just saying that those teenagers "'are bad, they're good for nothing.'" Adults "brand" such young people, he explained. "They are really driven out of the society and . . . that's not right." Even if the actions of the right wing are reprehensible, Martin seems to suggest, they are still a part of the larger society and can best be reached by addressing them as part of that society, rather than by shutting them out.

Mehmet, a Turkish-German hotel trainee, agrees, arguing that putting bans on political parties or on ways of thinking doesn't make any sense. "They need resocialization processes," he said, and suggested that offenders should be made to have a meal with a Turk every day for a week. Another student said that schools should be less segregated and suggested that classrooms be deliberately structured so that all classrooms had a mix of foreigners and Germans. One of the teachers also noted that students need more cultural interaction across different groups, pointing to the lack of interaction and fear of the other among Turkish students from Kreuzberg (a district in Berlin) and students who live in east Berlin.

Carola, a cook apprentice who is the ex-girlfriend of an active right-wing radical youth, suggested that the state create projects to bring right-wing radicals and foreigners together. Because she thinks it would be difficult to force people "off the street" to do this, she suggests starting programs in prisons:

> If for example some skinheads were in prison, you could take them out and lock them up with [foreigners]. Then they should really talk to each other. Then of course they shouldn't take a foreigner who can't speak any

German or something, rather that they could really have a good conversation with each other.

Many students felt that the state's closure of youth centers and after-school clubs, particularly in east Berlin (see Weaver 1995, 147), had caused an increase in right-wing extremism. Young people don't have anything to occupy their time, they observed, and the right wing becomes a social group and an activity base from which they engage in fights or general troublemaking.

Some students said that teachers' approaches were hegemonic and overly narrow. For example, Michael, a construction apprentice, reported:

> I have the feeling that the teachers try to convince us that [right-wing extremism] is bad . . . and that one shouldn't engage in it if one wants to be a good member of society or do good for the country . . . but you have so few opportunities to learn why they think that . . . you're sort of cornered in to a thought . . . you're just pushed into this societal picture but you can't really see what the other side, what's behind the other side.

Kai, an information-technology apprentice, observed that it would help if schools tried to introduce more intercultural work or teach about international issues or multicultural concerns in a more positive way. It would help, he suggested if

> people were taught earlier that the other cultures are worthy, I'd say . . . in school you only learn that the other countries are there and that we harmed all the other countries, that's what you learn in school. But one should also [teach] people . . . I don't know, one should talk more about the positive aspects of countries.

Some of the most insightful comments came from the students I interviewed who identified themselves as having been formerly a part of the right-wing radical scene. During my initial interviews and focus groups, I encountered several young men who told me that they had been a part of the right-wing scene in their early teens, but were no longer involved. While all of the young people I interviewed identified a range of factors they thought influenced youth to engage in the right wing, including schools, family, and peer groups, the young men who told me they were or had been a part of the radical right were more specific about what attracted them. These young men were attracted to the right wing through their exposure to what they perceived as a "cool" right-wing subculture and their personal connections to right-wing radical members, especially close male friends or older siblings. In addition, right-wing rock music played a significant role in many of these young people's experiences. This music is aggressively racist, couching xenophobic, proauthoritarian, fascist lyrics in aggressive heavy metal music that has proven appealing to alienated youth. Claudio, who identifies himself as a former hooligan, says that he got involved in the scene after he started going to professional soccer games with a friend of his:

> And you make friends there, and there was also a former friend of mine, he also became right-wing, and then you are a part of a big group and have a bomber jacket and everything . . . and at some point you get really involved, vandalize and loot, getting up in people's faces, getting drunk.

Finally, the explanations offered by former right-wing young people about how they got away from the scene are also informative. One student told me that while he was still an active part of the right wing, he was randomly assigned a seat next to a foreign student (from the former Yugoslavia) in his new vocational school class. As they became friends, he began to recognize the contradictions in his beliefs and was gradually able to pull away from the right wing. Students who had never been involved with the right wing also emphasized the importance of cultural interaction. A student whose family moved from east to west Berlin right after the wall fell, for example, told me that he thinks the reason why he never got involved in the right wing is because he grew up and went to school with so many Turkish youth. His childhood friends from the east, he explains, were socialized into a different scene.

Pride, Desire, and Extremism

In just one generation, a radical transformation in the demographic base of the right wing has meant that popular support for the right wing is largely cemented in working-class youth, rather than in lingering Nazi party members from World War II. The causes for this shift are multiple and complex. In this chapter, I trace an additional mechanism that has been overlooked by scholars who study the German right wing, arguing that a younger generation of Germans' resistance to the taboo on national identity and pride has created a space in which the radical right-wing becomes more appealing. This is particularly true for alienated working-class youth, many of whom are likely to end up un-employed upon completion of their apprenticeships and who see the radical right as a ready site in which to break social taboos and lash out at parents and teachers. And it may be even truer for youth from east Berlin, who sense that national pride—which was encouraged in the east—has been taken away from them in the post-unification era.

This isn't to suggest that young people's desire for pride necessarily leads to participation in the extreme right-wing. But for a small num-ber of youth, their desire to be proud can lead them toward the radical right-wing, whose aggressive marketing with national pride slogans has created virtually the only space in which national pride can be expressed. More broadly, it may be the case that a younger generation's resistance is helping to transform the prevailing narrative about national identity, revealing how nations are continually re-imagined over time.

Educators may be able to help students engage in dialogue about national issues, including national pride, while simultaneously prevent-ing them from latching onto the nation in virulent and violent ways. Whether they are successful depends, at least in part, on what happens in the classroom when topics such as national pride are raised. It is to this question that we turn in chapter 5.

five

Teaching and Unteaching
National Identity

Studying citizenship and national belonging as cultural practices means taking seriously the ways in which ordinary people understand and interpret these concepts in their everyday lives (Fox and Miller-Idriss 2008). Moreover, studying these concepts in isolation is not adequate; such understandings need to be situated within the context of the institutions and structures with which ordinary people interact on a daily basis—such as schools, workplaces, the media, or government offices. Studying such sites—and the ways in which ordinary people live and interact with them—reveals how ordinary people may mediate, interpret, resist, or potentially transform the official versions of citizenship and national belonging that elites introduce (see, e.g., Smith 2008).

Schools are a particularly well-suited site for such an investigation because they sit at a key intersection of elite and non-elite interactions, particularly in educational systems with state-mandated textbooks or curricular frameworks that specify what future citizens are expected to know and be able to do. Moreover, they are an ideal site to study these kinds of interactions across generations since, by their nature, schools are structured so that younger and older generations formally interact around questions of what it means to be a citizen or belong to a nation. In most places, such interactions happen through civic education courses, and in this regard, Germany is no exception.

Civic Education and German Vocational Schools

Civic education in Germany has evolved over time, in large part due to frequent and significant political changes over the course of the past century. Although there are some indications that German civic education can be traced back to the seventeenth century, formal civic education programs did not receive widespread attention until the mid-nineteenth century, when the German monarchy began to shift attention from the political education of the ruling classes to that of the ruled classes, with the idea that they might be socialized to be more patriotic, obedient, and to serve the state (Kuhn et al. 1993, 13). Schools gradually began to play a stronger role in this regard; by 1890, a speech by Kaiser Wilhelm II argued that history and German instruction should focus on the founding of a national identity and the strengthening of a sense of the fatherland (Kuhn et al. 1993, 16-17).[1]

Although the goals of civic education in the democratic Weimar Republic included a focus on "the careful consideration or tolerance of those who think differently" (*die Schonung der Empfindungen Andersdenkender*) (Kuhn et al. 1993, 53), schools and teachers were later accused of being unprepared to educate or socialize German young people to support a democratic state. This failure was one among many that may have helped open the door to the fascist state that emerged in the early 1930s (Kuhn et al. 1993, 55). Under Hitler, in turn, civic education meant indoctrination to a nationalistic, racist ideology and to the totalitarian state (Händle 1999, 20; Wegner 2002). This took place largely through an emphasis on emotional and psychological factors rather than on critical thinking skills (Kuhn et al. 1993, 81-83). The focus of instruction within the school system was on the development of a national identity grounded in a race-based notion of the German people and of the purity and superiority of the Aryan race over all others. German youth were supposed to be ingrained with a sense of race until it became instinctive (Kuhn et al. 1993, 81).

After World War II, the denazification programs organized by the Allied powers focused on a complete break with the German past, a total reeducation of the German public and a reorientation to democratic principles. The Allied powers developed reeducation programs focused on "healing" the damaged and sick psychological character of the German people (Gagel 1995, 32). The focus and methods of each of the Allied reeducation plans varied somewhat, however (for an overview, see Gagel 1995, 31-48; Kuhn et al. 1993, 109-17). For example, Gagel (1995, 34) reports that the Americans emphasized the development of "basic values," in particular tolerance, and Händle (1999, 21) points out that in U.S.-occupied zones, certain topics were forbidden from curricular plans. Among others, forbidden topics included "exclusion on the basis of racism, nationality, religion or political attitude." Despite these variations in emphasis, the Allies were united "in their belief that the democratization and moral re-education of the German people was just as essential as fundamental political and economic reform" (Rathenow and Ehmann 2000, 24). The French, British, and Americans all shared an emphasis on denazification and civic reeducation (Thelen 2004). Vocational schools became a particular target because it was argued that the lack of civic or political education in vocational schools had ultimately opened the door for Hitler and the National Socialists.[2] Strengthening civics instruction in the vocational schools was therefore a particular area of focus during educational reconstruction in the postwar period (Thelen 2004).

It was during this period that civic education was introduced into the vocational schools, which until this point had focused primarily on occupational training.[3] The vocational schools, which educated a significant portion of the German population, were now viewed as an important site for the socialization and indoctrination of German youth to democratic attitudes and beliefs. The "Allies concentrated effort on convincing the West Germans of the necessity to include a larger element of character and personality training in the vocational school curriculum" (Taylor 1981, iii).

There is not complete agreement about the role that individual teachers played during this period, however. While Rathenow and Ehmann (2000, 33) argue that teachers in both the western and Soviet occupation zones became actively engaged in curriculum revision in an effort to "deal critically with the Nazi past and the nationalist traditions of Prussian and German history," some of the teachers I interviewed pointed out that teacher practice in the post–World War II era was characterized more by silence and avoidance of the Nazi era than by critical engagement. For many teachers, discomfort with teaching the Nazi era in the immediate aftermath of World War II led to emotional distance and avoidance of much of the detail of Germans' participation in the atrocities (Marcuse 2001). As Sabine Reichel (in Marcuse 2001, 306) describes, when the time came for her teacher to talk about Hitler and the Third Reich, "she seemed embarrassed and distraught, biting her lip and looking down at her orthopedic shoes while trying to summarize the Third Reich in fifty minutes."

There are three points of particular relevance to this book that can be drawn from the history of civic education in the post–World War II era.[4] First, it is important to note that the emphasis on emotional ties to the nation that was so prevalent in the Third Reich's efforts to develop national identity was noticeably absent in the post–World War II era.[5] Second, in the explicit efforts that education reformers made in the postwar era to deal critically with both the National Socialist *and* Prussian and German nationalist past (Rathenow and Ehmann 2000, 33), we can begin to trace the emergence of the link between national pride/nationalism and right-wing extremism that would become a part of a prevailing West German narrative on national identity. Finally, however teacher practice is characterized, the German state was clearly engaged in the postwar period in utilizing the school system to try to create more democratic, tolerant citizens.

Civic education in Germany's post-unification era (since 1990) has continued along much the same lines as it had in West Germany since 1949. After reunification, east German teachers were retrained, and curricula, textbooks, school structures, and the organization of the entire educational system in the east was replaced with west German versions of the same (see, e.g., Phillips 2000a). Today, civics is a required school subject for vocational school students in Germany, the majority of whom are training in full-time, three-and-one-half-year vocational programs and are required to complete 280 hours of civics instruction as part of their occupational certification. In Berlin, the official goals of civic education, as laid out in Article 1 of the Berlin school law, include the development of individuals who resist the ideology of National Socialism and authoritarianism and who can help to establish a state and society based on "democracy, peace, freedom, human rights, and the equality of the sexes" (Senatsverwaltung für Schule, Jugend und Sport 1999, 3).

Improvising in the Classroom

Teachers are thus formally charged with the task of socializing future citizens, although they do not receive very much assistance in terms of how to go about this. In Berlin, each school's curricular plan is adapted from a state curriculum framework for civics, which focuses heavily on institutional and structural aspects of citizenship and democratic systems, covering topics such as the principles of democracy, the functions of the parliament, and systems of checks and balances, among others (Senatsverwaltung für Schule, Jugend und Sport 1999).[6] There is room within the framework for teachers to discuss issues related to national identity, especially in units on National Socialism, the division and unification of Germany, and European integration, as well as in subunit areas and subtopic recommendations that focus on minorities and migrants, xenophobia, prejudice, problems of integration, neo-Nazism, and right-wing extremism (Senatsverwaltung für Schule, Jugend und Sport 1999, 23). Aside from listing learning goals and topics for instructional content, however, the state curricular framework does not provide further guidance on how teachers ought to address these issues. Instead, each teacher decides how he or she will address those topics, designs the content, chooses the instructional materials and assessments, and determines where to place particular emphases. Freedom to design instructional content is somewhat curtailed, however, by the centralized comprehensive examination that all students in each vocational field must pass at the end of their three-year program. In addition to content exams in all of their professional subjects, students must pass the civics part of the exam in order to become certified in their respective fields.

Given that there is very little formal curricular structure for teachers who wish to address the topic of national identity in their civics classrooms, I began my observations by simply asking do teachers delve into the topic at all, and if so, how do they approach it? What are their strategies and emphases? One of the most significant gaps in policymakers' and researchers' understandings of the schools' role in socializing students to their future roles as citizens is understanding what actually takes place within classrooms. This is particularly true for the German case. While there have been several large quantitative studies in civic education in Germany (e.g., Oesterreich 2002; Oesterreich, Händle, and Trommer 1999), there have been few qualitative or ethnographic studies on civic education, especially in vocational schools, where research is lacking more generally (Bacher 2001).

Teachers at all three of the schools I studied struggled with what they perceive to be a general political apathy among young people. Interest in politics is generally down among youth in Germany (Deutsche Shell 2000b, 263; Händle et al. 1999b, 266), as is trust or confidence in institutions and views about democracy and the German political system in general (Gaiser et al. 1998). It is important to note, however, that young people remain engaged or supportive of nongovernmental social action and groups such as Greenpeace (Gaiser et al. 1998, 153). A series of political scandals in the late 1990s, particularly related to financial misconduct and abuse (e.g., Cohen 2000), seems to have had an impact on young people's views as well. One vocational school teacher remarked that students have told him that they didn't feel it was worth being interested in politics since "it's all corrupt anyway."

In general, I found that despite a lack of formal curriculum to support their efforts, teachers addressed issues of national identity and national pride in all three schools, although these issues were rarely the focal point of their classroom lessons. Instead, their efforts were typically subtle and informal, taking the form of conversational asides, side comments, jokes, and spontaneous remarks that were interwoven into lessons about other topics. Thus, teachers' efforts took place outside of the formal curriculum and largely in the absence of official guidance. They improvised on the spot as opportunities arose in which they could address national identity or in which they felt compelled to respond to students' antiforeigner or xenophobic comments. In the following sections, therefore, I focus on classroom discourse, examining in particular how teachers inserted comments and asides about national identity into their instruction on related or unrelated topics. Through these efforts, teachers sometimes directly mediated prevailing public and social narratives about national belonging, but in other cases, they avoided, sidestepped, or transformed these same narratives. Overall, the picture that emerges of teacher practice is one of teachers struggling to influence youth who they worry will veer toward xenophobic nationalism, but having to do so in a variety of ways, often improvised in lieu of formal guidelines, curriculum, or training (see Miller-Idriss 2006b).

Dismantling the Nation

One of the attempts through which teachers worked informally to affect students' opinions about citizenship and national identity focused on efforts to dismantle the existence of a collective German identity or to deconstruct German national identity more generally. Teachers favored logic-based, rational arguments in their approach to this topic, often grounding their arguments in historical facts to present logical arguments to students that there is no such thing as "being German"—instead, Germans were ethnically mixed due to centuries of immigration and shifting borders. They emphasized the historical absence of a

German "nation" and the primacy of regional identity until very recent times.

One day in the late fall, I observed Herr Prost's civics class during a lesson focused on the Weimar Republic. During the discussion, Herr Prost tells the class that there are three important dates from the nineteenth century that are necessary for understanding the events of this century. He solicits dates from the class, and then settles on 1871, the founding of the German empire. He explains to the class that "before that, Germany was never an empire—before 1871, one could never be called a German—the concept, that one could be a German just didn't exist back then." He continues to ask the class for important dates in German history and succeeds in soliciting 1848, the March Revolution, and 1813, referring to the Wars of Liberation (*Befreiungskrieg*). At the mention of 1813, Herr Prost interjects:

> This is where the ideology of the German state begins—and the notion that whoever lives there is a German. Before that this didn't exist—one was from Saxony, the Rhineland, and so on. In this time, as the Prussian king issued a call for all men to take up weapons against France—from then up to Hitler there was a consequential strengthening of nationalistic ideas. Today, those people who talk about a German consciousness, they don't know what they are talking about.

During this discussion, the students are attentive, listening. Herr Prost then distributes a short text by Goethe that has a reference to a fatherland as something new, an invention of the Prussians. Herr Prost speaks to the class of the "invention of the ideology of the Fatherland" and then draws a brief comparison to Spain and the United States, pointing out that there is no "fatherland" feeling in the United States.

Herr Prost's dismantling of the notion of the nation is subtle at times, overt at others. He uses history and literature to argue that the fatherland is a myth based on a misunderstanding of history and an invented ideology that is not grounded in real German history, and contends that the notion of "fatherland" is nonexistent in many other industrialized nations. By using the word "ideology," Herr Prost makes clear that the German state is something that is constructed. Such strategies draw on the argument that until the mid-nineteenth century Germany could never be categorized as a state or an empire, and emphasize the primacy of regional identity vis-à-vis anything that might have been called "Germanness." But he also links this historical lack of nationhood with contemporary national identity, telling the students that people today who speak of a German national consciousness "don't know what they are talking about."

Herr Prost was not alone in this strategy. Herr Jaeger, another civics teacher in the same school, also told students that "Germany" is a recent concept, emerging in the late nineteenth century, implying that there is no historical basis for a German national identity. Until then, he argued, only regions existed, not a country: "Before then, there was no Germany—there was Saxony, there was Prussia . . . but you couldn't call Germany 'Germany' before 1871." Like Herr Prost, Herr Jaeger then links this historical claim with the contemporary situation, shifting immediately into a discussion about skinheads and foreigners in Germany. He turns to the class and says, abruptly, "OK, let's take the skinheads from this class," and calls on three students by name, all of whom have shaved heads. He then asks, "what if the three of you were walking down the street, wearing your bomber jackets and your big black boots, but without the ideological thoughts that go with that—what if you just looked like that and were walking down the street together, how would people react?" When one of the students replies, "We'd be attacked!" Herr Jaeger counters, "I don't really think so," and tells the students that people would be afraid of them, explaining that a lot of right-wing extremists are not actually committed to the ideology, but rather are right-wing because it gives them a sense of power, a feeling of power. "They need to feel more powerful," he suggests.

Both Herr Prost and Herr Jaeger work to dismantle the notion of a German nation by arguing that Germanness is a relatively new construct that was created out of more regional affiliations. But immediately after making this argument, both teachers raised the situation of the contemporary resurgence in nationalism. Herr Jaeger did this overtly, shifting the discussion from Germany's founding in 1871 directly to a hypothetical discussion about what students would do if they were attacked as right-wing extremists, finally working to devalue right-wing ideology entirely, claiming instead that many right-wing extremists are engaged in the scene because they need to feel powerful. Herr Prost, whose link to the contemporary situation was more subtle, nonetheless directly argued against the current increase in observed nationalistic behaviors and attitudes. He argued that "those people" who talk about a German consciousness are wrong because they are unaware of their own history.

By linking the historical absence of a German nation with the current situation of increasing right-wing extremism, both teachers worked to deconstruct national identity among their students. Coupled with many teachers' stated aims to "reach" the students in their classrooms who they deemed "at-risk" for participation in right-wing radical groups, which were made clear to me during faculty meetings, in interviews, and during informal conversation with teachers, it seems especially clear that these side remarks and instructional "moments" have deeper intentions. But their rational approaches to the subject may not resonate very well with what might be a more emotionally laden desire on the part of students—namely, a wish to express a sense of national identity and pride.

Debunking the Myth of German "Ethnicity"

A second set of arguments observed among teachers relates to the historical context of German ethnicity, as teachers made explicit attempts to invalidate a blood-based conception of national belonging. For example, teachers told students that "Germanness" is much more complicated and diverse than one might expect. "We are all foreigners ourselves, really," Herr Jaeger argued in one lesson, pointing out that Germans today are the product of centuries of intra-European intermarriage through widespread migration and immigration. He explained that much of German and Berliner slang was influenced by French as a result of the Huguenot migration: the slang word for goodbye (*Tschuss*), comes from the French word "Adieu," as does a Berlin slang word for pub and a few other slang terms. In an interview in 2004, Herr Jaeger reported that he works to deconstruct his students' view of Germanness as based on genetic factors:

> I always try to [approach this] with my students in connection with "who is foreign [*fremd*], what is a German." I tell them, well, if one looks at your genes, if one could tell from genes which nation you belong to, . . . I say, one would probably find very little left that could be characterized as German or the old Teutons [*den alten Germanen*], as they were always called, yeah, there one would also find a little of the French, a little of the Roman, a little Scandinavian. . . . Yeah, well it's, the German nation is actually pretty mixed (laughs) . . . also through the Napoleonic wars, everything . . . the typical German actually doesn't exist, there are very, very many differences.

Herr Meyer, a civics teacher in his mid-thirties, remarks that "the German nation is a hodge-podge of different peoples. With phases of immigration, so that we, so that I wouldn't dare to cite German blood. Because it doesn't exist. It's also a construct." The emigration of Huguenots from France during the persecution of Protestants was a popular example, both in classrooms and in interviews. Teachers also pointed out that whole populations immigrated from Sweden and other border countries during historical periods in Germany when the population was low and workers were needed. Frau Stein, a teacher in her early fifties, reports:

> The German nation for me is a mix [*Mischform*] of people of diverse heritages. Well, for example the debates about immigration and so on, for me they are actually incomprehensible because there have always been a lot of people who immigrated to Germany, whether it's the Huguenots who came to Berlin, also from Poland and so on, well, right with Berliners' names . . . it's very clearly recognizable.

As we sat in the teachers' lounge in the spring of 2004, Frau Dann, a civics teacher in her mid-fifties, explained how she uses this strategy intentionally with her students:

> And I really try to pass on to the youth that we always have to be courageous. And I do that, for example . . . by having them tell oral histories from home. How was it in World War II, where did the parents come from, where did the grandparents come from, in order to point out the multicultural in every family, and that is my thing, that I am very happy to point out this diversity and basically always try to point it out here at school, [to point out that] Berlin was always a melting pot, and this "Aryan" doesn't exist here. And I am always the best example of an Aryan, and I say, I have Italian blood in me, lots of it, only one can't see it, and they wouldn't know it, eh?

Frau Dann points out that she works to show students that all Germans are "multicultural," that all families are of mixed ethnic background. The notion that there is such a thing as an "Aryan," she argues, is absurd: it "doesn't exist." As proof, moreover, she offers students her own mixed ethnic background. One would never notice her "Italian blood," implicitly referring to her own light skin tone, eyes, and hair. Such teacher interactions clearly reinforce a narrative that devalues a German national identity that is based on blood-based heritage.

These interactions may not have the effect that teachers intend, however. In trying to deconstruct an ethnic idea of Germanness by focusing on the "mixed" character of Germans (due to centuries of intra-European migration), for example, teachers could potentially—though unintentionally—have the opposite effect, by reinforcing the notion that national communities are grounded in blood-based ties (e.g., by referring to one's "Italian blood," for example). And again, a rational approach to deconstructing Germanness may not be very effective at reaching students whose appeals to German identity and pride appear to be grounded in more emotional claims. Some of Frau Dann's students, she admits, "totally resist" her efforts. When that happens, she gives them a homework assignment to

> ask your mother and your father, grandfather, grandmother, where, who still knows something. Who comes from where, and you tell us about it here. Yeah? Simply so that it will become clear to them, and many [of them] want of course to be good, pure Germans and then have a problem with it. But when they notice then, that actually everyone is really a mixture, um I don't want to claim that I can change their thinking, but I want to place something beside it. I want to open up the closed [minds].

Other teachers used discussions about the complexity of Germanness to confuse students' thinking about national identity and national pride. As Frau Cordner, a civics teacher in her early forties, observes:

> Well, the students that I have, they are frequently right-wing. I think it is sort of in fashion, that it's cool to be right (wing). How well grounded it might be, that's questionable. Thank God it is not always so well grounded. . . . But in any case it is apparent that a high percentage of students have this oppositional attitude, according to the motto "we are always made responsible for what happened then, in the Third Reich, and we don't have anything to do with that," and "the others have committed crimes that were just as terrible," these kinds of arguments are very frequent. And there are also very often phrases like, in the direction of, "I am proud to be German," even if it is not exactly this phrasing. . . . But then they find out, when we talk about it, what is German, that it is very difficult to ascertain [based on] particular attributes.

Frau Cordner introduces several important issues in this brief statement. First, she acknowledges that some young Germans are attracted to the right wing as part of an oppositional culture (Willis 1977), in reaction to a perceived pressure to feel guilt, shame, and responsibility for the crimes of their grandparents' generation. Second, she notes that the right wing is attractive as a fashion statement, intuiting that some of the appeal of the right wing is due to its popularity as a youth subculture (which, in turn, may be linked to the oppositional elements of this same culture). Finally, she reports that her reaction to such students is to have a discussion about Germanness, forcing them to realize that Germanness is complex and difficult to define based on particular (racial or cultural) attributes.

Maintaining the Taboo on National Pride

Because the timing of my research in one school coincided with a parliamentary debate about national pride, the topic emerged as a primary discussion topic in two classrooms taught by Herr Bach, an experienced civics teacher, and was raised in other classrooms as well as in casual conversations and interviews with students. While one teacher's views on national pride cannot be generalized to all teachers, Herr Bach's approach is consistent with students' reactions to a perceived taboo on national pride, which I discussed in chapter 3. The detailed discussion in these two classrooms offers rich detail about how this taboo is discussed by teachers and perceived by students.

When the parliamentary debate about national pride broke out during the spring of 2001, Herr Bach decided to discuss the topic of national pride with his classes. At the start of the discussion in each of the two classes I observed on this topic, Herr Bach put up an overhead of a newspaper picture depicting a collage of famous Germans and German things: Goethe, German countryside scenery, the German Basic Law, Katharina Witt, Mercedes, Bridgestone, and Beethoven, among others, with the caption: "Yes! Bild-Readers are Proud of Germany!" and asks the students what they thought of the picture. During the ensuing discussion, Herr Bach's comments were unapologetically anti-pride, as the following excerpt illustrates:

Herr Bach: I can't be proud that I was born in a country . . .
Markus: I don't think it's bad to be proud of your country as long as it doesn't mean that you think your country is better than others.
Herr Bach: But can you always make that distinction clearly?
Robert: If I say I'm proud, it doesn't mean I'm proud of everything.
Susanne: Being proud doesn't mean that you're blind.

Herr Bach: But national pride is a totally overgeneralized feeling.

Robert: We don't even know what pride is — because during the past years national pride was such a taboo — I think we can start to be proud now.

Martin: But with the EU now, each country can't start to have its own individual national pride.

Marena: I think you can because each country has to retain its own identity. . . . I think we should also [have] our own culture.

Herr Bach: But in order to achieve that, do we need national pride?

As the discussion continues, Herr Bach tells the students that a country can have an identity and a culture without national pride, and pride carries a dangerous connotation, in the sense that it is not possible to distinguish between an expression of national pride that is "internal" and one that necessarily views other countries as lesser.

A few minutes after the previous exchange took place, a student brought up the example of other countries' flags, and how in many other countries, flags are hung out on national holidays. He asked Herr Bach what he thought about this practice, and Herr Bach said that he finds it odd. The following dialogue then ensued:

Klaus: Flags are just a sign that one belongs . . .

Herr Bach: [He] gives up his individualism and joins a community.

Klaus: What's wrong with a community?

Marena: It wouldn't work if everyone just lived for himself — one is only stronger in a group, in order to change something, you can't do it alone. That's why humans have lived for centuries in groups.

Herr Bach: But this group feeling gets sacrificed to the national . . .

Here, Herr Bach emphasizes that national pride (as expressed by the display of a national flag, for example) necessitates a loss of individual freedom and a sacrificing of individual will for the good of the community. Even as his students argue with him that a community is a good thing, Herr Bach remains firm that identification with or pride in a national community is something dangerous. During the remaining classroom discussion as well as in the other classroom discussion I observed, Herr Bach pointed out that Hitler came to power through the abuse of the feeling of national pride, and observed that he (Herr Bach) was born into a generation where you couldn't ever say you were proud to be German. "I think national pride is a sickness," he lectured to one class matter-of-factly:

I can't be a nationalist because I place a great value on my individual freedom. Some people say there is a difference between healthy patriotism and unhealthy patriotism, but I don't really think so—there are just different levels of nationalism, whereby the weaker forms are less of a sickness.

In a later interview, Herr Bach described his personal goals in his classroom instruction to me:

I would like to educate the students to become self-confident individuals, so that they don't just fall into being "followers" or something. I mean they should express themselves, and they should react humanely in the sense of humanity, and then of course I'd also like them to become good democrats.

In his own stated goals, Herr Bach does not say that he is trying to shape students' political opinions (about national pride or anything else) in any particular way. Indeed, he did not actually tell students that they could not be proud of being German; most of his explanations of why he thought national pride was unacceptable centered on his own opinions, telling students that he thought national pride is a sickness. His insistence that pride is unacceptable could be interpreted as a consistent effort to "play devil's advocate" and encourage debate. But his efforts were characteristic of the general taboo on national pride that students hear repeatedly from adults and authority figures.

In an interview in 2004, Herr Bach elaborated on his views about nationalism and patriotism, supporting the views that he shared with his classes:

But in the end I do have a little bit of difficulty in differentiating all these expressions, for me patriotism is only a varnished form of nationalism. Of course I also love my Heimat and would like to see that the people there are doing well, but in and of itself, with all of these expressions there is always the danger, conscious or unconscious, that they, that one holds oneself up higher than other patriots of other nations, that one looks down on them, or that one separates oneself off from the others through patriotism and the result, I think, can be conflicts. . . . And I think that is one of the basic problems of European history, that there is much too much nationalism and patriotism.

Moreover, Herr Bach feels that his students are more nationalistic than he is. He reported to me during the same interview:

This is always so poorly generalized, eh, . . . but for the majority of my students, I think, nationalism is meaningful. . . . I always notice it if, I don't know, there are soccer games or, what's that program called with the hit [songs] . . . Grand Prix de Eurovision or something . . . well, I always am not able to comprehend that at all, how one can kneel right down like that [*wie man sich da so reinknien kann*], but I think, they overwhelmingly have . . . other opinions about that.

Upon further prodding about what might lie behind these differences between himself and his students, however, Herr Bach rejected the notion that this might be a generational difference. Instead, he notes, laughing, "in the end I am convinced that also in my generation, most [people] think (laugh) like my students." He sees himself as part of a vanishing minority of nonnational thinkers, but still holds out hope that others will come to identify more as Europeans than as Germans:

I fall a little bit out of the frame, although of course I hope that I don't only belong to a disappearing small minority, and my hope is that it will grow in some way, that it will become more natural to think European, that . . . but it's just a wish . . . I am still very skeptical about whether it will come to that, because at the moment [I see] rather the tendency for it to go in the opposite direction.

In fact, Herr Bach is less of an outsider than he perceives. In an interview in the spring of 2004, Herr Weiss, an experienced civics teacher in his mid-fifties, observes that his generation consciously rejected identifying with Germany or with the German nation, choosing instead to confront their parents and other adults about their roles in the Nazi era. He notes that Germany does not mean much to him personally: "patriotism . . . fatherland is also of no value for me. It's the country in which I was born, not more." But the younger generation, his students, he has noticed, have a different relationship to the nation. In the classroom, he reinforces the taboo on pride with his students:

This expression "pride," I always criticize it because one can only really use "pride" for something that one has achieved oneself. That is my firm conviction, and "I am proud to be a German," I think something like that is moronic [*Schwachsinniges*]. I always tell the students, I am proud to live in [name of a local district] or something . . . in order to develop it ad absurdum, many [of them] don't understand when I criticize it this way. . . . Well, they apparently need it, they must be allowed to react to their nationality somehow emotionally . . . and for them that's pride, then.

This excerpt is revealing in several ways. Herr Weiss acknowledges that he has an unapologetically antinational pride stance, which he conveys to students. His use of the phrase "ad absurdum," moreover, indicates how ridiculous he finds the possibility of a sense of collective pride grounded in the nation. But he also understands that his stance on national pride may shut down discussion among his students. Earlier in the interview, during a discussion about right-wing radical tendencies among adolescents, I asked Herr Weiss how these kinds of conversations come up in his classes and whether opinions based on nationalism or national pride appear to be limited to his right-wing extremist students. His reaction is key to understanding how discussions of national identity or national pride may be silenced in classrooms: "Well, of course they always already know that I react to that in a pretty allergic or critical way and in that sense, I think, they don't all say what they think."

Alternative Approaches

Not all teachers I observed mediated an antinational approach to Germanness and German national identity, and the presence of alternative approaches illustrates the ways in which multiple narratives about nationhood coexist. During a discussion about identity and the European Union, one civics teacher spoke about German national identity in relatively positive terms, discussing the sense of German unity and referencing a sense of German identity. He contrasted the feeling of unity felt in Germany to that of the European Union, and claimed that even though Germans have internal divisions, in the end there is a sense of Germanness that connects everyone: "We make jokes about people from Saxony, or Bavaria, but really we are convinced that they are also Germans and that there will be a unity."

There were also instances where teachers challenged the prevailing narrative prohibiting national pride. As I was observing her class one late spring day, Frau Schmidt, a young teacher of civics and English, told her students that she feels it is time for Germans to be able to express pride. Frau Schmidt and her class had recently taken a field trip to the new Jewish Museum in Berlin and had spent a day viewing the exhibits, architecture, and historical displays in the museum. When the class next met, Frau Schmidt engaged the students in a reflection session about the trip. During the discussion, one student argued that he didn't feel that this generation should be made to feel guilty for the Holocaust and that it should be acceptable to be proud of being German. Frau Schmidt agreed, telling the class that she believes that this generation can be proud of what Germany has accomplished in the post-1945 era. As one of the youngest teachers I observed, however, Frau Schmidt is closer in age to the younger generation of students than she is to most of the teachers, and thus her efforts to support national pride are also reflective of generational transformations in the meaning of Germanness and German national identity.

In an interview in 2004, Frau Schmidt reiterated her earlier views, arguing that Germany needs to develop a stronger sense of national pride:

> Yes, I think . . . that Germany is perhaps at the moment, just after unification, um, a little bit on the way to finding itself again, to developing a consciousness for the nation, to developing a healthy patriotism, somehow we still haven't managed to do that and are always still searching for it and um, that, I think, will be a process that takes years. Decades probably. . . . Yes, I find that it's not at all a scandal if one says, one is gladly a German or one is happy to live here. On the contrary, we probably need more of . . . a normal relationship to our country, what unfortunately through the Third Reich um, is seen very critically, and it is, yes, we are lacking a normality with our patriotism, still. Unfortunately.

Unlike Herr Bach, who thinks that most of his students are more nationalistic than he is, Frau Schmidt finds that her students do not find their national identity particularly important:

> Frau Schmidt: Many of the younger people or students don't see it as important and say, "yeah, it doesn't matter whether I'm a Pole or a German or a Turk or a Spaniard" and "one mustn't be proud of his country," and I think that my parents' generation was happy to be pr-, well, to formulate it even more precisely, are happy to be German, but one doesn't really trust oneself here completely. . . . I think for a lot, a lot of [young people], it doesn't matter at all to them if they are, for example, German citizens or not, they just live here, and that is a sort of indifference that they develop, and I also think that, among young people, among those who are not somehow right-wing, no particular patriotism is prevailing. Well, it is almost negative to be patriotic.

CMI: And how do you notice that during instruction?

Frau Schmidt: I notice it in conversations, when one speaks to them, when one introduces this theme, then you get a response like, "yeah, that's all the same [to me]" and "that's just on a piece of paper, that doesn't mean anything, what kind of citizenship I have" and . . .

According to Frau Schmidt, her students largely support the anti-nationalist narrative that is mediated in textbooks, political debates, and in a broader public discourse. She finds that they resist her efforts to talk about national pride and that they are not interested in identifying with the nation. Even Frau Schmidt, however, stumbles over the actual word "proud," interrupting herself during her characterization of her parents' generation as proud. Before she even finishes saying the word "proud" (*Stolz*), she rephrases, suggesting instead that the older generation was simply happy to be German.

Frau Schmidt was not the only teacher who argued that Germans should be permitted to express pride. Across town, in a civics class of thirteen third-year construction school students, Herr Hahn led a discussion one day about what is "typically German." The class worked in small groups for a few minutes to discuss and complete five sentences on a handout, all of which dealt with issues of German identity, foreigners, and national pride. For example, the third sentence on the handout read: "In comparison to many other countries, in Germany there is no general national pride. A) I agree with this statement and think that . . . ; or B) I disagree with this statement and think that . . ."

After students worked in groups to complete the handout, a discussion began. When one student interjected a comment about national pride, saying that one can't have it, Herr Hahn corrected the student, saying "everyone can have it, the question is how you deal with it." A brief discussion then ensued with this particular student, who expressed anti-German and antinational pride opinions.

Although he defended the possibility of expressing national pride in this situation, however, Herr Hahn's own views about German national identity were rather complex. In another class discussion, he tried to persuade students that nationality is not something important. Instead, it could be viewed as merely one of many identities that individuals use to distinguish themselves from others. "Why does everything have to go in the direction of German or foreigner?" he asked, arguing that human behavior isn't always divided up this way and pointing out how when he was young, people from different towns would fight with young people from other towns instead of with foreigners.

In an interview three years later, Herr Hahn again revealed the complexity of his own views about national pride and national identity, showing that even though he defended the possibility of feeling national pride to his class of civics students, he personally was raised to believe otherwise:

> And I also think that Germany is simply too hard on itself. And therefore it is difficult for national consciousness to be raised, y'know? [*Und deshalb kommt da auch so ein äh . . . Nationalbewußtsein sehr schlecht hoch, ja?*] Because one is always in danger of tipping over and then perhaps too strong, to have too strong of a national consciousness. And that's the way I was raised, that one doesn't [have] such a strong, yes, that one sees oneself perhaps rather as, I don't know, as a human being and not at all as in the state.

Although Herr Hahn was quick to encourage his students in the classroom to view national pride as something not entirely taboo, he acknowledges that his own feelings on pride are more complicated. He does not personally feel a strong sense of attachment to the nation, preferring instead to identify as a "human being" rather than as a member of a national state, and sees the potential for national consciousness to be a slippery slope, in which the risk of developing a strong and exclusionary form of nationalism is always present.

Avoiding or Sidestepping Public Narratives

We can learn quite a bit about how public, official, or state narratives about national belonging are engaged in schools by paying attention to the silences in classrooms around issues of national identity. Most of the teachers I observed experienced some discomfort in broaching difficult subjects, such as those dealing with race, nationalism, national belonging, or the legacy of the Third Reich. Particularly in cases where students assert right-wing extremist or neo-Nazi attitudes and behaviors, teachers may feel uncomfortable discussing difficult, politically laden topics in the classroom, especially those that have been social taboos for so long, such as national pride.

Some teachers may also avoid such topics because they haven't fully resolved their own feelings about Germany's changing cultural landscape. Some of the teachers I interviewed and observed revealed prejudices about foreignness or a sense of insecurity about cultural transformations in Germany, particularly in terms of the increasing population of Muslim residents and foreigners. In two separate interviews, Herr Jaeger referred to the fact that his Turkish students do not know "their own history," although it is likely that many of them were born in Germany. Another teacher referred to the "foreign temperament" of his students. One teacher reported that she would not like to see a majority Muslim population in Germany because "that would make me fearful." She expressed concern that in such a scenario, her rights as a lesbian might not be protected. Herr Metzer discussed the problem of girls who are not allowed to do certain things "only because they had the bad luck to grow up in an Islamic-oriented (*islamistisch geprägten*) family." Herr Preuss, a teacher in his early thirties, said that potential citizens should have to take some kind of test "because they would [then] logically assimilate (*sich anpassen*) to the German [way]."

It is important to note that these comments were exceptional and do not reflect the entirety of these particular teachers' views. On the contrary, the comments are noteworthy because some of them were made by teachers who expressed some of the greatest concern with the perceived xenophobic leanings of their students and who seemed most dedicated to addressing these sentiments in their classrooms. They are included here to illustrate the extent to which even teachers who are deeply motivated to address their students' xenophobia may be struggling with Germany's increasing diversity, and because they offer a possible clue as to why so many of these teachers' peers may have chosen to avoid the issue altogether. The struggle to come to terms with Germany's rapid cultural transformation is thus not limited to right-wing students. Teachers, like students, are in need of further education and training to help them reconcile the transformations they are experiencing in their classrooms, their neighborhoods, and their nation.

The examples I have drawn upon thus far in this chapter rely on cases where teachers did directly raise and discuss issues related to national identity with their students, either by mediating or resisting narratives about national identity and national pride. But most of the teachers I observed did not address issues of national identity directly, instead remaining focused on topics related to less controversial ideological issues, such as the mechanics of voting, the reaction to the mad cow disease epidemic that year, and technical discussions of legal policies and regulations related to their future occupations, thereby avoiding direct discussions of national identity. In describing such classroom interactions as instances where national narratives were avoided, I do not mean to imply that the nation itself was disregarded. On the contrary, such topics also provide potential opportunities in which the nation is constructed—as teachers and students talk in national terms, reify national categories, and discuss the ways in which their lives are regulated and monitored by national authorities. In my observations, however, teachers did not use such conversations to address broader questions of what it means to be a German, of how Germanness can be understood, or of whether it is acceptable to be proud of being German. In other words, for most teachers, the prevailing public narratives about Germanness were overlooked, while they kept civics classroom topics within a range of less ideological and less controversial topics.

There were also teachers who found a middle ground—neither directly raising controversial narratives about Germanness nor avoiding them entirely. These teachers raised discussions of national identity or nationalism through metaphors or vague descriptions. Herr Prost, for example, made a veiled reference to the radical right, as described above, when he referred to "those people" who talk about a German consciousness. Another civics teacher, Herr Krug, as I discussed in chapter 4, referred to right-wing extremists as those "with very short hair," as he worked to shift students' opinions about black market labor by redirecting blame for the problem to Germans. By using the phrase "those with very short hair," Herr Krug's veiled reference to the shaved heads of right-wing radicals enables him to invoke the right wing while sidestepping an actual discussion of it.

Sidestepping discussions of the nation is not an uncommon tactic for the oldest generation of Germans—most of whom were active participants in World War II in some way or another. For nearly twenty years after the end of the war, German public discourse remained essentially silent about the atrocities committed by fellow Germans. It was not until the 1960s that a broad public discussion about the Holocaust began, as television specials and debates about the politics of various memorials coincided with a younger generation calling their parents to account for the war. Herr Mais, a civics teacher in his early fifties, who was born in the west, offered a lengthy discussion of how the three generations deal with the trauma of World War II. While his parents' generation ignored their crimes, his generation actively worked to force an older generation to be accountable. Meanwhile, a younger generation no longer feels the pressure to force this national accountability onto the public agenda because

> for the younger generation, it's totally clear that it's different. They didn't live through this time, which we lived through, where this confrontation with the crimes of National Socialism first of all practically didn't take place for twenty years. . . . Because we couldn't forgive our father's generation, they weren't even prepared to come to terms with their crimes . . . and that problem doesn't exist for today's generation . . . and they want to feel and live again this unbroken national identity, like other countries too . . . from their perspective it is certainly understandable. . . . In the meanwhile there has been a lot of working through, also in the schools in the meantime, in my time [issues about the war] were completely dead silent in the schools . . . and it was only the teachers-in-training and the younger generation of teachers who came into the schools in the 60s, who began to make this a topic in instruction. And the old teachers didn't agree with that.

Moreover, Herr Mais believes that young people's frustration with the taboo on national identity results from their lack of understanding about the degree to which an older generation's relationship with the nation was destroyed in their attempts to confront their parents with the crimes of the Holocaust. "This broken relationship that my generation has to Germanness . . . and so on, that's not there for [my students]. They perceive that many people have this [broken relationship] in Germany, . . . but for them that creates a lack of understanding and, in part, also anger."

Students' Views of Civic Education

Students may not have a very clear understanding of why an older generation has a "broken relationship" with Germany, but they certainly sense that teachers have clear ideas about how they should relate to the nation. During the interviews I conducted with students, a significant number told me that they felt pressured to adopt certain political opinions. Nearly a third said that they felt social pressure *not* to express their opinions openly about certain topics in general—especially those related to national pride, belonging, immigration, or identity. Several students had the perception that teachers only provided some of the story of the Third Reich. Even when these complaints came from students whose political opinions were right-wing, they still reveal a sense of resistance to a perceived hegemonic discourse about World War II. As Jan, a construction apprentice, complains, teachers

> only portray us as the bad, the evil ones, and everything else is glorified . . . there are bigger injustices and worse things than what happened in our history, what we did, and maybe some of that shouldn't be silenced . . . but that is all taboo, taboo topics . . . the main thing is to only talk about our guilt, but nothing else is allowed to be brought up.

While Jan expressed views that were openly sympathetic to the right wing and even suggested that National Socialism was not completely bad, similar opinions were voiced by students whose political views were more moderate or liberal.

Ten students felt that pressure was exerted by teachers to think in a certain way or said that they felt censored or restricted in class from expressing opinions openly. Two students complained about teachers' "left-wing" opinions and approaches, while others talked more about the lack of open discussion in classrooms.[7] An antinational feeling was also perceived to come from *outsiders* (from other countries or from foreigners) and from other Germans. Maria, a twenty-two-year-old hotel-worker trainee who had already attended an academic *Gymnasium*, observes that the topic is a constant issue, whether in high school classrooms or while visiting other countries:

> I was at an academic high school (Gymnasium) and there, I'd say at least every other year the topic—whether it's in religion, German, or history—of the second World War is brought out again. . . . And sometime, I have to say that our generation can't do anything about that . . . and especially because, what I've noticed is that the prejudices against Germans throughout Europe are still there . . . and it's a little shocking, when you go there and are then called a Nazi, although you can't do anything about it.

Several students complained, often with a good deal of bitterness, that there was too great of an emphasis on the Third Reich and the Holocaust. As Markus, a scaffold-builder apprentice remarks, referring to how classroom time is allocated, "I was told for a year straight how shitty and how horrible the Second World War was, but I see that already all day long . . . how shitty it was, I don't need to be told that anymore."

Another lengthy excerpt from Jan, the eighteen-year-old construction apprentice quoted above, captures the emotions that I heard from many students about their civics classrooms and about the sense they have that Germans are held to an unfair standard compared with other nations that have committed atrocities in the past. In this excerpt, Jan is responding to the question of what he would do differently if he were a civics teacher:

> Jan: And then I wouldn't present this politically one-sided instruction and force certain opinions onto students, which is done though in civics instruction in every school, actually, that there are certain standpoints that are not at all . . . if somebody has a certain standpoint, he's made laughable and isn't listened to anymore, can't even get a word out, is always interrupted and . . . that certain texts are always only pushed in one direction and actually all of the students are only pushed somehow, yeah, it's like that, it is, and not at all somehow to critically engage certain texts, but rather always only, um, politically very much in one direction.
>
> CMI: And which direction is that?
>
> Jan: Um, the left, yeah the far far left.
>
> CMI: And do you mean both from the teachers and in the textbooks, that it's one-sided?
>
> Jan: Yes, of course . . . only texts from certain authors are selected, that then only deal with certain topics, mostly it's like that, whether it's German civics . . . always the evil National Socialism, and um, evil, evil, we started all the wars and so on and finally it's not, I mean, it doesn't matter where you go, it's always only these topics and, well, that one could engage divergent [views] somehow . . .
>
> CMI: Which topics do you think would be better?
>
> Jan: Well, you could . . . I see that, well the Americans have committed a lot of war crimes and actually every . . . every country has and . . . and there are other bigger war crimes that other countries committed . . . you have to look at the Russians also and . . . that one could also discuss our history and the suffering that our people experienced . . . and that one also could discuss that.

Jan is a typical example of the kind of student about whom teachers in the construction school expressed concern. Although he did not openly admit to being part of the right wing or to having right-wing extremist opinions, many of the statements he made during the interview placed his political opinions clearly within the range of right-wing radicalism. Yet his reaction to the ways national identity and pride are taught and discussed in schools is typical of how many students felt about their generation and the continuing legacy of World War II, and is also illustrative of the ways in which teachers' efforts can backfire. Jan appears to be yearning for some kind of positive engagement with his own national identity, or at least for a sense that Germany is not the only country which committed evil and horrible acts. His comments illustrate the appeal that right-wing extremist groups may have for young people like him, who express such frustration with the prevailing narrative that Germanness is something to be ashamed of, that it is not possible to be proud of being German, and that there can be no sense of national identity, particularly one based on an ethnic or cultural notion of Volk. In this context, radical right-wing groups whose recruiting tactics include efforts to provide young men a space to express a positive sense of national pride may become all the more successful.

Another student also suggested that teachers' efforts may be backfiring. Kai, a nineteen-year-old information-technology apprentice, argues that teachers spend too much time talking about World War II and believes this focus ultimately leads to the deterioration of German identity and increased hate for other countries: "At some point the people ask themselves if it all even makes sense anymore, to be German . . . or you get the mentality then that all the other nations are bad, as a result of this total focus on one issue."

Some students also felt that the complete focus on Germany and its history took away time that could have been better spent. Mehmet, a Turkish-German hotel trainee reports:

> [If I were a civics teacher] I would try to give the people more about other peoples and other cultures, as a required subject. That everyone would have to learn how a Chinese and an Indian and an Arab greet one another. That's what it's actually about, in civics it's not just about problems that are in Germany, or only what's going on here.

Conclusion

This chapter detailed the various ways in which civics teachers mediate, resist, avoid, and potentially transform prevailing public narratives about nationhood in their classrooms. A prevailing narrative about national identity and national pride in Germany has presented an antinationalist approach to collective identity and has invalidated national pride as a legitimate expression of national belonging. Although in interviews an older generation of teachers is, by and large, quite supportive of the prevailing antinationalist narrative, this chapter illustrates that more divergent viewpoints are evidenced in the classroom. While some efforts reinforce the prevailing narrative, at other times they reveal how competing narratives about nationhood can coexist.

Most often I found that prevailing narratives about nationhood are avoided by teachers, many of whom may be uncomfortable with the social taboos surrounding national identity and national pride in Germany. The teachers who did reinforce a prevailing narrative about national belonging in Germany that invalidates national pride and discourages national identity more broadly did so in a variety of ways. These included attempts to deconstruct a "German" identity by showing that Germanness is something relatively new (historically), or that it doesn't "really" exist—especially if it is based on a biological or ethnic conception of national belonging—due to decades of intermarriage among immigrant and German populations. Other efforts aimed at invalidating national pride by arguing that it is not possible to be proud of "just" being born somewhere, or that national pride is dangerous, inevitably leading to the quest for power and the destruction of other peoples, as illustrated by Germany's own history. There were also teachers who resisted or rejected these prevailing narratives about nationhood, however. Two teachers made statements that directly contradicted the prevailing narrative about national pride, for example, both resisting and potentially transforming that narrative. The range of approaches taken by teachers in the classroom reminds us that the terrain of nationhood is contested and that multiple narratives can coexist and be mediated simultaneously, even to the same students in the same school.

By focusing on teachers' intentional efforts to directly address national identity, we should not overlook the fact that the nation is mediated and constructed in classrooms in a myriad of mundane ways that may be wholly unrelated to teachers' intentions. The nation can be reified or constructed, for example, in students' quotidian interactions with textbook titles that emphasize Germany, with curricular topics that focus on national retirement or health care systems, or during fieldtrips to former concentration camps or other historical sites, to name just a few examples. The focus of this chapter has been on teachers' attempts to directly transmit messages about national identity and Germanness to students, but these efforts are a small part of students' everyday interactions with the nation.

Finally, it is also significant that most teachers were aware of generational differences between them and their students, although they also pointed out that differences of opinion stem not only from generational differences but also from political and educational differences and, as one teacher succinctly observed, from experience: "They simply don't have as much life [experience] behind them, within one specific society." Teachers are also aware that schools are not the only (or even the most important) site where their students experience socialization. Frau Cordner, for example, notes that she thinks it is possible to achieve something through schooling, but says there is always too little time. "It's also a long-term thing. I always hope . . . that it starts some kind of thinking process for them. Well of course I can't transform (*umkrempeln*) the students in an hour."

Teachers' efforts to shape the ways in which their students relate to the nation are tempered by the reactions of their students to their civics classes. Students' views about civic education reveal a perceived hegemonic pressure to relate to the nation in a particular way. Even those students who do not sense such pressure, however, may not have received the narratives that teachers mediate in the same way in which teachers intended. For example, teachers who argue that Germany needs foreigners to support its social welfare state because Germans aren't reproducing enough—an argument I heard in classroom observations—could inadvertently fuel the paranoia of right-wing extremists who fear that Germans will be overrun by foreigners.

Teachers are aware of generational differences between themselves and their students, just as they are aware of their own generation's efforts to confront their parents' generation with the crimes of the Holocaust. But they may not be aware of the extent to which the same exact statement can be interpreted quite differently by different people, depending on each individual's worldview or standpoint. Statements that teachers make to try to convince students that they should be more open to cultural diversity, then, may actually confirm students' fears because they hear and interpret such statements through a different lens or worldview. And finally, the rational approaches taken by many teachers may not be effective at addressing what appear to be more emotionally rooted calls for a national identity and national pride.

six

Blood, Culture, Birthplace

Determining how ordinary people think about nationhood requires more than an investigation of how they relate to prevailing national narratives. We must also consider how they think about the very definition of nationality, what it means to belong to the nation, and who is permitted to become a part of it. According to literature which presents Germanness as grounded in a blood-based understanding, we might expect ordinary Germans to limit their understanding of who belongs in the national community to those who share German "blood," having descended from German forefathers. However, neither the older generation nor the younger generation of Germans I interviewed supported a blood-based conception of national belonging, with only a few exceptions. Instead, my interviews with both generations reveal that both the older and the younger generation of Germans formally deviate from the official conception of Germanness that was in place up until 1999, as evidenced in citizenship and naturalization law. Instead, most of the teachers and students I interviewed support a view of German national belonging in which anyone can become German, providing that they assimilate culturally. I analyzed teachers' views on this matter in chapter 5 and documented their explicit efforts to deconstruct a blood-based conception of Germanness in their classrooms and in interview discussions. In this chapter, I turn to students' conceptions of Germanness, relying on teacher interviews to a lesser extent to draw out generational comparisons, similarities, and contrasts.

Although the vast majority of the young people I interviewed conceive of Germanness as determined primarily by cultural criteria, for a few students, citizenship and national belonging is actually something determined by blood. It is this data which I address first in this chapter. Of the sixty students I interviewed, four privileged blood over culture as a condition for German citizenship, linking citizenship to a community of descent (jus sanguinis) or to a national group's physical appearance, as several quotes below illustrate. Three of these four students were born in east Germany, while one was born in west Germany. Two of these students were training in information-technology trades, while the remaining two were training in construction trades; in other words, the four students who expressed a blood-based view of citizenship were evenly divided between occupations with excellent labor market prospects and those with poor labor market prospects. Three additional students generally defined citizenship in terms of filiation, showing that they conceive of citizenship directly linked to the citizenship of a parent, and two more students expressed understandings of citizenship that were classified as "ethnic" because they referenced the German term "Volk" while defining the term "citizen."

Jan, an eighteen-year-old training in a construction field, had the most clearly racialized view of citizenship among all of the students I interviewed. He used adjectives like "absurd" and "sick" to talk about the notion of non-ethnic Germans identifying as German and expressed his views quite clearly during a discussion about the possibility of dual citizenship:

> What I think about [dual citizenship]—it is absurd. . . . Because if you put a Hungarian salami in a refrigerator and then look at it after six years, it's still a Hungarian salami and not a little German sausage. And that's the way it is also, that one can just say, I am indeed a Turk, but now I'm a German, or I will perhaps be both, simply, rather one is born into a community of fate [*Schicksalgemeinschaft*], and one has to accept that, you can't just write "sheep" on a pig and have it then be a pig. I mean, that's oversimplifying a little, but I mean, that makes the point then.

It is important to note students' responses could not always be clearly identified as having a "racial" or an "ethnic" or a "cultural" understanding of citizenship because several students expressed multiple viewpoints throughout their interviews or contradicted themselves at some point in the interview, as some of those who initially focused on ethnic elements in talking about national identity later emerged as having a stronger cultural approach, and vice versa. Jan, whose extreme views on Germanness and race became increasingly clear as the interview progressed, for example, stated in one of the first responses in the interview that "the term 'citizen' is not connected to any particular heritage," thus initially indicating that he does not understand citizenship in ethnic terms. Over the course of the next several interview questions, however, his responses revealed just the opposite, showing that he conceives of citizenship as an essential and biologically embedded part of an individual. According to Jan, it is no more possible to change one's citizenship than it is for a pig to become a sheep.

Some students simply seemed to be confused about which elements were more important to them, demonstrating that ethnic and racial characteristics, for them, are important in combination with cultural issues. One example is Benjamin, an information-technology apprentice. Early in the interview, Benjamin defined citizenship as linked to rights and duties and explicitly argued that it should not be understood in ethnic or religious terms:

> Citizenship . . . if I live in a state, I have as I said rights and duties accordingly, and this citizenship symbolizes, in principle, that I belong to a particular state, and in my opinion that shouldn't have anything to do with whichever . . . origin or religion or so . . . rather, it has only in principle [to do with] also things under international law, that a specific differentiation exists regionally, they are also OK, one should accept them, and that would be in my sense citizenship.

Although Benjamin initially stated, in this part of the interview, that origin should have nothing to do with citizenship, he later notes that cultural assimilation is important to his understanding of who constitutes a German:

> I don't know, well just because someone has a German passport or so, [he] is not exactly in that sense or in my eyes necessarily a German, rather . . . it always still depends how you view the context, well for example, I know here somewhere in Brandenburg there is an Indian mayor here for a number of years already. He . . . feels comfortable there and at home and is there for the people and so, there I wouldn't necessarily say he is a German, but he simply belongs, if he was elected there, he appears to have, um, competencies and he belongs there and he appears to have mostly integrated there, so why shouldn't he live or work and what, I don't know, have a family here in Germany, I see no reason that would speak against that, although I probably wouldn't exactly say to him, "that is a German" in that sense, that . . . I don't know, whether . . . whether one can say that so simply, just because someone has a passport, is one that automatically, that is surely also an attitudinal question for each individual, how he integrates . . .

Finally, as the interview continues, Benjamin becomes more specific in his criteria for what constitutes a German, stating that it would be easier for him to perceive someone as German if they have a "European appearance." He explains that someone who has German citizenship (from another ethnic group)

> has the same rights and duties. . . . I don't see any problem with that at all, that he can have that . . . [and can] be a respected member of society. . . . And I don't know if he is . . . [if one] must definitely say "that's a German then," rather, he is then, I, what do I know, someone who lives in Brandenburg, he's just a Brandenburger or . . . is just a nice person or . . . but I don't know . . . there, I find, it's hard to say, if it is then definitely a German, probably it would be easier for me, I'd say, if he . . . also had more of the European appearance [*europäisches Aussehen*].

Here, after his initial argument that citizenship, in the abstract, should not be linked to origin or religion, Benjamin shows that in the German case, Germanness is something separate from citizenship for him and implies it is linked to race, at least in terms of phenotypical attributes and physical appearance. Having German citizenship does not mean one is a "German." Benjamin's understanding of Germanness became more muddled elsewhere in the interview, however, when he defined the German Volk as an ethnic group, but stated that other ethnic groups can still become German—thereby defining Germanness as something other than ethnic heritage. But in the above quote, he explains that it would be easier for him to think of a "non-ethnic" German as a German if the person "looked" like a German or European.

Like Benjamin, Henning, a scaffold-builder apprentice, appears to view Germanness as something separate from citizenship, as he complained about the number of foreigners in Berlin: "When I'm [in Berlin], I only see Turks instead of Germans." By stating that he "sees" Turks instead of Germans, Henning reveals that he understands Germanness as linked to physical or phenotypical appearance rather than to citizenship status. Rene, a nineteen-year-old information-technology apprentice, was even clearer about how his understanding of Germanness is linked to race and phenotypical appearance:

> CMI: Does that mean, then—there are foreigners who have been in Germany for many generations—where do they fit in relation to the German Volk?

Rene: For me they are still foreigners. OK . . . with some of them, you can't see it, but . . . for example, with the Russians you can see it, with the Turks you can see it, with the Negroes[1] you can see it . . . with the whites here you can't really see it, that they come from somewhere else . . . there are just particular ethnic groups [*Völkergruppen*] . . . where you can recognize that they were foreigners and are still foreigners.

According to Rene, even foreigners who have been in Germany for many generations cannot be called Germans—and this is because Germanness is clearly identifiable on the basis of genetic or physical cues. Moreover, these groups and individuals are "still foreigners," according to Rene, even if "with some of them, you can't see it."

It is also important to note that there were occasions when culture appeared to function like race in students' thinking. This was particularly the case when certain cultural and religious practices were viewed as incompatible with German cultural norms, which betrays a view of culture as bounded and impermeable (Anthias 1995; Wren 2001). Other scholars have argued that racism can be expressed without any mention of "race" per se (Balibar 1991, 23; also see Gilroy 1991, 1996, 2000; Salecl 1994; Wieviorka 1996). In other words, culture sometimes "acts" like race, and "race is coded as culture" (Goldberg 1993, 73). For example, Henning, an eighteen-year-old scaffold-builder apprentice, believes that it is impossible for Muslims to be both Muslim and German:

Henning: It's just my opinion, for example, if all of the Muslims are supposedly Germans now, with their passports that have "German" in them. Then they should . . . for example, when you drive through Berlin, then you see all the mosques that they built extra for the Muslims, so that they can run in there with their headscarves and pray "ha la salam." Well, then they're not Germans, then they're still Muslims, Muslims, I'd say, or?
CMI: So in order to be German, one must then—
Henning: —assimilate to the Germans. Exactly.

According to Henning, being Muslim is incompatible with being German. Henning's view of cultural and religious difference as a closed or bounded entity (where it is impossible to be both Muslim and German) implies that at least for some, religion may pose a barrier to being perceived as "really German."

Germanness Defined by Citizenship,
Birthplace, and Language

At the beginning of the interview, I asked participants to define the words "citizen" and "citizenship" as they would to an alien who had just landed in a spaceship. In the analysis of their responses, I found that most of these young people define citizenship—both in the abstract and as applied to the German case—primarily by birth or residence in a geographic region. The most frequent abstract definition of citizen referred to someone who lives within the borders of a given state and is a part of the society within that state. A third of the students (twenty) defined the term "citizen" by explaining that there are multiple states in the world and that the people living within each of those states are citizens of that state.

Citizenship, in other words, is primarily understood in terms of birthplace and geographic residence. Citizenship is also, however, deeply intertwined with understandings of Germanness. For the majority of these students, "German" refers primarily to anyone with German citizenship. For example, Martin, a twenty-year-old information-technology apprentice, argues that the German nation is to be equated with the German Volk, which in turn includes anyone who has German citizenship:

> CMI: When you say that the German nation is the same thing as the German Volk, what does German Volk mean for you? . . . Who belongs to it?
>
> Martin: Well, everyone who lives in Germany, the German Volk, . . . no difference if someone has moved here, I mean from outside, from whichever foreign country or so . . . and has German citizenship, whether he has only gotten it recently, [he] is also a German, I would say.

The term "German," for Martin, refers to anyone who has German citizenship, even those who have obtained it only recently. Other students also revealed that their conceptions of citizenship are deeply intertwined with their sense of who belongs to the nation. Jens, an information-technology apprentice, suggested that the German nation is made up of the German citizens—which include the citizen-children of former guest workers:

> The German nation? Yeah, from the people, from the German citizens, the ones that have a German passport, were born here, yeah . . . the for-

eigners, who were brought here earlier, as workers, as manual laborers . . . the children that are being born here now, are also German citizens.

Although recent scholarship has made a compelling argument for the decoupling of citizenship from identity in studies of citizenship law and policy (Joppke 2004, 2005a, b), the evidence in these interviews suggests that for most ordinary people, understandings of citizenship are often inseparable from their understandings of national identity. Peter, a twenty-five-year-old information-technology apprentice, volunteers that his understanding of who a German is relies on an individual's citizenship status, along with language fluency:

> If someone doesn't speak especially good German, then one automatically assumes it is not a German, although German actually would mean that he has the German citizenship, which he certainly can have. We had that in our class, yeah, [another student] is somehow German or so . . . and came, I think, from Kosovo and we first assumed, that that is just someone from Kosovo, but no, he was a German, because he had a German citizenship.

Peter defines Germanness quite clearly with reference to German citizenship when he states that "German actually would mean that he has the German citizenship." Tina, a twenty-year-old who is training to be a drafting apprentice at the construction school, also conceives of Germanness as something determined by citizenship, as her discussion about foreigners in Germany shows:

> But what can one take as the standard, what are too many foreigners? You actually can't say either. I mean, if they have German citizenship, then they are not foreigners. What does one know, when one sees people on the street, is that a German, or is that a foreigner, one doesn't know at all either. One can't say, I'd say now, just because I have been hit on by them, it could also be someone who has German citizenship, who was born here, or something.

For Tina, the acquisition of German citizenship—which for her is linked to birthplace—eradicates foreignness. Once one has obtained citizenship, one is no longer a foreigner. Visible or auditory cues—such as the physical appearance or the accents of men "hitting on" Tina on the street—do not, for Tina, indicate foreignness. She argues that these men on the street are just as likely to be Germans.

Perhaps most surprisingly, this was even the case for some of the young people whose views tended to be right-wing or antiforeigner. By and large, if foreigners are born in Germany, then most of these young people consider them to be Germans. For example, Paul, a concrete-worker trainee, reported that "foreigners who are born in Germany are Germans." Paul expressed a number of views consistent with right-wing extremism during the interview and described himself politically as having a "little rightist opinion." Yet he views anyone born in Germany as being German, clearly expressing a view of citizenship and national belonging that is consistent with jus soli principles.

In addition to geography and birthplace, language emerged as a critically important factor in these young people's discussions of foreigners and naturalization. Language was mentioned in nearly every interview in the context of discussions about national belonging or the criteria for naturalization. This finding about the importance of language to conceptions of national belonging is consistent with research on younger students in Europe. In interviews with children aged six to eleven in England, Cullingford (2000, 186) found that language was more significant than skin color or the shape of the eyes in determining differences between people. According to the young people I interviewed, language is the primary means of integration for foreigners as well as one of the central ways in which they identify with Germany. Language proficiency is closely linked in these young people's minds to their understandings of what constitutes Germanness. Michael, who was born in Honduras and moved to Germany when he was seven years old, suggests:

> Maybe that's the main thing . . . the German language, I also have a German passport, but there are lots of others who have a German passport and aren't as typically German, they don't have anything culturally in common with Germany or anything else, so . . . that's how they identify . . . through [the] German [language].

Finally, it is worth noting that while most students were not very clearly versed in current citizenship and naturalization law, at least one student who did know more about the law (albeit with some factual errors) stated a clear position in favor of a jus soli reform. According to Sven, a twenty-four-year-old information-technology apprentice, born in the East:

> Sven: Here in Germany it's the case, at this time it's still the case, it's still the law . . . um, that whoever has a German as a relative is automatically a German. Well, from blood, from genet- or not from genetics,

but from the, being related. For you [in the United States] it's the case that . . . well, you know that, yeah . . .

CMI: Yes, when one is born there. What do you think of that?

Sven: I think your variant is better. . . . Because it is more flexible. Well . . . now one really just gets an [official] stamp from the law here, so one is a German now because . . . his parents are German . . . and the people who come here and want to be German have to fight for that forever or wait until they can become [German].

The previous sections have shown that citizenship, for these young people, is a concept understood in terms of birthplace and residence within a geographic set of borders, combined with language proficiency. But how do these young people determine who counts as a German—who belongs?

Behavioral and Attitudinal Criteria for Naturalization

As the interviews progressed, it became clear that these young people do not view citizenship as being merely about birthplace, residence within the German borders, or the flawless mastery of the German language. As I probed more deeply, I found that their understandings of citizenship encompass a much more specific *behavioral* definition of what it means to be a citizen. Almost all of the students I interviewed talked about issues of belonging and membership when they defined the terms "citizen" and "citizenship" and talked about the criteria for membership in Germany as hinging on issues of commitment to Germanness and the choice to become German, rather than on biological or ethnic criteria. While they did explain that belonging to a country means being born there, living there, and adhering to the laws set out by that country, also key to their explanations was the notion that belonging means "feeling" like one belongs. As Kai, a nineteen-year-old male information-technology apprentice, suggests, a citizen "is someone who feels like they belong with a certain mentality, you don't have to be born in the country in order to . . . belong there and to feel like [you belong there]." Lennart, a twenty-five-year-old cook apprentice, reported what it meant to him to be a citizen in Berlin, Germany, and the European Union: "Everyone has to know for himself where he feels at home. I always say, you're 'at home' wherever you feel comfortable, and I don't let myself get put into any category, just because I was . . . born into a place."

Citizenship, for these young people, appears to be a choice of membership in a place where you feel like you belong, and the notion of commitment to this place where you feel you belong was a key element in how these young people conceived of citizenship and national belonging. But they also view citizenship in terms of commitment to a particular community in other ways, particularly when they discussed their understandings of "good" and "bad" citizens. Good citizens, according to these young people, are most often defined as people who improve Germany or Germany's image. As Enno, a twenty-one-year-old who is training to be a drafter states, "A good citizen is a citizen who manages to bring his state, his country, somehow to bring his country forward." Good citizens are also people who help others, who are a part of society, pay their taxes, have or raise children, try to "do good," and don't engage in criminal activity. Markus, a scaffold-builder apprentice, volunteered that a good citizen is someone who "thinks about his fellow citizens. About the next (person). Is not an egoist." Similarly, Patrick, a seventeen-year-old who is training to be a computer assistant, noted: "A good citizen, for example doesn't just take care of himself, for example rather lives for society, well, for other citizens, and when they are in need, he also supports them." Students were particularly insistent that one of the characteristics of a good citizen is that he or she helps others or is an active part of the community. Bad citizens, then, were just the opposite. As Nico, a cook trainee, volunteered:

> Bad is simply people who really don't want to accept anything, who simply have no sense of community, who are simply egoistic, I find, those are actually bad citizens. Bad people, people with whom you can't work together, because they always have to profile themselves, exactly. Yeah, those are actually the people who tend to be bad citizens for me. People who only see themselves . . . people who want to have a lot, but don't want to give a lot in return.

"Bad" citizens were most often defined as people who "live off the state" or who are otherwise "against society" in some way, especially if they hurt others: a "bad" citizen is someone who doesn't pay her taxes, is egoistic, criminal, radical, doesn't care about society, doesn't help out, lives off the support of the state, is a terrorist or works against the state, or doesn't take responsibility for her actions. Alexander, a hotel-worker trainee, commented: "And a bad citizen doesn't take any responsibility, he just shirks, so to say . . . how can you say it? . . . Probably someone who only wants rights but no duties."

Students' conceptions of "good" and "bad" citizens illustrate that they think of citizenship in terms that are behavioral rather than innate. Belonging to Germany, according to them, means being committed to the country, assimilating and adhering to its legal and cultural norms for behavior. These students have an expectation that citizens will not only participate in the formal rights, duties, structures, and institutions related to citizenship—such as voting—but rather, that citizens will actively help fellow citizens and work toward improvement of the country. Citizenship is not only a *status* for these students—it is also a *practice* (Miller 1999). How citizenship is lived, for these young people, in other words, is as much about issues of belonging and engagement as it is about state membership. The behavioral aspects of being German were also evident among "non-ethnic" German participants. Mehmet, a twenty-five-year-old Turkish-German student, born and raised in Germany, is a German citizen. He talks about his perception of what Germanness is and how it relates to him:

> There are of course the virtues of the Germans . . . the German punctuality, there is the German sense of order, there is the German, this precision in work, the German bureaucracy, the German order. I find these really good . . . they are deep in myself . . . but only because I'm in Germany. It's not a natural part of the character, it actually comes from the education that I have had. It is because, in this country . . . we have accepted it, it is good. . . . here that's the way it is and in the meantime, we've also come to find it the right way and I think, that's German.

Mehmet states clearly that he feels German and has a clear sense of what that is. For him, the key elements of Germanness, or of German virtue, are punctuality, order, precision, and bureaucracy. He also clearly indicates that he has adopted these attributes, arguing that they are acquired elements of his character rather than innate ones.

Frau Cordner, a teacher in her early forties, confirmed the importance of behavioral criteria for her students' understandings of Germanness. She suggests that for her students, "actually this Germanness is rather [determined] in opposition to negative characteristics that one attributes to foreigners. So [German is] . . . to be not criminal or [laughs] yeah, or to be not asocial, such things . . ." Other behavioral aspects of citizenship emerged during the interviews. For example, several students raised economic concerns in the context of their explanations of citizenship and national belonging. Rather than focusing on ethnic or racial characteristics to determine who belongs, according to these young people, foreigners who contribute to society, pay their taxes, work, and are economically solvent "belong," while those who are "living off of the state" do not belong. This understanding is particularly relevant when one considers that the homeless are often targets of right-wing hate crimes and that a persistent misconception about foreigners in Germany is that they overwhelmingly are abusers of the social welfare system. According to these students' understandings of belonging, individuals who do not contribute economically to society do not belong. Most of these students would not see this view as particularly right-wing, however. Carola, a nineteen-year-old cook trainee, points out the difference between her view and the right-wing's ethnic conception of belonging:

> CMI: Do you mean that in that sense there are two different German nations?
> Carola: Clearly, I mean we have a lot of right-wing radicals here, that's totally clear.
> CMI: And for some people, for them the German nation is this—
> Carola: Racially pure German. Definitely.
> CMI: And for you?
> Carola: For me everyone is German who can stand on their own two feet, who earns their own money and doesn't live off of the state's pocketbook.

Later, she reiterates and expands on this view, offering that Germans are "those who were born here. Those whose home [Heimat] is here. And in any case definitely not those who live off the state's pocketbook, for whom I go and work and so on."

Other students consistently emphasized the importance of not living off of the state when they discussed citizenship and national belonging. Those who do live off the state, then, are not considered German and do not belong to German society. In other words, there are economic conditions for belonging in Germany. Foreigners who fulfill those conditions are a part of German society, but those who do not fulfill them do not belong. Herr Hanson, a civics teacher in his early forties, believes that while some of his students view genetic heritage as the most important factor in determining national belonging, this does not make them more receptive to "ethnic German" returnees from eastern Europe or the former Soviet States. Instead, it is economic criteria that seem to matter most:

There are students, who actually want the genetic expression, the genetic conception of nationality, and simultaneously go home and criticize those [Germans] of Russian origin . . . for them they are . . . outsiders who represent a threat, because they are using resources. . . . That always creates fear. Someone comes from the outside and sits down at the same communal dinner table. . . . It's about a fear of resources being divided up.

Moreover, these views were not limited to students. Frau Schmidt, a civics teacher in her early thirties, believes that behavioral criteria matter to her in understanding Germanness but also thinks that an older generation of Germans views this differently:

I believe that Germany sometimes has a problem giving citizenship to people who don't, who have no German roots, who weren't born here, or who come from somewhere else and live here maybe ten, twenty years and then want to have this citizenship, and sometimes, we make it a very big deal to recognize foreigners as Germans, even when they act practically like Germans and also pay their taxes here. . . . I think that whoever makes a conscious decision for it and says, "I would like to have German citizenship because I live here, because I work here, because my family is here, because I pay taxes here . . . and because I can speak German well and because I see this somehow as my home [Heimat]," that would be dumb to refuse such people this citizenship because they are also an enrichment for the country. . . . For example, I don't think my parents' generation, [those who are] fifty and older, would necessarily say, "ok, just because someone lives here for twenty years, he should get German citizenship, I think there is rather this . . . one is only a German if one is born here and has German ancestors, that dominates in the older generation, while I think that my generation and especially those who are even younger, see it differently.

In addition to behavioral criteria, *attitudes* toward German citizenship also turn out to be an important aspect of students' conceptions of citizenship, particularly when students discussed what they thought should be the conditions for naturalization. Their responses also reveal how important culture and cultural assimilation are to their conceptions of Germanness. When students discussed the reforms in naturalization laws that had recently taken place, many of them expressed concern that the process was now made too easy for foreigners. Eighteen of the students felt that naturalization should be made more difficult (as opposed to eight who felt it should be easier, and six who felt the process is currently appropriate—the others did not have an opinion). Their reasons for wanting it to be more difficult, however, illustrate deeper feelings about diversity and belonging in Germany.

In particular, students felt strongly that one of the most important conditions for naturalization should be a desire to be German—in other words, foreigners should truly want to live in Germany and become German, assimilating to German cultural norms—in contrast to foreigners who want to become Germans just to benefit economically from living in Germany, but then would continue on with their own cultural traditions. Markus, a twenty-one-year-old scaffold-builder apprentice, believes that a condition for obtaining German citizenship should be:

> that he wants to become a German and doesn't just want to live in Germany. That he wants to become a German and not [just] live here, rather . . . wants to become one of us. And that's not the way it is. Here it's starting to be just the way it is with you [in the United States], in your big cities with Little Chinatown and Little this and that, and yeah, that's nice and multicultural, but then every city district gets into wars with every other district, and that's probably not the sense and point of multiculturalism. Then they could just as well stay in their own country.

Although Markus implies that he is espousing a redefined conception of multiculturalism, his view of multiculturalism is that all cultures blend into or assimilate to German culture. As his response illustrates, the young Germans I interviewed are mostly opposed to a multicultural society in the sense of diverse cultures living side by side. They don't want to have sections of cities broken up into ethnic ghettos, don't want to see street signs with a foreign language on them, and don't want people to have hyphenated identities. But Markus's response also reveals that he believes becoming German is in fact possible—and that Germanness, in turn, is not something which is only obtainable through the inheritance of a certain set of genetic characteristics. The cultural characteristics of Germanness are, for Markus, the defining elements. Martin, a twenty-year-old information-technology apprentice, believes that, in order to get citizenship, foreigners "shouldn't be allowed to say 'I just want my money, and then I'm getting out of here.' . . . A condition [should be] . . . that they actually will become *German* citizens, and not German-Turkish, or . . . Turkish, or whatever." Becoming a German citizen, in other words, means wanting to be German, committing to German cultural norms, being an economic contributor to the German economy, and essentially, leaving one's other cultural identities at the door. In addition to birthplace and language ability, behavioral factors appear to be important criteria for citizenship and naturalization for these young people. According to the young people I interviewed, if foreigners fulfill these conditions of cultural and economic assimilation, they are German. The results of interviews with nine young people who were "non-ethnic" Germans or were born outside of Germany offer a different perspective on these claims, however.

The Limits of Cultural Assimilation

Despite the fact that the young Germans I interviewed overwhelmingly defined Germanness in cultural terms, there appear to be limits on how this understanding is actually extended to "non-ethnic" Germans or foreigners in practice. Table 3 shows that over a third of the students I interviewed feel that there are too many foreigners in Germany and that this feeling is strongest among students with the worst labor market outlooks. The "non-ethnic" Germans I interviewed, moreover, report that they have difficulty feeling like they belong in Germany. Of the sixty students I interviewed, nine were either born outside of Germany or had one or two parents who were not "ethnically" German. Six of these nine students were born outside of Germany, in Poland, Russia, the Philippines, Israel, and Honduras. One of these students is Jewish and has Israeli citizenship. Of the remaining three, two are of Turkish background, born in Germany, and one is Afro-Deutsch (one parent is African American, living in the United States, and the other parent is German). All but one student (who has Israeli citizenship) were German citizens.

Julia, whose background is Palestinian-Israeli and who came to Germany when she was nine, is training to be a skilled restaurant worker. She is a German citizen and describes her sense of belonging in the following excerpt:

Julia: I actually feel like a foreigner.
CMI: Like a foreigner, although you have a German passport?
Julia: Yes. How can I explain it. Actually, my habits are actually German, because I've been living here since I was nine. But people separate you off in a lot of ways. "Yeah, what are you doing here."

Table 3. Students' views on number of foreigners in Germany by labor market prospects[a]

Labor Market Prospects	Need more	Too many	Number OK	Total
Improving (information technology)	4	6	6	16
Stable (hospitality and cooking trades)	1	4	1	6
Declining (construction trades)	0	14	4	18
Total	5	24	11	40[b]

Note: Forty students responded; the remaining students had no opinion or did not respond in a clear category; e.g., as one student explained, "There are exactly the right amount [of foreigners] who work, and there are too many of those who don't work."

a. ~ ($p < .10$)
b. Two students responded in more than one category; only their first response is counted here.

Mehmet, who is studying in a special one-year program in the hotel and hospitality school, was born in Germany to Turkish parents. He is a German citizen and volunteers that he feels like a German, but is not accepted by Germans as one of them: "I . . . say that very often and very—, a lot of people laugh at that also, I mean, Germans do . . . How can *you* feel like a German. Yeah, how can I not feel like a German? I was born here."

Mehmet says that although he was born in Germany, people laugh at him for saying that he feels like a German. According to the statements of the students I interviewed, Mehmet should be regarded as just as much of a German as any other individual born and raised in Germany. He says that his habits are very German. Yet he perceives that his feelings of Germanness are met with incredulity: "How can *you* feel like a German," demonstrating how improbable Germans actually find the prospect of a "non-ethnic" German really being German.

Mehmet was not alone in his feelings about this matter. Although young Germans said that foreigners who "act" German and "want to be German" are in fact German, the "non-ethnic" Germans I interviewed mostly report that they are not accepted by Germans as Germans. These claims from "non-ethnic" Germans sharply contradict the young Germans' conceptions of citizenship and national belonging described above. This provides compelling evidence for the continuing role of racial and ethnic characteristics, such as skin tone, in patterns of xenophobic or racist behavior, even if race and ethnicity are not discussed in young Germans' explanations of national belonging.

Two examples from civics classrooms in the construction school offer support for the reports from the "non-ethnic" Germans I interviewed that they are still viewed as foreigners, even if they assimilate. The first observation, which I made on a day late in the fall of 2000, reveals the ways in which biological criteria continue to be an important component in at least some of these young people's conceptions of Germanness. Since I was running late from a meeting with the school headmaster, I did not walk to the civics class with the instructor, as was generally my habit in this school. Class had already begun when I snuck open the front door and quietly entered a classroom full of fifteen future masons, being taught by Herr Jaeger. The students were all male and several had shaved heads—which is often a sign of membership in, or sympathy with, the radical right-wing. Because Herr Jaeger had already begun his prepared lecture, he simply nodded at me, and I took a seat in the back of the classroom without being introduced.

The topic of discussion was the financing of political parties, and gradually, the discussion shifted to the NPD (the National Party of Germany)—a right-wing political party that appeared to be on the verge of being banned formally in Germany. Herr Jaeger asked the students to name one of the goals of the NPD, and a student immediately called out, "Foreigners out!" Herr Jaeger responded by explaining why this goal would hurt Germans—because of inevitable repercussions from the European Union and other countries. "What would happen in Germany?" he asked rhetorically, "Daimler Benz would go bankrupt." Herr Jaeger then paused for just a moment, as if something had just occurred to him, and caught my eye briefly. The following dialogue then ensued:

> Herr Jaeger: How can one recognize a foreigner?
> Hans: Dark hair, the mentality, and so on.
> Herr Jaeger: Look around the class, is anyone here a foreigner?
> Students: (looking around) No, no one here.
> Marcus: (in a joking tone, pointing to a classmate who has dark hair) Klaus looks like a foreigner. (Draws much laughter from class.)

Herr Jaeger then pointed to me, saying, "Yes, we have a foreigner here," and introduced me as a guest from the United States. This drew several responses from the students, who made comments ranging from the

United States being different than Germany to questioning whether the Ku Klux Klan was comparable to the radical right-wing in Germany or not. One student remarked that the United States is different, explaining that "they are a nation of immigrants, and none of the original Americans are really left—they were all killed." This brief observation was intriguing for several reasons. The students did not know who I was and obviously assumed—on the basis of my light skin and hair color, most likely—that I was a German. Their initial reactions to Herr Jaeger's question about whether there were any foreigners in the room showed this clearly—they did not even consider me as a possible foreigner. The only person they focused on was Klaus, a student who has black hair. Their subsequent response to Herr Jaeger's revelation that, indeed, there was a foreigner in the class, was denial—Americans are different, so I didn't really count as a foreigner. Moreover, again we see here evidence that foreignness is "recognizable" both in cultural (the mentality) and biological (dark hair) ways.

A second interaction that took place that same fall between two students in another civics classroom illustrates the complexity in the relative weight attributed to biological versus nonbiological criteria in determining who belongs to the nation. During a classroom discussion, a student of German ethnic descent, who has dark hair, related an incident when he was insulted by a German woman who thought he was a foreigner. His tone, as he related this incident, was indignant; he was shocked that he was perceived as an outsider. A classmate who was of Turkish descent called out, "Hey, you should have shown her your German passport!" This response indicates that this student believed that the woman would not have insulted the German student if she knew he was German—or at least that his German status would have made a difference in her opinion of him. In this case, it is the German passport—German citizenship—that symbolizes belonging and guards against exclusion. But this brief interaction also reveals that biological characteristics, such as hair color or skin tone, continue to serve as markers for racism and exclusion among the broader German public. It was the "ethnic" German student's dark hair and dark eye color that led the woman to believe he was a foreigner and to insult him.

The data analyzed here cannot determine the causal factors at work in the contradiction between the emphasis on cultural criteria for citizenship in the vast majority of student responses and the experiences of "non-ethnic" Germans who report that cultural assimilation does not lead to their being accepted as Germans. It may be the case, for example, that young Germans' verbal responses in interviews do not reflect how many Germans behave when they encounter foreigners, particularly those who don't fit their physical image of Germanness. As the evidence above demonstrated, at least a small percentage of Germans view Germanness as directly tied to ethnic and racial characteristics, and interactions with such individuals by "non-ethnic" Germans could also account for some of the experiences these young people had. This would suggest that in practice, racist behavior still relies—at least in part—on biological cues such as hair color and skin tone, even if the articulation of exclusionary beliefs is shifting to cultural forms. Alternatively, this contradiction could reflect generational differences in Germany, as younger Germans who are growing up in an increasingly diverse community exhibit more tolerance for difference and conceive of national identity in multicultural ways, while older generations remain wedded to ethnic conceptions of Germanness. Finally, this contradiction might be explained by transformations within cohorts as they grow older, which would mean that although these young people's responses now indicate a genuine openness in defining Germanness, they may become more exclusionary and xenophobic as they age. More research is needed to examine these and other potential explanations of this contradiction.

Rethinking the Blood-Based Nature of German Belonging

At least some of the research on German citizenship has assigned Germans a static and uniform notion of citizenship that is rooted in blood-based conceptions of national belonging. The findings in this chapter, however, reveal that younger Germans define Germanness primarily in cultural, economic, civic, and geographic terms rather than by ethnic or racial criteria. Most of the young people I interviewed clearly expressed an understanding of Germanness based on jus soli principles, arguing that anyone who is born in Germany and assimilates to the "German" way of life is a German.

It is important to acknowledge that the experiences of a small number of respondents cannot be generalized to the experiences of Germans more generally. Because so few quantitative surveys have included questions that directly ask about citizenship and naturalization, more research is needed to determine how and whether these patterns hold for larger numbers of participants. It is also significant that reliance on cultural rather than racial or ethnic criteria in conceptualizations of citizenship was not completely uniform among the sixty students interviewed for this research. There were dissenting views, both from a minority of students who viewed citizenship in "blood-based" terms, as well as from "non-ethnic" Germans who pointed out that even if they assimilate culturally, they are not accepted by Germans as Germans. Even with a clear consensus among a majority of respondents about the importance of culture and cultural assimilation, the continued salience of racial and ethnic heritage for even a small minority of interviewees shows that it is problematic to assume a uniform conception of citizenship for all the members of a single nation, as has been done in the German case, and that it is important to acknowledge a range of definitions of citizenship and national belonging across national populations.

The findings from this German case therefore reveal that citizenship cannot be thought of as a unified and static concept whose meaning for individuals can be understood by examining citizenship policies or naturalization laws. Unlike the literature on nations, which generally views nations as entities that are actively imagined by the individuals living within them, the scholarship on citizenship has overwhelmingly focused on institutions, structures, and legal policies. Although the theoretical literature on nations has argued with some consistency that state policies cannot be equated with citizens' views of the nation (Hobsbawm 1990, 11), most research on citizenship has neglected the perspectives of ordinary citizens. This chapter therefore emphasizes the importance of a sociology of everyday experiences of citizenship. While laws and policies are clearly important, it is also important to understand how those policies are interpreted, reacted to, and acted upon in everyday life. This chapter's interpretive approach to examining everyday practice in the conception and interpretation of citizenship reveals that relying solely on institutions and policies to determine how national populations view themselves is problematic. Ordinary citizens may experience and understand citizenship in ways that may not be reflected in the policies that regulate access to the national community.

seven

Generational Change
and the Re-imagining of Nations

At the end of a book focused on nations and national attachments, it is worth reminding ourselves that in the scope of human history, nations—and the predominant form of the nation-state—are relatively recent phenomena. It was not so very long ago that individuals' lives were more deeply rooted in, and regulated by, much more local forces: clans, tribes, extended family networks, or feudal systems, to name just a few.

The importance of local connections and relationships hasn't disappeared entirely, but the power of the local today is matched—or even, potentially, surpassed—by the global. This is true even for people who spend their entire lives in the same place and lead decidedly local lives. Grocery aisles are packed with produce from Mexico and South America, eradicating the notion of seasonal fruits and vegetables from most western and industrialized communities. As recent controversy over imported Chinese product ingredients shows, even products made within one country may include ingredients imported from places much further away. Phenomena from across the political, social, and economic spectrums—from YouTube to al Qaeda—are organized in nonnational ways and exist without national boundaries. Schools and universities are increasingly internationalized through changes in curricula, study abroad programs, faculty scholar exchanges, and the expansion of western universities into satellite or branch campuses overseas. Other examples abound: the deterritorialization of the workplace through the use of e-mail, telecommuting, and videoconferencing; the eradication of local currency in Europe in favor of the euro; patterns of cyclical transnational migration in which diasporic communities remain deeply and emotionally attached to—and financially supportive of—their homeland communities. Such examples reveal the ways in which the boundaries between the local and the global have become blurred: many people's local lives, today, are embedded in the global.

None of this is especially new. Scholars have been writing for quite some time about the transformations posed by globalization, about patterns of transnational migration, about the expansion of multinational corporations, and about the emergence of a macronational political entity in Europe. But our scholarly interest in globalization or in the blurring of the local and the global should not make us lose sight of the national. The national remains salient in the lives of most ordinary people, even if they do not wear it on their shirt sleeves or wave it in a flag on their front lawns.

The extent to which and the ways in which the nation is salient for particular national populations varies, however, and it is this variation which is the subject of this book. Until recently, we did not know very much about how ordinary people related to the nation; most of what we knew about nationhood was derived from studies of elite interactions, distilled through policy briefs, legislation, and parliamentary debates (Olick 1998; Levy 1999). The recent turn toward the study of everyday nationhood (Fox and Miller-Idriss 2008) offers a more specific focus on ordinary perspectives. But existing scholarship has focused primarily on whether and how ordinary people think about the nation (Fox and Miller-Idriss 2008; Brubaker et al. 2006), or it has focused on the relationship between the nation and other types of identifications, such as religion (Zubrzycki 2006), leaving open the question of variation across societal groups—such as generations. Scholars who have looked in depth at the differences in interpretations of national and state narratives across generations (Borneman 1992), on the other hand, do so without delving into the potential impact of such differential interpretations on social change. Most scholarship which looks more specifically at generational change, in turn (Mannheim 1952; Pilcher 1994; Schuman and Rieger 1992; Schuman and Scott 1989; Griffin 2004) has not focused on the nation as the object of inquiry (for an exception, see Moses 1999).

Generations are not monolithic entities, of course. Their members share diverse opinions which likely contradict and challenge one another, based at least in part on individuals' affiliations and identities as men and women, as residents of cities or rural areas or of particular regions, as conservatives or liberals, as parents or siblings, as survivors of illness or tragedy, or any one of a myriad of other factors. The opinions voiced by the members of the two generational subgroups in this book—namely, middle-class, university-educated teachers and their younger, working-class vocational students—are not necessarily representative of all members of their respective generations. But because this particular interaction of generational subgroups occurs repeatedly, for the large percentage of German youth enrolled in vocational schools across the country, it is a particularly important intergenerational interaction to investigate.

The theoretical claims presented in this book—which I summarize below—are therefore suggestive. Because so little work exists which focuses specifically on the intersection of generational change and nationhood, we sorely need more empirical work to tell us whether these patterns hold up in other places and specifically to integrate generations as a variable in the study of transformations in collective identities and meanings. This is true both for national idioms as well as for other powerful forms of collective identity, such as religion or gender. Additional work in Germany—in other regions, in other time periods—would help reveal whether the generational dynamics I trace in Berlin are more limited than I have presented here. Even if I am wrong about the importance of generations as a mechanism in the transformation of the nation, however—and despite the fact that these findings are not generalizable to everyone within the same generation, they nonetheless point out the ways in which change can be generated in the meaning of the nation. They are an important example of how nations and their meanings are renegotiated over time. Nations, I contend, are not only imagined once; they are re-imagined again and again by different groups of individuals, as different versions of, and narratives about, nationhood potentially compete, coexist, or succeed one another over time.

Being German in Germany: National Narratives and Generational Change

Young Germans, born several decades after the end of World War II, still face the question almost daily of whether it is acceptable to be German. Again and again, in the politics of memorial establishment, in political debates about immigration and naturalization, in newspaper articles about asylum, in policy decisions about integration, in class-room discussions about retirement and foreigners, Germans are faced with a horrific past which calls into question the very acceptability of their national identity. In tracing the resistance of young, working-class Germans to the taboo on national identity and pride, this book makes several arguments.

First, I show that a younger generation's efforts to reclaim the nation clash with an older generation's instinctive rejection of it, as manifested both in interviews with, and observations of, teachers and through a prevailing public and social narrative about Germanness within German domestic political culture and public life. This narrative—although contested—is characterized by a continuing sense of institutionalized shame resulting from the Holocaust and an accompanying antination-alist consensus that invalidates national pride as a legitimate expression of national belonging. Teachers' well-intentioned efforts to enforce the illegitimacy of national pride and German identity, I argue, coupled with resistance to the taboo on pride among younger Germans, have the unintended consequence of increasing the appeal of radical right-wing groups. Young Germans' resistance, moreover, reveals a mechanism that facilitates the re-imagining of nations, explaining how continuing transformations in understandings of nationhood take place.

Second, I reveal how a new cultural understanding of national belonging is emerging among German young people, in which cultural attributes—rather than genetic or "blood-based" criteria—take precedence in determining who belongs in Germany. This cultural understanding contradicts the story told about Germanness by many academics who study Germany—namely, that German identity is shaped by a blood-based sense of national belonging that is tied to an ethnic conception of Volk and to the jus sanguinis principles that characterized German citizenship and naturalization policy until 1999. Although this narrative also has been contested—particularly by historians who argue that Germany has always had a deep cultural element in its construction of national belonging—it has stubbornly persisted.

The group of young people I interviewed clearly express an understanding of Germanness based on jus soli principles, arguing that anyone who is born in Germany and assimilates to the "German" way of life is a German. Young Germans are thus actively re-imagining the nation, as understandings of who can be a German evolve. While German citizenship and naturalization law up through 1999 made it very difficult for "non-ethnic" Germans to naturalize, the young working-class Germans I interviewed do not see biological or genetic heritage as important criteria for establishing Germanness. Instead, their view of German identity as determined by cultural assimilation to a German way of life is, in many ways, more open and tolerant of biological difference than the dominant view about German national belonging would lead one to expect. At the very least, the cultural conception of Germanness that I reveal among young, working-class Germans shows that there are multiple conceptions of German identity among Germans. This radically redefines the dominant understanding about German national belonging, showing that it can no longer be characterized as employing a blood-based definition. As Erwin K. Scheuch observes, "The Germans are—in an astonishing way—much less Germanic in their thinking than is normally thought" (in Holzer 1992, 346). Taken together, both of these findings refine theories of nation-formation to incorporate patterns of change, suggesting that generational shifts can act as a mechanism in the re-imagining of nations.

Nations and National Identity Revisited

For all of our collective research on the nation and national identity, we still understand very little about how, exactly, national identity is formed. Most theoretical work on the nation—at least since Benedict Anderson suggested that the nation is an "imagined" community of individuals—has acknowledged that nations are socially constructed entities rather than something primordial or given. We also recognize that there are dominant and alternative constructions of the nation and that these constructions are not necessarily static, but change over time. Indeed, when Napoleon once complained that "the trouble with the Germans is that they are always becoming, never being," he captured the heart of the matter. The nation—and the collective identities attached to it—are always changing, always becoming. What we don't have a very good understanding of is how these inventions, imaginings, re-imaginings, or reconstructions of the nation might take place.

This isn't to say that there aren't any clues to how the process of nation- and national-identity-formation happens. Some scholars argue that it is intellectuals who "appear to have the greatest agency in the shaping of national understanding" by doing "the imaginative ideological labor that brings together disparate cultural elements, selected historical memories, and interpretations of experiences, all the while silencing the inconvenient, the unheroic, and the anomalous" (Kennedy and Suny 1999, 2). But it is not only intellectuals who are involved in the imagining of the nation. Other scholars have focused on the role that ordinary people—including subordinated groups—play in interpreting and constructing alternative versions of the nation (Gelvin 2002, 99; Göçek 2002). As ordinary people construct their sense of national identity, they interpret, react to, and in particular, interpolate intellectuals' views with their own lived experiences. The young people I interviewed crafted their own sense of national identity and national belonging out of a complex set of criteria that developed as a result of their own experiences with nationhood and which emerged, in many cases, in opposition to an older generation's views on the nation.

With regard to the notion that Germanness is determined by a blood-based sense of national belonging, the lived experiences of a younger generation are shaping their beliefs in ways that deviate from an older generation's official conception of Germanness. Previous generations crafted laws and policies carefully designed to privilege German heritage in naturalization decisions, making it very difficult for foreigners without German heritage to naturalize. However, neither the older generation nor the younger generation of Germans I interviewed supported a blood-based conception of national belonging, with only a few exceptions.

Instead, what I found is that both the older and the younger generation of Germans support instead a view of German national belonging in which anyone can become German, providing that they assimilate culturally. This became clear in classroom observations and interviews with teachers, for example, when they aimed to emphasize the mixed ethnic heritage of all Germans, pointing out that due to centuries of intra-European migration, there is no such thing as a "blood-based" German ethnicity. Chapter 6 detailed the conceptions of a younger generation of working-class Germans, which overwhelmingly emphasize cultural, behavioral, and economic criteria for Germanness. The deviation of both generations' understandings of German national belonging from more typical academic characterizations of Germanness, as well as from the conception of Germanness evidenced in citizenship and naturalization law until 1999, reveals the importance of a sociology of everyday conceptions of national identity. It is not sufficient to rely on institutional and structural accounts of citizenship and naturalization policy in order to determine how national populations understand themselves.

With regard to the notion that Germanness is forever tainted by World War II and the Holocaust and that national pride is an illegitimate expression of national belonging, there were differences between the older and the younger generation featured in this book. The younger generation's resistance to the national pride taboo is a reflection of differences in lived experiences compared with older generations and reveals a mechanism through which nations are re-imagined.

The first generation to come of age after World War II explicitly and consciously rejected national identity and national pride, psychologically linking national pride to racist and exclusionary beliefs, the Holocaust, and the radical right-wing. But for the younger generation—the grandchildren of those involved in the war—the signification of pride has shifted. These young Germans resent being made to feel guilty for the legacy of World War II and are deeply resistant to the notion that they can never be proud of being German. They argue that they are held to a different standard than citizens of other nations, feel entitled to express pride in the nation's accomplishments before and since World War II, and reject the taboo on national pride. The resistance by young working-class Germans to the conception of nationhood offered by their teachers and other adults preceded significant changes in the broader public opinion on the nation—and it is this phenomenon that reveals a mechanism that may aid in the transformation of national meanings over time. Divergent and alternative constructions of the nation—whether from a new generation or from a subordinated group—can push change in the dominant version of the nation, potentially transforming the way that elites, intellectuals, and a broader public view the nation. The waving of German flags and the singing of national anthems in Berlin streets during the 2002 and 2006 World Cups and the renewed debates about whether it is acceptable to "love" Germany are just two examples. This book, therefore, demonstrates that nations are not static entities that are imagined at one time in the distant past, but are rather continually re-imagined, and it reveals that generations can play an important role in this process. As historical circumstances change, new generations actively re-imagine nations.

Beyond the German case, my findings suggest that the interpretation by ordinary people of public narratives about the nation, and intellectuals' views on it, are grounded in the cultural context in which individuals live their lives. Even if people absorb and internalize elites' efforts, they may not react to them in anticipated ways, at least in part because individuals interpret the social world through their own standpoint or lens (D. Smith 1987). Indeed, my findings suggest that the same statement can be interpreted quite differently by different people, depending on what each individual's worldview or standpoint is. Statements that German teachers make to try to convince students that they should be more open to cultural diversity may actually confirm their students' fears because they understand and interpret such statements through a different lens. When young people hear that Germany needs foreigners because Germans are not reproducing fast enough, for example, their existing insecurities that Germans may be culturally overrun by foreigners may only get worse. The young people I interviewed may hear the words that teachers say quite accurately, but they do not necessarily interpret them in the way that teachers assume will be the case.

These findings, therefore, refine theories of nations and national identity to incorporate patterns of change across generations, revealing that the imagination of national identities and their relationship to citizenship is never complete. In addition to being imagined and constructed, nations and national identities are transient, contested, and dynamic. The state's efforts to shape national identity, even when intentional, are always tempered and potentially transformed as each generation reacts to the official conception of what the nation "ought" to be. It is because these reactions are potentially transforming that the construction of nations cannot be understood as a linear process, or one that is ever complete.

Confronting Cultural Forms of Exclusion in Teacher Practice

My interviews with young Germans also illustrate what the German state's project to create democratic and tolerant citizens in the post–World War II era may have overlooked. On the one hand, the striking absence of blood-based elements in young people's discussions of criteria for national belonging demonstrates the success of official efforts to end the descent-based conception of Germanness. Moreover, if the testimony of the young people I interviewed can be taken at its word, teachers' efforts to transform the xenophobic, anti-Semitic, and racist attitudes and behaviors of young Germans—especially in terms of invalidating genetic heritage or "blood" as criteria for Germanness—are meeting with some success. The young people I interviewed do not view Germanness as a concept bound by blood. On the contrary, their notions of Germanness, at least initially, seem quite open, accepting, and inclusive since by their own definitions, virtually anyone can be German, regardless of their race, ethnicity, or national background. But the interviews also reveal that the criteria for belonging are often ethnocentric and prejudiced. The evidence I uncovered in my analysis of conceptions of Germanness showed that the initial multicultural conception of Germanness articulated by the young Germans I interviewed is layered over a deeper, exclusionary understanding of German identity. Germanness is not an all-inclusive concept for these young people, but rather implies a very specific adherence and assimilation to a set of cultural and religious norms, behaviors, and attitudes. Yes, a Turk born in Germany is considered a German, according to these young people, as long as she lives in a neighborhood with other Germans (not just with other Turks), shops in German grocery stores, cooks German food, speaks German at home with her children, and does not wear a headscarf or pray in a mosque five times a day.

The seemingly democratic and tolerant nature of the conception of Germanness being created by young Germans masks subtle and underlying forms of prejudice based on cultural exclusions. The young people I interviewed do not, by and large, accept cultural difference within a German national identity. Moreover, young people's seemingly open conceptions of Germanness carry implicit assertions that they are not racist, even as they articulate conceptions of national belonging that are exclusionary. This perception contributes to the sense that the real racists (i.e., the right wing) are the students who really need schools' and teachers' attention, as opposed to acknowledging and addressing a potentially broader problem. In their focus on biological racism, teachers and other state actors overlook the extent to which cultural forms of exclusion are a part of many young Germans' articulations of national belonging.

This may be the state's—and the school system's—most significant failure in their attempts to transform xenophobia, prejudice, and racism in Germany. Educators overlook the potential for culturally exclusionary beliefs and practices to be dangerous, whether independently or for their potential to serve as a foundation for more extreme and racist ideologies and doctrines, such as those propagated by the extreme right-wing in Germany. At the same time, an older generation of teachers inadvertently helps to make the right wing more attractive to alienated youth when they insist that a collective identification with, or pride in, the nation is illegitimate, particularly in the context of increasing resistance among young people to what they perceive to be an unfair standard for their generation. Because the organized radical right markets itself so aggressively with national pride, I have argued, the continued taboo on national pride now means that the extreme right provides the only space where young Germans feel they can express a sense of national pride at all. Here an alienated and frustrated group of working-class youth can easily lash out at adults, in part by latching onto an expression of national identity that has persisted as the ultimate taboo in German society. The pride taboo, in this sense, may help to maintain the attractiveness of right-wing extremist groups, where young people's culturally exclusionary beliefs may be transformed into more virulent and violent practices. Thus, these findings point to the potential consequences of generational and political differences between teachers and students for the ways in which schools can inadvertently create conditions for the appeal of right-wing extremism among a younger generation.

This is taking place, moreover, while the state is simultaneously expecting a younger generation of Germans to accept the new criteria for naturalization that it has implemented, shifting to a jus soli understanding of Germanness and citizenship. Teachers were not ignorant of the contradictions inherent in some of these demands. As Herr Martin, a teacher in his late forties, explains, problems with the integration of foreigners "are perhaps connected to the fact that we ourselves don't want to have an actual national identity. And how should I expect to convey [an identity] to someone who wants to naturalize, if I don't have it myself?"

Methodologically, these findings suggest that in order to understand the complex processes that go on in the construction of the nation and national identity, we need to structure research on the nation in a way that examines both the official narratives to which ordinary people are exposed (e.g., policies, structures, laws, or statements and efforts made by intellectuals) and the reactions, resistance, and responses of those ordinary people (Fox and Miller-Idriss 2008; A. Smith 2008). This book therefore joins a growing sociology of the everyday practices of nationhood, examining the experiences of individuals in the construction of their national and ethnic identities. The education system is, I suggest, an especially fruitful site to investigate how ordinary citizens—such as the working-class students I studied—respond to and potentially affect official and unofficial narratives in their everyday lives.

The young people I interviewed were at an age—early adulthood—when many young people make decisions and have life experiences that help them form who they are. Identity formation does not stop with the end of childhood; rather, it continues after adolescence, into young adulthood, and across the life course (Arnett 2000, 469). Studying citizenship education in public schools, community colleges, and universities, among a population whose identities are solidifying and being formed seems an excellent place to begin to develop a more comprehensive understanding of how the formation and re-formation of national identity takes place.

Integration, Inclusion, and Exclusion in Europe and Beyond

Any critique of an exclusionary model of national belonging quite obviously relies on an implicit alternative political community, a Germany that is inclusive and celebrates diversity instead of rejecting it (Mandel 1989, 45). These are not only German concerns. The renegotiation of national identity and citizenship among younger generations is taking place in changing historical circumstances across the globe. European countries in particular are facing tremendous change as they struggle to construct a new European identity, define their own national identities, and learn to incorporate millions of immigrants from predominantly Muslim societies into their national cultures. How and whether previously rather homogenous societies will come to terms with their new and increasingly multicultural communities will play a large part in determining the extent to which the inequalities and resentment experienced by alienated youth—as evidenced in Parisian riots, German neo-Nazism, or British "home-grown" terrorism—can be reversed.

Official state and public definitions and understandings of the national community set a powerful example for youth and send important messages about who can belong to the nation and how one should relate to it. In France, for example, where candidates for naturalization can "be rejected on the grounds of insufficient assimilation" (Bowen 2007, 196) and young women are barred from wearing headscarves in school, the French state sends a clear message about "what is acceptably

French" (Bowen 2007, 248). Schools are one place where such messages are transmitted, but they are not the only such site. Legal policies about citizenship and naturalization, presidential speeches, media coverage of antiforeigner violence, parliamentary debates about dual citizenship, or local and national disputes over religious practices—such as the building of mosques, religious attire, or the state's right to perform autopsies—all have an impact on how ordinary people think about citizenship, national belonging, and foreignness.

These are relevant concerns for European communities, indeed, but they are also salient for all communities and societies dealing with the blurred boundaries of globalization and the challenges of widespread migration. Should Starbucks be kept at bay so as to preserve a local Main Street coffee culture? Is it justified to implement policies to protect national languages? Isn't some measure of immigrant assimilation—a degree of language mastery and awareness of the constitutional principles and practices of any given democratic society—a necessary starting point for participatory engagement in democratic processes? All nations and societies will struggle with how to develop more inclusive understandings of citizenship and national belonging that can incorporate the experiences of ethnic minorities, learning to balance diversity with national identity.

In these efforts, it is neither practical nor desirable to suggest that we do away with national citizenship, especially in the absence of any compelling or feasible alternative. At the very least, citizenship is an important organizational tool for states. But citizenship is also a means of fostering national identity, which if used in a positive way, can inspire and encourage citizens to care about matters beyond their own families and communities. Viewing oneself as a part of a community larger than neighborhood or city boundaries or of one's own racial, cultural, or religious identity, I submit, is part and parcel of engaging constructively in the increasingly diverse world in which we all live.

As nations, communities, and individuals respond to widespread transformations in ethnic and racial diversity within countries, they will face challenges resulting from the desire of some to resist change and preserve familiar traditions, histories, cultures, and customs. This book's story, therefore, matters for our understandings of how indigenous Europeans and immigrants will negotiate national and cultural identities in the new Europe. But it can also teach us a great deal about what can happen when there is not room for members of a younger generation to rethink how they relate to the nation and how they can express their sense of national identity.

Thus, there is a lesson here about how young people are attracted to extremist movements more generally. In Germany, teachers' and public officials' efforts to repress national pride may be further driving young people to right-wing groups—who actively recruit with slogans about national pride—where their cultural xenophobia may be transformed into more virulent forms and violent expressions of racism. Educators, parents, and other adults who are concerned about adolescents' participation in extremist movements would do well to consider whether generational shifts in the meaning of collective identity can play a role in the appeal of such groups. As young people actively re-imagine their sense of what a nation should be, educators and other adults may find themselves competing with extremist groups for legitimacy in how the nation is understood. When a collective identity, whether national, ethnic, or religious, is suppressed by society, extremist groups become the only space in which these identities can be expressed. But by creating space for all young people to openly discuss the meaning of the nation, a broader society can engage youth before the extremists do it for us.

Overview of the Case Studies

For readers interested in additional details about the schools I studied in Berlin, the following case study overviews provide contextual information about each site's facilities, students and staff, the economic outlook of occupations for which students at each school are training, and a general assessment of the social and political culture of the student body, particularly as these relate to right-wing extremism or radicalism.

*The Comprehensive Vocational School
for Construction Trades*

Although for much of the 1990s and into the new century, Berlin has been ranked as the city in Europe with the most ongoing construction, employment prospects for construction trainees are dismal. In the city of Berlin alone, nearly forty thousand German construction workers were unemployed as I began my research.[1] At the Comprehensive Vocational School for Construction Trades (cvct) in the outskirts of Berlin, the impact of the job market on students' and teachers' moods and motivation is tangible.

The school, a sprawling complex of several buildings, offers academic and practical training for about 2,500 students in five construction fields: drafting, masonry, scaffolding, roofing, and concrete work. With bleak facades of faded and peeling paint, the school grounds are representative of the 1960s East-German building styles and are awaiting promised renovations. Inside, the school buildings and atmosphere are not much cheerier than the school grounds. In one of the rare instances where student work is displayed in a classroom, a closer look reveals that the posterboard presentation is hung sideways on a window, serving as a makeshift curtain to replace the broken blinds.

Many students are at the CVCT because it was the only apprenticeship that they were able to secure, having failed to obtain an offer in their first-choice field. Estimates of job placement upon completion of the apprenticeship range from 10–30 percent, which is a radical change from ten years ago, when the vast majority of students found work in their field upon graduation. Today, teachers and the principal explain that some of the school's pathways "unofficially" have become social programs for disadvantaged youth. During the course of an apprenticeship, about 25 percent of the students in the school drop out, according to the principal's estimate.

Most students enter the school with a lower-school certificate (*Hauptschule*), although some have graduated from middle school (*Realschule*). The roughly seventy-five "non-ethnic" German students at the school are mostly concentrated in the masonry and drafting classes, which have the highest enrollments, at about five hundred students apiece. Although official statistics are no longer collected on whether students come from east or west Berlin, the principal estimates that students in the dual system are evenly divided between those from east and west. For students in the full-time, school-based training programs, about 75 percent of the students come from the east.

About 30 percent of the one hundred teachers at the CVCT are female. Most teachers teach in two subjects, and about 50 percent of the teachers have to teach subjects for which they were not trained, mostly as an addition to their main subject. Approximately two-thirds of the teachers come from the east and the remainder from the west, although this has become increasingly mixed since some teachers who were born in the east now live in the west and vice versa. The student body at the CVCT is a challenging one for teachers, and this has an impact on classroom culture and dynamics. The students are mostly large, physically strong young men, many of whom do not view school or education in a positive light. Male and female students alike tend to dress simply and conventionally, in sweatshirts, jeans, and sneakers, neither exceptionally trendy nor displaying any of the youth "punk counterculture" that had been popular in the past. Many of the young men sport shaved heads, and teachers talked quite a bit about the need to ban bomber jackets and *Springerstiefel* (black boots)—symbols of radical right-wing groups.

Teachers and the principal openly discuss the problem of the radical right in the school, although the actual number of students who belong to radical-right groups is difficult to estimate, for reasons that were more fully elaborated in chapter 4. By any definition, however, students with radical-right views or memberships were a presence in many of the classrooms I observed, and in some classrooms they represented the majority view of students.

The Vocational School for Hotel and Cooking Trades

Also on the outskirts of Berlin, a brand-new, eighty-million-dollar structure houses Berlin's 4,300 students and apprentices training for hospitality trades (hereafter referred to as the Hotel and Cooking School).[2] The school building and grounds, recently renovated, are modern and cheerful. The main building's three floors surround an open central courtyard with several benches, where students sit in the breaks between classes. Behind the main building, there are three additional classroom buildings and a modern sports hall, complete with basketball court, soccer field, and a hundred-meter track and long jump pit. In the foyer of the main building, there is a display of student trophies from regional and national cooking competitions, framed artwork lining the walls, and a large sign pointing visitors in the direction of the main office. Outside of the main office, a long glass case displays wine bottles and place settings used in formal restaurants, and three bulletin boards provide information about job offers, union membership, and school and community events.

The Hotel and Cooking School trains students for one of six occupations: hotel employee, restaurant employee, hospitality employee, cooks, hotel businesspersons, and hotel gastronomes. Cooks and hotel-employee trainees count among the ten largest apprenticeship occupations in Berlin and are also the occupations with the highest enrollments at the school. The number of apprenticeship placements in hotels and restaurants in Berlin has increased by more than a third over the past several years, and the total number of students training for hotel, cooking, and hospitality trades in Berlin has doubled since 1990. Half of the students enter the school with a middle-school (Realschule) certificate, 30 percent have the lower-school (Hauptschule) degree, and 16 percent have earned an *Abitur*. Three percent have no previous degree. Gender in most of the occupations is balanced, with the exception of cook apprentices, who are overwhelmingly male.

Employment prospects for most of the hotel and cooking occupations are favorable, particularly in the wake of the construction of several new hotels in Berlin following the move of Germany's capital from Bonn to Berlin. The occupations tend to be relatively unpopular, however, due in large part to the long hours and the comparatively low pay,[3] and the fact that the jobs require weekend and holiday hours. This results in a high drop-out rate in many of the occupations, as well as high numbers of students who complete the apprenticeship but do not seek employment in the field.[4] About 20 percent of the students drop out of their apprenticeship program before completion.

With about 130 teachers (80 of whom are female), the school is still short several full-time instructors, creating class sizes upward of thirty students. The school was fused together from two previously existing schools in east and west Berlin, and the majority of the teachers in the combined school originally come from western Germany. Among students, there is a balanced mix of students from east and west Berlin (58 percent from the west, and 42 percent from the east), and about thirty students per semester come to Berlin from somewhere else in Germany to study hotel and cooking trades. Student dress at the school is fairly conventional; male and female students alike tended to wear jeans and simple shirts or sweaters.

There is a perception among the teachers that the radical right is a presence in the school, especially among certain occupations and pathways. Since many cook apprentices shave their heads to stay cooler in the kitchen, one of the most common identifying characteristics of radical-right youth (shaved heads) cannot be interpreted in this manner in this school, so it is not easy to estimate how large a presence right-wing students are. Occasional comments in some classrooms indicate that some students do express right-wing political views, but they seemed to be in the minority among their peers in the classroom.

The Vocational School for Communication and Information Technology

Across the city from the CVCT and the Hotel and Cooking School, 2,800 apprentices and full-time students train for over ten different occupations in communications, information, and media fields at the vocational school for communication and information technology trades (hereafter referred to as the IT school). The school grounds reflect the growth of the field over the past several decades: wings have been added hastily upon other wings, resulting in an architectural mélange from the 1950s, 1970s, 1980s, and early 1990s. A central courtyard is flanked by architecture from all four decades, with a pathway leading to another classroom building, the sports hall, and outdoor athletic courts. Inside the main entrance, there is a pleasant entryway with several cases displaying student projects as well as flyers on school course offerings and a few posters advertising upcoming community events.

Student work is on display prominently throughout the school in public spaces—in the cafeteria and in nearly every hallway there are cases with student projects or framed prints of student artwork and class projects. There are also displays of students' successful participation in regional and national competitions, including photographs of the students and local newspaper clippings, a permanent display of student artwork and class projects, framed photographs from a recent school play, and a display of student school records in track and field events. In the basement of the main building, there is a large student cafeteria and a student theater, and a school play is held in cooperation with another upper secondary school each spring. The hallway leading up to the student theater is lined with large displays of photographs from previous plays.

The school employs roughly 150 teachers, of whom about 20 are female, and two-thirds are originally from western Germany. The occupations with the highest enrollments are IT-systems electricians, software and hardware technicians, and communications and telecommunications electricians and information technicians. All students have graduated with at least a middle-school (Realschule) diploma (except for a few classes of students in special programs), and many have already graduated from Gymnasium with an Abitur, having decided to gain practical experience during an apprenticeship before making the decision whether or not to enter further study at a university. Employment prospects are extremely strong in most of the fields offered, especially in the information technology (IT) branches. Apprentices report they expect to have their choice of job offers upon graduation.

Less than 10 percent of the student population is female, and female students tend to be concentrated in the media occupations. The principal reports that most of the students of "non-ethnic" German heritage have German citizenship and that exact information on the percentage of "non-ethnic" Germans is not available. Foreign students tend to be concentrated in the computer and media occupations, however. Statistics on percentages of students from east and west Berlin are no longer collected. The drop-out rate for students in a traditional apprenticeship at the school is very low. Students dressed conventionally, wearing jeans and T-shirts or sweaters. In this school, I saw very few of the shaved heads or other symbols that might be indicative of a presence of radical right-wing students.

Notes

1. According to Berlin's State Statistics Office, in 1999 there were over thirty-seven thousand people employed in construction in Berlin, which reflected a loss of over two-fifths of construction jobs from 1992. Between 1992 and 1999, over twenty-seven thousand jobs in construction in Berlin were lost. As possible reasons for the decline, state authorities cite the decline in construction after the construction boom of the mid-1990s as well as problems with black-market labor (Statistische Landesamt Berlin 2000; also see Senatsverwaltung für Stadtentwicklung 2000).

2. The new school building was opened in the 1999–2000 academic year, and was 80 percent financed by the European Union as part of a special set of funds for east German education and training improvements (the remaining 20 percent of the costs were paid for by the Berlin Schulsenat, the equivalent of a Ministry of Education).

3. Cook apprentices in Berlin are paid significantly lower than bakers or butchers, for example.

4. A union representative from the Berlin union for hotel employees and cooks estimated that 50 percent of cook apprentices in Berlin drop out before they complete their apprenticeship, and an additional 25 percent choose not to seek employment in the field. These numbers, he explained, are not quite as high for hotel employees, although retention is still a problem.

Methodological Overview

In setting out to investigate conceptions of citizenship and national belonging among ordinary Germans, my initial research design used mixed methods, combining qualitative and ethnographic fieldwork in schools with an analysis of a large-scale, national survey dataset. After initial analysis of the student interviews, however, I discovered that a disconnect existed between the ways in which a younger generation thinks about issues related to national identity and the ways in which an older generation has designed survey research questions. This was most obvious in questions about national pride, where national surveys use the phrase "I am proud to be a German" as a measure of right-wing extremism. After hearing such overwhelming resistance from young Germans to the taboo on national pride and their desire for a more normal relationship to the nation, I determined that the available national datasets were not asking the right kinds of questions for this study. As a result, my project shifted to an examination of generational differences, relying exclusively on ethnographic and qualitative data. It is my hope, however, that this research will inspire revisions in survey instruments so that they more accurately reflect how a younger generation conceives of concepts related to the nation and particularly, national pride.

Qualitative Research Design and Access

My methodological design in the schools used intensive observation in schools and classrooms combined with semistructured interviews and focus groups. I conducted all of the observations, interviews, and focus groups myself. Because I originally set out to investigate differences in conceptions of citizenship and national identity among various groups of young people, I selected case studies in order to maximize differences on a number of variables. Among these variables were (1) apprentices' employment prospects, (2) the sector of the economy into which the occupations fell and each sector's relationship to global, national, or local economic changes, (3) students' and teachers' east or west German background, (4) students' ethnic heritage, and (5) gender. I gained access to schools through a combination of references from academics and educational experts in Berlin and cold calls to schools. I narrowed an initial list down to seven schools, and following preliminary research in 1999 and a pilot study in 2000, narrowed the schools to three cases: a school for construction trades, one for information-technology trades, and one for hotel and cooking trades.

I spent a concentrated period of five to six weeks in each school in consecutive case studies over the course of one academic year, but spent significant amounts of time at all three schools before and after each "concentrated" case-study period, as well as during two two-month follow-up trips in 2002 and 2004. I conducted over 170 hours of classroom observation in the three schools. My access to teachers varied quite a bit from one school to the next, based on the preference of the school principal, and ranged from informal, direct recruitment to principal-facilitated recruitment of teachers. The structure of classroom observations was based on a desire to observe a range of challenges, methods, and strategies in civics classrooms and as broad a spectrum of students as possible. Students in German vocational schools attend their civics classes only with other students training for the same occupation, meaning that I could observe civics classrooms where all students were future masons, cooks, scaffold-builders, and so forth. Based on advice from my key contact person in each school (the principal or civics department head), I selected classes of students that they characterized as stronger, weaker, and average, which typically corresponded with specific occupations for which the students were training. This turned out to be a fairly straightforward process since administrators and teachers in each school openly discuss the range of academic abilities, disciplinary difficulties, and motivational challenges in various classes. Once I had selected the occupations for study, I applied several additional criteria to guide my selection of observations. As much as possible, I hoped to observe both female and male teachers as well as teachers who had grown up in either east or west Germany. Whenever possible, I observed teachers in multiple classrooms, with diverse groups of students training for different professions. I used a graphic representation of these criteria to manage observations during each case study, making

Table 4. Frequency distribution, students by age, east/west birthplace, and gender

Age	East	West	Male	Female	Total
17–18	11	4	12	3	15
19–20	16	5	15	6	21
21–22	7	5	11	1	12
23–25	6	5	9	2	11
Total students	40	19	47	12	59[a]

Note: Students born outside of Germany are included in each category according to the location in which they grew up after immigrating.

a. Due to a missing value for age, one male student participant has been removed from this table.

sure that I had a range of observations that fulfilled each of the criteria. I interviewed each teacher as soon as possible after completing the last observation with him or her. During the teacher interviews conducted in 2000–2001, I asked questions that focused on gaining further knowledge about teachers' goals, strategies, methods, challenges, and views about civic education generally, as well as questions directly related to classroom observations with each teacher (see tables 4, 5, and 6).

Data Collection and Analysis

During classroom observations, whenever possible I sat in the back of the classroom so that I could observe and record the teachers' instruction as well as students' reactions and the dynamics within the classroom community. In classroom field notes, I recorded both the sequence of events and the content of the discourse, noting in a separate section of field notes my own interpretation of events when I felt it was immediately necessary. This was particularly important in terms of noting facial gestures, the tone of students' and teachers' voices, and the actions of students that went unseen by the teacher. For more on the methodological issues involved in classroom observation, the specific challenges of overseas research, and ethical and reflective concerns about qualitative research, see Barrett and Cason (1997), Weis and Fine (2000), and Wragg (1999).

Table 5. Teacher interviews and observations

Age on 12/31/04	Sex	Region of birth	Pseudonym
51	Female	East	Frau Jacobs
60	Male	East	Herr Jaeger
52	Male	West	Herr Hahn
56	Female	West	Frau Dann
49	Male	East	Herr Krug
49	Male	East	Herr Kirsch
68	Male	West	Herr Prost[a]
55	Male	West	Herr Weiss
53	Female	East	Frau Schwartz
28	Female	East	Frau Klein[b]
42	Male	West	Herr Wiener
	Male		Herr Berg[a]
	Male		Herr Grass[a]
54	Male	West	Herr Franz
47	Female	West	Frau Licht
48	Male	West	Herr Martin
62	Male		Herr Wilke[a]
51	Male	West	Herr Mais[b]
	Male		Herr Tort[c]
	Male		Herr Herman[c]
33	Male	East	Herr Preuss
50	Female	East	Frau Wasser
33	Female		Frau Neuman[a]
53	Female		Frau Turner[a]
61	Male	East	Herr Bach
36	Male	West	Herr Meyer
39	Male	West	Herr Plaut[b]
29	Female	East	Frau Main[b]
33	Female	West	Frau Schmidt[b]
43	Female	West	Frau Cordner[b]
42	Male	West	Herr Hanson[b]
51	Female	East	Frau Stein[b]
41	Male	West	Herr Metzer[b]

a. Interviewed in 2001 only (due to retirement, relocation, or illness).
b. Interviewed in 2004 only.
c. Observed but not interviewed.

Students were recruited for interviews at the end of classroom observations through a verbal announcement. I aimed to recruit three to
five students from each of the occupational clusters I observed. Student
interview questions focused on their conceptions of citizenship and national identity, their feelings about Germany, their opinions about their

Table 6. Student/apprentice interviews

Gender	School[a]/Year[b]	Age[c]	Citizenship	Region of birth[d]	1st degree[e]	Pseudonym
Male	Construction[f] 1st yr	18	German	West	Realschule	Jan
Female	Construction 1st yr	23	German	East	Realschule	Kristina
Male	Construction 2nd yr	22	German	West	Realschule	Klaus
Male	Construction 3rd yr	20	German	East	Realschule	Bernd
Male	Construction 1st yr	22	German	Honduras (7)	Realschule	Michael
Male	Construction 2nd yr	18	German	East	Hauptschule	Toby
Male	Construction 2nd yr	18	German	East	Hauptschule	Thomas
Male	Construction 2nd yr	19	German	East	Realschule	Christian
Male	Construction 2nd yr	21	German	East	Hauptschule	Stefan
Male	Construction 2nd yr	17	German	East	Realschule	Magnus
Male	Construction 2nd yr	18	German	East	Realschule	Dirk
Male	Construction 2nd yr	19	German	East	Hauptschule	Daniel
Male	Construction 2nd yr	19	German	East	Realschule	Christof
Male	Construction 2nd yr	21	German	East	Realschule	Markus
Male	Construction 2nd yr	18	German	East	Realschule	Frank
Male	Construction 2nd yr	18	German	East	Realschule	Henning
Male	Construction 2nd yr	21	German	East	Realschule	Enno
Female	Construction 2nd yr	20	German	East	Realschule	Tina
Male	Construction 2nd yr	18	German	East	Hauptschule	Paul
Male	Construction[f] 2nd yr	18	German	East	Hauptschule	Claudio
Female	Construction 2nd yr	20	German	East	Realschule	Sarah
Female	Construction 2nd yr	18	German	East	Realschule	Heike
Male	IT[g] 2nd yr	25	German	East	Realschule	Peter
Male	IT 2nd yr	22	German	West	Realschule	Joerg

(*Table 6. Continued*)

Gender	School[a]/Year[b]	Age[c]	Citizenship	Region of birth[d]	1st degree[e]	Pseudonym
Male	IT 2nd yr	22	German	East	Abitur	Andreas
Male	IT 2nd yr	22	German	East	Realschule	Benjamin
Male	IT 2nd yr	19	German	East	Realschule	Rene
Male	IT 2nd yr	20	German	East	Realschule	Martin
Male	IT 4th yr	19	German	East	Realschule	Marcel
Male	IT 4th yr	20	German	East	Realschule	Matthias
Male	IT 4th yr	20	German	West	Realschule	Frederick
Male	IT 2nd yr	18	German	Poland (5)	Realschule	Mario
Male	IT 3rd yr	23	German	East	Abitur	Lars
Male	IT 3rd yr	24	German	East	Abitur	Sven
Male	IT 2nd yr	18	German	Poland (2)	Realschule	Erik
Male	IT 2nd yr	17	German	West	Realschule	Patrick
Male	IT 4th yr	19	German	East	Realschule	Kai
Male	IT 4th yr	24	German	East	Abitur	Enrico
Male	IT 4th yr	19	German	East	Realschule	Jens
Male	IT 2nd yr	19	German	East	Realschule	Karsten
Male	IT 2nd yr		German	East	Realschule	Karl
Male	IT 3rd yr	23	German	East	Abitur	Georg
Male	Hotel/Cook[h] 3rd yr	21	German	East	Hauptschule	Jochen
Male	Hotel/Cook 2nd yr	20	German	West	Hauptschule	Helmut
Male	Hotel/Cook 3rd yr	24	German	West	Abitur	Alexander
Male	Hotel/Cook 3rd yr	20	German	East	Hauptschule	Hans
Female	Hotel/Cook 3rd yr	19	German	East	Realschule	Carola
Male	Hotel/Cook 2nd yr	25	German	West	Abitur	Lennart
Female	Hotel/Cook	22	German	West	Abitur	Maria
Female	Hotel/Cook 2nd yr	20	German	West	Abitur	Michaela
Male	Hotel/Cook 2nd yr	23	German	West	Realschule	Detlef
Female	Hotel/Cook 2nd yr	20	German	East	Hauptschule	Clara
Male	Hotel/Cook 2nd yr	19	German	West	Realschule	Nilo
Female	Hotel/Cook 2nd yr	20	German	Philippines (7)	Hauptschule	Gesine
Female	Hotel/Cook 2nd yr	24	German	Israel[i] (9)	Realschule	Julia
Female	Hotel/Cook 2nd yr	18	German	East	Realschule	Anja

(*Table 6. Continued*)

Gender	School[a]/Year[b]	Age[c]	Citizenship	Region of birth[d]	1st degree[e]	Pseudonym
Female	Hotel/Cook 2nd yr	18	German	East	Realschule	Claudia
Male	Hotel/Cook 1st yr	21	Israeli	Israel[j] (7)	Realschule	Kurt
Male	Hotel/Cook 1st yr	22	German	East	Realschule	Dieter
Male	Hotel/Cook 1st yr	25	German	West	Realschule	Mehmet

Notes
a. Specific occupations for which students were training included scaffold builder, mason, roofer, concrete worker, drafting apprentice, information-technology systems electrician, information-technology communications electrician, cook, hospitality worker, and hotel trainee. Participants' specific occupations are not identified in this table, in order to reduce the likelihood that they could be identified.
b. Year refers to the student's year in the training program.
c. Age on 12/31/00.
d. Refers to participant's birthplace in either West or East Germany. Students not born in Germany indicated prior citizenship or country of origin, as noted. The number in parentheses indicates age at immigration.
e. Refers to student's highest degree prior to entering vocational school (Hauptschule, Realschule, or *Abitur*).
f. Construction school apprentice or student.
g. Information technology school apprentice or student.
h. Hotel/cooking school apprentice or student.
i. Student identified herself as having been Palestinian-Israeli.
j. Student's parents are or were Russian.

civics classes, and their views about foreigners and right-wing radical-ism. Before finalizing the interview instruments, I asked several people to read the questions, including two native German speakers, with whom I discussed issues of cultural meaning in order to be sure that the questions conveyed the same meaning as I had intended. Student interviews ranged widely in length, from under thirty minutes to over three hours, but typically took about an hour. Interviews usually took place after school, during students' free time, on the school grounds. Students received the equivalent of about ten dollars for participating in interviews during their free time. In instances where students were released from class to participate in an interview, they were not com-pensated. Teachers did not receive compensation for participating in the research.

In April through May 2002, I returned to the three schools to conduct follow-up interviews and life-narrative interviews with nine selected students from the original study. This part of the data collection focused specifically on developing a better understanding of the life narratives and explanations of political consciousness among radical right-wing youth as compared to youth who are not members of the radical right (or who do not express radical right-wing views or attitudes). My design for this follow-up research was based on narrative methods and qualitative and ethnographic interviewing and observation. These participants also took part in an interview during which they reviewed transcripts of their original interviews and discussed whether anything had changed since they were first interviewed. Eight of the nine students were available for these interviews (one was doing his mandatory military service at the time), and seven participated in both the transcript review and the life-narrative interview. Students received about the equivalent of twenty dollars for each interview, provided the interview took place during their free time and not during school hours.

In May through June 2004, I returned to the three schools for a final two months of data collection, reinterviewing, and expanding teacher interviews. During this period, I conducted twenty-five semistructured interviews with teachers, during which teachers were asked the same questions that I had asked of their students three years earlier, in order to compare their responses to questions about citizenship and national belonging with those of their students. Finally, I gathered curriculum, textbooks, instructional materials, and other school informational materials from all three schools. School principals were not formally interviewed, although I met with each of them several times before and during data collection.

My ethnographic work also included significant amounts of research gathered outside of the schools. Discussions and information-gathering trips with representatives from teacher-training organizations, unions, and other institutions in Berlin, Bonn, and Nuremberg helped me to understand the role that policymakers and other relevant state and local agencies play in the civic education of vocational youth. I also reviewed at least one local newspaper nearly every day during primary fieldwork and read more than one local or national newspaper as much as possible. I collected hundreds of newspaper articles and analyzed them for media discussions about the radical right, foreigners, the school system, and employment prospects in the occupational fields I was studying, as well as various debates about national identity, national pride, immigration, naturalization, and assimilation. These newspaper articles helped me gain an understanding of the cultural, social, political, and economic context within Germany and Berlin, offering illustrative details for my analysis and depiction of public and political debates, such as the parliamentary debate about pride that took place in the spring of 2001.

Field notes, interviews, and focus groups were all fully transcribed. Transcripts of student interviews from 2000, 2001, and 2002, teacher interviews from 2004, and classroom observations from 2001 were coded line-by-line in a qualitative software program, following inductive data analytic strategies outlined in LeCompte and Schensul (1999). Codes were developed from the "bottom-up," with the final code book ultimately including over 350 codes (see table 6 for sample coding categories related to "citizen" and "citizenship"). I exported collections of the codes to separate files for pattern-level analysis (LeCompte and Schensul 1999, 98), which involved repeated review and analysis of collections of quotations organized by code, as I established patterns within the collections of quotations. In some cases, I wrote analytical memos as an intermediate step to help further analyze particular trends in the data. I also quantified the frequencies of some of the codes and examined them according to various categories (e.g., occupational cluster, generation, east or west birthplace, etc.), and performed chi-square tests to determine the significance of various patterns. The focus groups served the purpose of either confirming or indicating a deviation from the patterns that emerged from the analysis of student interviews, and the teacher interviews in 2001 helped to triangulate classroom observations.

Outsiders and Insiders in Ethnographic Research

It is important to note the ways in which my status as both an outsider and an insider in Germany may have affected my access to schools, the willingness of students and teachers to participate, and my own interpretations of the data. On the one hand, as an American, being an outsider gave me the freedom to ask seemingly banal questions about what it "feels like" to be a part of Europe. Unable to reference a common feeling, participants were forced to be explicit with me in their explanations, offering greater detail than they might have done otherwise. As an outsider, I could also ask politically charged questions about foreigners, the radical right, national pride, or continued tensions between

Table 7. Sample coding categories and descriptions for citizenship and citizen

Domain	Code	Description
Geography and birthplace	multiple states	reference to many states in the world, and each state has citizens
	birth	reference to, or definition of, citizenship in terms of birthplace
	residence	definition of citizen or citizenship as residence in a state or within borders
Learned behaviors	accept culture	naturalization linked to acceptance of, or assimilation to, cultural norms
	language	naturalization or citizenship as linked to language proficiency
	not criminals	in order to naturalize, foreigners should not have criminal history
	registered	citizen is someone who is registered in the country, not "illegal"
	person's use	naturalization should be linked to a person's "use" for the country
	adhere to rules	citizens (or foreigners in country) should adhere to rules, laws, etc.
	taxes	reference to citizenship as linked to paying taxes
	well-being	reference to a citizen as taking care of his own well-being
	choice	notion that one can choose one's citizenship
	work	citizenship linked to work and economic behavior
Belonging and desire	desire	reference esp. with naturalization on wanting to become German
	part of society	citizens are a part of society
	part of state	citizens are a part of the state
	shared interests	citizens are people who have shared interests
Ethnic and racial	filiation	related to parents' citizenship, independent of ethnicity
	ethnic	descent or heritage, e.g., terms *Volk, Ursprung, Herkunft, Vorfahren*
Geography and birthplace	racial	explicitly racial or genetic terms, e.g., refers to physical differences

(*Table 7. Continued*)

Domain	Code	Description
Other	system	citizenship is a system
	family	reference to family as connected to citizenship
	gender	reference to gendered aspect of citizenship
	human	reference to a citizen as a "human" or to humanity

Note: The full codebook includes over 350 codes. Only a sample of those related to citizenship is included here.

east and west Germans with more freedom than a German would have had.

On the other hand, being non-German means that I may have missed some cultural cues or linguistic subtleties in conversations. My German is fluent but not native, and not having grown up in Germany, there are always cultural references that escape me. I addressed this concern by asking for feedback by native Germans on my findings during formal presentations on trips back to Germany in 2003 and 2004 and during meetings over coffee and meals with scholars, university students, and teachers on those trips. I also hired two native German speakers to translate portions of the findings into German and discussed the findings with both translators. Finally, being an American likely played a role in students' willingness to talk with me. Many teenagers and young adults in Germany, while increasingly critical of U.S. policy, are enamored with American pop culture and have the perception that economic opportunities are better in the United States. So many of the students I interviewed asked me how to apply for a green card in the United States that I eventually found the number in Germany that one should call for information, and began bringing it with me to interviews.

However, I was also an insider in Germany in ways that may have affected my data collection and research more generally. As an American whose own ethnic heritage is partially German, I occupied a status somewhere between a German and a foreigner. One school administrator introduced me to her colleagues on more than one occasion by noting that my last name "was formerly *Müller*," a common German surname. Moreover, I was likely privy to negative comments about foreigners, primarily from students, that they might not have shared with a foreigner who was not of "ethnic German" heritage. It was clear to me that in such moments, participants did not classify me in the same category as the "foreigners" they were discussing.

In other ways, my insider-outsider status was not always clearly defined. As a middle-class academic, I had much in common with many of the teachers and administrators, who embraced me warmly and invited me to their homes for meals and celebrations and brought me along on various cultural excursions in Berlin and elsewhere in Germany. I felt—and still feel—extremely sympathetic toward the teachers, who I felt were trying, with little official support and with almost no professional training on this particular issue, to affect these young people's views. I had less in common with the students, whose lives and viewpoints diverged sharply from my own, but for whom I continue to feel a sense of compassion. I often had the sense that students were pleased, and surprised, to have their opinions asked. Some of their views disgusted and offended me. But mostly, I was saddened by their exclusionary views, by the lack of opportunities in many of their lives, and by the contradictions and misunderstandings in their resentment of foreigners and foreignness.

notes

introduction

1. Throughout this book, when distinguishing between categories of Germans who have descended from German forefathers as compared to those who have become German citizens via naturalization but have another "ethnic" heritage, I use the terms "ethnic" German and "non-ethnic" German. I place the two terms "ethnic" and "non-ethnic" in quotation marks, however, to indicate that these are contested terms.

2. For figures on the increase in right-wing crimes, see reports of the *Verfassungsschutzbericht* (*Erziehung und Wissenschaft* 2000: 10; Krupa 2001).

3. For a thorough discussion of the development of right-wing extremism and radicalism in Germany after World War II, see Harnischmacher (1993), Kreutzberger (1983), Miller and Ready (2002), Pfahl-Traugber (1999), Rojahn (1996), and Schubarth and Stöss (2001). Also see Paul (1995, 40) and Steinmetz (1997). For an elaboration of the skinhead and neo-Nazi scenes and subcultures, see Pfahl-Traughber (2000).

4. Peck cites Morley and Robins (1990, 11), referring to Kreutzner (1989), for the phrase "free of ideological taint."

5. For more on the use of the term "foreign cocitizen," see White (1997, 761).

6. See White (1997, 761) for a discussion of the shifts in German vocabulary about foreigners over the past 40 years, from *Fremdarbeiter* (foreign workers) to *Gastarbeiter* (guest workers) to *Ausländer* (foreigner) or *ausländische Arbeitnehmer* (foreign employees), to the more politically correct *Migranten* (migrants) or *ausländische Mitbürger* (foreign cocitizen).

7. For more on the controversies surrounding the reform in German citizenship law, especially regarding the different positions taken by Germany's various political parties, see Hogwood (2000).

8. It is also important to note that class divisions in Germany tend to be quite clearly defined. Terms such as *Arbeiter* (worker) and *Angestellte* (employee) have clear meanings in the class structure. I am grateful to Steve Hamilton for reminding me of this point.

9. I use the terms *student* and *apprentice* interchangeably. Technically, some young people were apprentices (spending three to four days/week learning on

the job) and some young people were students learning in a simulated full-time setting on-site at the vocational schools, or were in full-time, school-based programs to earn a degree enabling them to continue on in higher education. All of these young people attended one of the three vocational schools for the school portion of their degrees, however. I use the terms *student* and *apprentice* interchangeably in order to confuse efforts to identify students by recognizing their occupational track and program in the school, which in some cases may have included a relatively small number of young people.

10. In thinking about how to interpret the data in this manner, I draw here on Michèle Lamont's (2000) book detailing interviews she conducted with working-class men in France and the United States, especially her description of her approach on p. 4 and in an earlier manuscript presented at a workshop in the Sociology Department at the University of Michigan. Lamont attributes the concept of "mental maps," which is the term she uses to describe her approach to the coding and interpretation of interview data, to Geertz (1973, 220).

1. Who Belongs to the Nation?

1. See Lisa Fein's ongoing dissertation work in sociology at the University of Michigan.

2. I am grateful to Fatma Müge Göçek for helpful discussions about these distinctions.

3. In the German case, for example, Dieter Gosewinkel (2002, 62) points out that diplomatic pressures, rather than a universal desire to preserve national homogeneity, led to the adoption of the most restrictive state model for naturalization—that of Prussia—as the model for national policy.

4. The seeming openness of the GDR's policies is, however, contradicted by the state's policy toward, and treatment of, its own guest workers. Although like its counterpart in the West, the GDR did recruit guest workers, largely from Vietnam, Cuba, Poland, North Korea, and Mozambique, the numbers were much smaller than in the West, and the integration of foreigners into East German society was discouraged or prohibited. Guest workers were segregated into dormitories and ghettos far removed from East Germans, and generally did not have social contact with outsiders. Officially, the presence of foreign guest workers was not acknowledged, so that eventually, their existence became a public taboo (Bade 1999, 19–20; Räthzel 1990, 43–44). Wolfgang Thierse, who would later become a prominent politician in unified Germany, characterized the situation as an "East German form of Apartheid" (Bade 1999, 20). Clearly, even if official citizenship policy allowed naturalization on ideological grounds, foreigners' access was more difficult than these policies imply.

5. Germany's asylum policies were also undergoing significant reform during the 1990s, although there is not space here to offer detailed discussion of these reforms. For a thorough analysis, see Joppke (1999b, 85–94).

2. Being and Becoming in Germany

1. I thank Hanns-Fred Rathenow and George Steinmetz for helpful discussions on this point.

2. Habermas (1992b, 89) also explains that the concept of constitutional patriotism in fact needed to be differentiated from three other possible bases for national identity that he calls "prepolitical": "the *Volk* as a historic community of fate," "the nation as a linguistic and cultural community," and the most recent West German alternative to national identity, "the social and economic system as a performance community."

3. For more on the debates about public memorials and memory, see Maier (1988) and Eley (2000, 25), especially n. 41, which offers a bibliographic overview of recent work on the politics of German Holocaust memorials.

4. Also see Olick (1999) for discussions of a move toward "normalization" earlier in West Germany.

5. See Fulbrook (1999) for a thorough account of the different approaches to dealing with the Nazi past in the FRG and the GDR and for a discussion of institutionalized shame and ritualized guilt. See Huyssen (1995) for comments on the leftist antinationalist position. For more on the differences between East and West German collective memory, see Verheyen (1999).

6. It is also important to point out that there are two kinds of teachers—state employees (*Angestellte*) and federal employees (*Beamte*). In Berlin, special legislation in 1996 gave state-employed east German teachers 100% of state-employed west German teachers' salaries. But federally employed teachers still experience the discrepancy (according to information provided during a meeting with a representative from the Berlin state school office's salary bureau, the *Landesschulamt Gehalts- und Lohnstelle* in 2001).

3. Germany's Forbidden Fruit

1. For example, the TV station n-tv hosted a show with CDU chairman Wolfgang Schäuble on the topic: "Are you proud to be a German?" on March 26, 2001.

2. Some public hesitancy to discuss national pride or national identity may have resulted from concerns from other European countries after 1990 about the potential strength of Germany as a unified country (see, for example, Greiffenhagen and Greiffenhagen 1993, 16–17; Olick 1998, 556).

3. I am indebted to Andreas Glaeser for the phrase "hegemonic moral dis-

course," which he used to describe the state and social narrative about national pride in a written text commenting on a draft of this chapter.

4. Quotes are taken from written comments provided to me by Andreas Glaeser when this chapter was presented at the American Sociological Association conference in Chicago in 2002.

5. Of course, national identity consists of many different and overlapping elements, of which national pride is only one. Others might include, for example, orientations toward territory, economics, citizenship, mass culture, nationhood, ethnicity, or "primordial ties" (for more elaboration, see Billig 1995, 7–9; Fulbrook 1999; Staab 1998, 8). While I address some of these aspects elsewhere, especially orientations toward territory, nationhood, citizenship, and ethnicity, this chapter narrows the focus to an examination of national pride more specifically.

6. The small sample size of teachers in this study means that I can only point toward trends here; further research is needed with a larger sample of teachers to tease out more significant patterns.

7. All names have been changed to pseudonyms. Several conventions are employed in the use of quotations from interviews. Square brackets are used for clarification; original German terms and phrases, in italics, are included in parentheses where an exact English translation is not available or when the original German is helpful for understanding the meaning. Following Straughn (2005), I note that grammatical errors and slang terms are retained wherever possible, but some linguistic nuance is lost in translation (see especially p. 1622, n. 48).

8. It is important to point out that the young people I interviewed who were either "non-ethnic" Germans or who were born in another country did deviate slightly from the pattern of complaints about the national pride taboo, although further research is needed with a larger sample in order to point to more significant trends.

4. Raising the Right Wing

1. There is still some uncertainty, however, as to whether the acts have actually increased in number or are rather simply being counted more accurately (see Homola 2001).

2. Although some studies suggest that unemployed youth are more likely to express xenophobic opinions, crime statistics show that most individuals involved in right-wing criminal acts are employed (see Heitmeyer 1999, 65). A 1991 study by Held et al. also showed that youth with secure employment prospects express greater xenophobia than youth with poor employment prospects (qtd. In Schnabel 1993, 806; also see Steinmetz 1997).

3. Steinmetz cites Heitmeyer (1988) and Heitmeyer et al. (1992).

4. This is my perception based on how students distinguished between the "politically organized" neo-Nazis and the "violent" skinheads. This does not mean, however, that neo-Nazis do not engage in racist violence. Skinheads, however, appear to be more focused on violence and less on political issues.

5. As advertised in the 2003 catalog of the right-wing National Democratic Party of Germany (NPD), *Kampf und Wiedergeburt* (published by the Deutsche Stimme Verlag), p. 127. The group sells fifty milliliter bottles of eau de toilette for 20 Euros. Archival materials accessed on May 26, 2004, at the Antifaschistisches Pressearchiv und Bildungszentrum Berlin e.v. (Anti-fascist Press Archive and Educational Center in Berlin).

6. I heard about the number "88" several times while in Berlin; the symbol "100-12" was reported by a representative from the Antifaschistisches Pressearchiv und Bildungszentrum Berlin e.v. The number "18" is reported to stand for Adolf Hitler in *PZ* (Politische Zeitschrift), no. 103, September 2000, 4.

7. According to information provided by a representative from the Antifaschistisches Pressearchiv und Bildungszentrum Berlin e.v.

8. "Aktiv handeln gegen Rechts—Handlungsmöglichkeiten für die Berufsschule" (Addressing the Right Wing Actively—Strategies for Vocational Schools), a weekend seminar from November 30 to December 2, 2001 at the DGB-Jugendbildungsstätte Flecken Zechlin.

9. Antifaschistisches Pressearchiv und Bildungszentrum Berlin.

10. The word *Neger* is translated as "Negro" and has a derogatory connotation.

11. As discussed with a representative from a teacher-training project in Berlin.

12. Current political reforms concerning retirement that were being debated in German parliament at the time of my research were a frequent subject of discussion in the civics classrooms I observed, although not all of the teachers made the link between the need to reform the retirement system and the need to have increased numbers of foreign workers.

13. From the 1993 album *Auslese*. Information in archival materials at the Antifaschistisches Pressearchiv und Bildungszentrum Berlin e.v.

14. Information in archival materials at the Antifaschistisches Pressearchiv und Bildungszentrum Berlin e.v.

15. The Pioneer groups were GDR youth organizations. See Wegner (1996) for further discussion of youth political socialization in the GDR.

5. Teaching National Identity

1. Political education was also seen as a means to counter socialist and communist ideas (Händle 1999, 14).

2. I am grateful to Steve Hamilton for reminding me of this point.

3. Civics, political education, or social studies classes were in fact introduced into all school forms during the postwar period as supplements to history instruction (Rathenow and Ehmann 2000, 33).

4. For more information on the history and development of civic education in Germany, see Gagel (1995); Händle (1999); and Kuhn, Massing, and Skuhr (1993). It is also important to note that civic education in German public schools represents just one aspect of the resocialization, reeducation, and reorientation programs that have taken place in Germany throughout the past century. Moreover, the goals of Germany's civic education programs are much broader than the issue of national identity, encompassing topics related to the functioning of a democratic government as well as social, legal, and economic issues.

5. See discussions of the French, British, American, and Soviet educational reform efforts in Gagel (1995); Händle (1999); and Kuhn, Massing, and Skuhr (1993).

6. The state's curriculum recommendations are based on the curricular frameworks developed by the Standing Conference of Cultural Ministers (Kultusministerkonferenz, or KMK), a federal body. For a more detailed explanation of this process, see Sekretariat der Standigen Konferenz der Kultusminister der Länder in der Bundesrepublik Deutschland (1999).

7. For more on the relationship between "leftist" teachers and "right-wing" attitudes among students in Berlin, see Bovier and Boehnke 1999.

6. Blood, Culture, Birthplace

1. The word "*Neger*" is translated as "Negro" and has a derogatory connotation. Also see chapter 4, n. 10.

bibliography

Achatz, Juliane, Wolfgang Gaiser, Martina Gille, Winfried Krüger, Corinna Kleinert, and Johann De Rijke. 2001. "Das Verhältnis Jugendlicher und junger Erwachsener zur Politik—Getrennte Wege im Vereinigten Deutschland? Ausgewählte Ergebnisse des DJI-Jugendsurveys." In *Jahrbuch der Jugendforschung*, edited by Hans Merkens and Jürgen Zinnecker, 211–42. Opladen: Leske and Budrich.

Alba, Richard, Peter Schmidt, and Martina Wasmer, eds. 2003. *Germans or Foreigners? Attitudes toward Ethnic Minorities in Post-Reunification Germany*. New York: Palgrave Macmillan.

Alexander, Jeffrey C., and Steven Seidman, eds. 1990. *Culture and Society: Contemporary Debates*. Cambridge: Cambridge University Press.

Almond, Gabriel A., and Sidney Verba. 1963. *The Civic Culture: Political Attitudes and Democracy in Five Nations*. Princeton: Princeton University Press.

Alter, Peter. 1992. "Nationalism and German Politics after 1945." In *The State of Germany: The National Idea in the Making, Unmaking, and Remaking of a Modern Nation-State*, edited by John Breuilly, 154–76. London: Longman.

Althusser, Louis. 1971. *Lenin and Philosophy*. New York: Monthly Review Press.

Amadeo, Jo-Ann, Judith Torney-Purta, Rainer Lehmann, Vera Husfeldt, and Roumiana Nikolova. 2002. *Civic Knowledge and Engagement: An IEA Study of Upper Secondary Students in Sixteen Countries*. Amsterdam: International Association for the Evaluation of Educational Achievement.

Anderson, Benedict. 1991. *Imagined Communities: Reflections on the Origin and Spread of Nationalism*. Rev. ed. New York: Verso.

———. 1999. "The Promise of Nationalism." *New Left Review* 235 (May/June): 3–17.

Anthias, Floya. 1995. "Cultural Racism or Racist Culture? Rethinking Racist Exclusions." *Economy and Society* 24 (May): 279–301.

Apple, Michael. 1990. *Ideology and Curriculum*. New York: Routledge.

Applegate, Celia. 1990. *A Nation of Provincials: The German Idea of Heimat*. Berkeley: University of California Press.

Archibugi, Danielle, David Held, and Martin Köhler, eds. 1998. *Re-Imagining*

Political Community: Studies in Cosmopolitan Democracy. Stanford: Stanford University Press.

Arnett, Jeffrey Jensen. 2000. "Emerging Adulthood: A Theory of Development from the Late Teens through the Twenties." *American Psychologist* 55 (May): 469–80.

Aronowitz, Stanley, and Henry A. Giroux. 1993. *Education Still Under Siege*. 2nd ed. Critical Studies in Education and Culture Series. Westport, Conn.: Bergin and Garvey.

Ausländerbeauftragte des Senats von Berlin, Die. 2000. *Die Reform des Staatsangehörigkeitsrechts: Hinweise zum Erwerb der Deutschen Staatbürgerschaft*. Berlin: Verwaltungsdruckerei Berlin.

Bacher, Johann. 2001. "In welchen Lebensbereichen lernen Jugendliche Ausländerfeindlichkeit? Ergebnisse einer Befragung bei Berufsschülerinnen und Berufsschülern." *Kölner Zeitschrift für Soziologie und Sozialpsychologie* 53 (2): 334–49.

Backes, Uwe, and Eckhard Jesse. 1996. *Politischer Extremismus in der Bundesrepublik Deutschland*. Bonn: Bundeszentrale für Politische Bildung.

Bade, Klaus J. 1996. "Einwanderung und Gesellschaftspolitik in Deutschland—Quo Vadis Bundesrepublik?" In *Die Multikulturelle Herausforderung: Menschen über Grenzen—Grenzen über Menschen*, edited by Klaus Bade, 230–53. Munich: C. H. Beck Verlag.

———. 1999. "Ziel Deutschland: Zuwanderungen nach 1945." In *Zuwanderungen-Auswanderungen: Integration und Desintegration nach 1945. Symposium des Deutschen Historischen Museums in Zusammenarbeit mit der Bundeszentrale für Politische Bildung*, edited by Hans-Martin Hinz, 14–34. Wolfratshausen: Verlag Edition Minerva Hermann Farnung.

———. 2001. "Immigration, Naturalization, and Ethno-National Traditions in Germany: From the Citizenship Law of 1913 to the Law of 1999." In *Crossing Boundaries: The Exclusion and Inclusion of Minorities in Germany and America*, edited by Larry Eugene Jones, 29–49. New York: Berghahn Books.

Balibar, Etienne. 1988. "Propositions on Citizenship." *Ethics* 98 (July): 723–30.

———. 1991. "Is There a 'Neo-Racism'?" In *Race, Nation, Class: Ambiguous Identities*, edited by Etienne Balibar and Immanuel Wallerstein, 17–28. New York: Verso.

Barrett, Christopher B., and Jeffrey W. Cason. 1997. *Overseas Research: A Practical Guide*. Baltimore, Md.: Johns Hopkins University Press.

Baumann, Jochen. 1999. "Staatsangehörigkeit und Citizenship: Das Deutsche Staatsbürgerschaftsrecht im Europäischen Vergleich." In *Blut oder Boden: Doppel-Pass, Staatsbürgerrecht und Nationsverständnis*, edited by Jochen

Baumann, Andreas Dietl, and Wolfgang Wippermann, 49–106. Berlin: Elephanten Press.

Baumann, Jochen, Andreas Dietl, and Wolfgang Wippermann. 1999. *Blut oder Boden: Doppelpass, Staatsbürgerrecht und Nationsverständnis*. Berlin: Elephanten Press.

Beauftragte der Bundesregierung für Migration, Flüchtlinge und Integration, Die. 2005a. *Daten-Fakten-Trends: Einbürgerung*. Berlin: Beauftragte der Bundesregierung für Migration, Flüchtlinge und Integration, in Zusammenarbeit mit dem efms- Europäisches Forum für Migrationsstudien, Bamberg. www.integrationsbeauftragte.de (visited July 5, 2005).

———. 2005b. *Wie werde ich Deutsche/r?* Bonn.

———. 2007. *7. Bericht der Beauftragten der Bundesregierung für Migration, Flüchtlinge und Integration über die Lage der Ausländerinnen und Ausländer in Deutschland*. Berlin: Beauftragte der Bundesregierung für Migration, Flüchtlinge und Integration.

———. 2008. *Wege zur Einbürgerung: Wie werde ich Deutsche—wie werde ich Deutscher?* Berlin: Beauftragte der Bundesregierung für Migration, Flüchtlinge und Integration.

Behnke, Andreas. 1997. "Citizenship, Nationhood, and the Production of Political Space." *Citizenship Studies* 1 (2): 243–65.

Beiner, Ronald, ed. 1995. *Theorizing Citizenship*. Albany: State University of New York Press.

Bellah, Robert, Richard Madsen, William Sullivan, Ann Swidler, and Steven Tipton. 1985. *Habits of the Heart: Individualism and Commitment in American Life*. Berkeley: University of California Press.

Bendix, Richard. 1996. *Nation-Building and Citizenship: Studies of Our Changing Social Order*. Enlarged ed. New Brunswick, N.J.: Transaction Publishers.

Benhabib, Seyla. 2002. *The Claims of Culture: Equality and Diversity in the Global Era*. Princeton, N.J.: Princeton University Press.

Berdahl, Daphne. 1999. "'(N)Ostalgie' for the Present: Memory, Longing, and East German Things." *Ethnos* 64 (2): 192–211.

Berliner Zeitung. 2001. "Auch Walter Jens ist Stolz, ein Deutscher zu Sein." March 29, 13.

Bernstein, Richard. 2005. "Germans Told to Cheer Up. 'Why Should We?' Some Say." *New York Times*, December 6, A4.

———. 2006a. "In World Cup Surprise, Flags Fly with German Pride." *New York Times*, June 17.

———. 2006b. "Soccer Good for the Psyche, Say the Winning Germans." *New York Times*, July 4.

Billig, Michael. 1995. *Banal Nationalism*. London: Sage Publications.

Birnbaum, Norman. 1990. "How New the New Germany?" *Salmagundi* 88–89 (fall–winter): 234–63.

Bohrer, Karl Heinz. 1992. "Why We Are Not a Nation—and Why We Should Become One." In *When the Wall Came Down: Reactions to German Unification*, edited by Harold James and Marla Stone, 60–70. New York: Routledge.

Borneman, John. 1991. *After the Wall: East Meets West in the New Berlin*. New York: Basic Books.

———. 1992. *Belonging in the Two Berlins: Kin, State, Nation*. Cambridge: Cambridge University Press.

———. 1997. "State, Territory, and National Identity Formation in the Two Berlins, 1945–1995." In *Culture, Power, Place: Explorations in Critical Anthropology*, edited by Akhil Gupta and James Ferguson, 93–117. Durham, N.C.: Duke University Press.

Bourdieu, Pierre. 1999. "Rethinking the State: Genesis and Structure of the Bureaucratic Field." In *State/Culture: State-Formation after the Cultural Turn*, edited by George Steinmetz, 53–75. Ithaca, N.Y.: Cornell University Press.

Bourdieu, Pierre, and Jean-Claude Passeron. 1990. *Reproduction in Education, Society and Culture*. 2nd ed. Thousand Oaks, Calif.: Sage Publications.

Bourdieu, Pierre, and Loic J. D. Wacquant. 1992. *An Invitation to Reflexive Sociology*. Chicago: University of Chicago Press.

Bovier, Elke, and Klaus Boehnke. 1999. "Do Liberal Teachers Produce Violent and Xenophobic Students? An Empirical Study of German Ninth Graders and Their Teachers." *Teaching and Teacher Education* 15: 815–27.

Bowen, John. 2007. *Why the French Don't Like Headscarves: Islam, the State, and Public Space*. Princeton, N.J.: Princeton University Press.

Breuilly, John. 1992. "Conclusion: Nationalism and German Reunification." In *The State of Germany: The National Idea in the Making, Unmaking, and Remaking of a Modern Nation-State*, edited by John Breuilly, 224–38. London: Longman.

Brinks, Jan Herman, ed. 2000. *Children of a New Fatherland: Germany's Postwar Right-Wing Politics*. New York: I. B. Tauris Publishers.

Brubaker, Rogers. 1992. *Citizenship and Nationhood in France and Germany*. Cambridge: Harvard University Press.

———. 2004. *Ethnicity without Groups*. Cambridge: Harvard University Press.

Brubaker, Rogers, Margit Feischmidt, Jon Fox, and Liana Grancea. 2006. *Nationalist Politics and Everyday Ethnicity in a Transylvanian Town*. Princeton: Princeton University Press.

Bude, Heinz. 1992. *Bilanz der Nachfolge: Die Bundesrepublik und der Nationalsozialismus*. Frankfurt am Main: Suhrkamp.

Calhoun, Craig. 1993. "Nationalism and Ethnicity." *Annual Review of Sociology* 19: 211–39.
———. 1995. *Critical Social Theory: Culture, History, and the Challenge of Difference.* Malden, Mass.: Blackwell Publishers.
———. 1997. *Nationalism.* Minneapolis: University of Minnesota Press.
Canefe, Nergis. 1998. "Citizens versus Permanent Guests: Cultural Memory and Citizenship Laws in a Reunified Germany." *Citizenship Studies* 2 (3): 519–44.
Carnoy, Martin. 1992. "Education and the State: From Adam Smith to Perestroika." In *Emergent Issues in Education: Comparative Perspectives*, edited by Robert F. Arnove, Philip G. Altbach, and Gail P. Kelly, 143–59. Albany, N.Y.: State University of New York Press.
Castles, Stephen, and Alastair Davidson. 2000. *Citizenship and Migration: Globalization and the Politics of Belonging.* New York: Routledge.
Cesarani, David, and Mary Fulbrook, eds. 1996. *Citizenship, Nationality, and Migration in Europe.* New York: Routledge.
Cherrington, Ruth. 1997. "Generational Issues in China: A Case Study of the 1980s Generation of Young Intellectuals." *British Journal of Sociology* 48 (June): 302–20.
Cohen, Roger. 1999. "Germany's East and West: Still Hostile States of Mind." *New York Times*, October 24.
———. 2000. "Head of Germany's Moderate Right Party Quits as Uproar over Corruption Scandal Grows." *New York Times*, February 17.
———. 2001. "Schroeder Joins Debate, Taking Side of Pride in Germany." *New York Times*, March 20.
Condor, Susan. 2000. "Pride and Prejudice: Identity Management in English People's Talk about 'This Country.'" *Discourse and Society* 11: 175–202.
Cooke, Miriam. 2002. "Humanist Nationalism and Lebanese Women's Texts." In *Social Constructions of Nationalism in the Middle East*, edited by Fatma Müge Göçek, 125–40. Albany: State University of New York Press.
Cooper, Alice Holmes. 2002. "Party-Sponsored Protest and the Movement Society: The CDU/CSU Mobilises against Citizenship Law Reform." *German Politics* 11 (2): 88–104.
Cullingford, Cedric. 2000. *Prejudice: From Individual Identity to Nationalism in Young People.* Sterling, Va.: Stylus Publishers.
Delanty, Gerard. 1997. "Models of Citizenship: Defining European Identity and Citizenship." *Citizenship Studies* 1 (3): 285–303.
Detwiler, Donald. 1999. *Germany: A Short History.* 3rd ed. Carbondale: Southern Illinois University Press.
Deutsche Shell, ed. 2000a. *Jugend 2000.* Shell Jugendstudie 13, vol. 1. Opladen: Leske and Budrich.

————, ed. 2000b. *Jugend 2000*. Shell Jugendstudie 13, vol. 2. Opladen: Leske and Budrich.

————, ed. 2002. *Jugend 2002: Zwischen pragmatischem Idealismus und robustem Materialismus*. Shell Jugendstudie 14. Frankfurt: Fischer Taschenbuch Verlag.

Diderot, D. 1994. "Citoyen." In *Citizenship: Critical Concepts*. Vol. 1, edited by Bryan S. Turner and Peter Hamilton, 318–20. New York: Routledge.

Dietrich, Stefan. 2001. "Kein Diener des Volkes." *Frankfurter Allgemeine Zeitung*, March 19, 1.

Dill, Marshall, Jr. 1970. *Germany: A Modern History*. Ann Arbor: University of Michigan Press.

Dirks, Nicholas B., Geoff Eley, and Sherry B. Ortner, eds. 1994. *Culture/ Power/History: A Reader in Contemporary Social Theory*. Princeton: Princeton University Press.

Eagleton, Terry. 2000. *The Idea of Culture*. Malden, Mass.: Blackwell Publishers.

Eley, Geoff. 1999. "Culture, Nation, Gender." Paper presented at the CSST Faculty Seminar, University of Michigan, Ann Arbor, October 28.

————. 2000. "Ordinary Germans, Nazism, and Judeocide." In *The "Goldhagen Effect": History, Memory, Nazism—Facing the German Past*, edited by Geoff Eley, 1–31. Ann Arbor: University of Michigan Press.

Eley, Geoff, and Ronald Suny, eds. 1996. *Becoming National: A Reader*. New York: Oxford University Press.

Etzioni, Amitai. 1995. "Too Many Rights, Too Few Responsibilities." In *Toward A Global Civil Society*, edited by Michael Walzer, 99–105. Oxford: Berghahn Books.

European Commission. 2001. *Eurobarometer: Public Opinion in the European Union*. Report Number 54. Brussels: Directorate-General Press and Communication. http://www.ec.europa.eu.

Fahrmeir, Andreas K. 1997. "Nineteenth-Century German Citizenships: A Reconsideration." *Historical Journal* 40 (3): 721–52.

Falk, Richard. 2000. "The Decline of Citizenship in an Era of Globalization." *Citizenship Studies* 4 (1): 5–17.

Farin, Klaus, and Henning Flad. 2001. "Die Texte." In *Reaktionäre Rebellen: Rechtsextreme Musik in Deutschland*, edited by Archiv der Jugendkultur, 35–92. Berlin: Archiv der Jugendkultur.

Flad, Henning. 2001. "Kleider machen Leute: Rechtsextremismus und Kleidungsstil." In *Reaktionäre Rebellen: Rechtsextreme Musik in Deutschland*, edited by Archiv der Jugendkultur, 99–116. Berlin: Archiv der Jugendkultur.

Fox, Jon E. 2003. "Nationhood without Nationalism: Being National in Everyday Life." Ph.D. diss., University of California, Los Angeles.

Fox, Jon, and Cynthia Miller-Idriss. 2008. "Everyday Nationhood." *Ethnicities* 8 (4): 536–63.

Frankfurter Allgemeine Zeitung Weekly. 2004. "'Biggest Problem Is Uncertainty': Presidential Nominee Köhler on Germany, Patriotism, and Religion." May 21, 3.

Fraser, Nancy. 1997. *Justice Interruptus: Critical Reflections on the "Postsocialist" Condition.* New York: Routledge.

Fried, Nico. 2001. "Schröder zeigt Jürgen Trittin 'Die Gelbe Karte.'" *Süddeutsche Zeitung*, March 21.

Fulbrook, Mary. 1990. *A Concise History of Germany.* New York: Cambridge University Press.

———. 1996. "Germany for the Germans? Citizenship and Nationality in a Divided Nation." In *Citizenship, Nationality, and Migration in Europe*, edited by David Cesarani and Mary Fulbrook, 88–105. London: Routledge.

———. 1997. "Myth-Making and National Identity: The Case of the G.D.R." In *Myths and Nationhood*, edited by Geoffrey Hosking and George Schöpflin, 72–87. New York: Routledge.

———. 1999. *German National Identity after the Holocaust.* Malden, Mass.: Polity Press.

Gagel, Walter. 1995. *Geschichte der Politischen Bildung in der Bundesrepublik Deutschland 1945–1989.* 2nd ed. Opladen: Leske and Budrich.

Gaiser, Wolfgang, Martina Gille, Winfried Krüger, and Johan De Rijke. 1998. "Youth and Politics in Germany: Interest in Politics, Confidence in Institutions, Value Orientations and Political Participation." In *Youth and Political Changes in Contemporary World*, edited by Jan Garlicki, 145–82. Warsaw: Dom Wydawniczy Elipsa.

Galston, William. 1995. "Progressive Politics and Communitarian Culture." In *Toward a Global Civil Society*, edited by Michael Walzer, 107–12. Oxford: Berghahn Books.

Geertz, Clifford. 1973. *The Interpretation of Cultures.* New York: Basic Books.

Gellner, Ernest. 1983. *Nations and Nationalism.* London: Oxford University Press.

———. 1996. "The Coming of Nationalism and Its Interpretation: The Myths of Nation and Class." In *Mapping the Nation*, edited by Gopal Balakrishnan, 98–145. New York: Verso.

Gelvin, James L. 2002. "(Re)Presenting Nations: Demonstrations and Nationalisms in Premandate Syria." In *Social Constructions of Nationalism in the Middle East*, edited by Fatma Mugé Göçek, 99–122. Albany: State University of New York Press.

Gilroy, Paul. 1991. *'There Ain't No Black in the Union Jack': The Cultural Politics of Race and Nation.* Chicago: University of Chicago Press.

———. 1996. "One Nation under a Groove: The Cultural Politics of 'Race' and Racism in Britain." In *Becoming National*, edited by Geoff Eley and Ronald Grigor Suny, 352–69. New York: Oxford University Press.

———. 2000. *Against Race: Imagining Political Culture beyond the Color Line.* Cambridge: Belknap Press.

Giroux, Henry. 1987. "Citizenship, Public Philosophy, and the Retreat from Democracy in the United States." In *In the Nation's Image: Civic Education in Japan, the Soviet Union, the United States, France, and Britain*, edited by Edgar Gumbert, 61–84. Atlanta, Ga.: Center for Cross-Cultural Education, Georgia State University.

Glaeser, Andreas. 2000. *Divided in Unity: Identity, Germany, and the Berlin Police*. Chicago: University of Chicago Press.

Göçek, Fatma Mugé, ed. 2002. *Social Constructions of Nationalism in the Middle East*. Albany: State University of New York Press.

Goether, Udo, Irina Mohr, Heinz Lynen von Berg, and Michael Rump-Raeuber. 1999. *Sackgasse Rechtsextrem: Argumente gegen rechte Sprüche.* Berlin: Berliner Institut für Lehrerfort- und Weiterbildung und Schulentwicklung.

Goldberg, David Theo. 1993. *Racist Culture: Philosophy and the Politics of Meaning*. Cambridge, Mass.: Blackwell Publishers.

Gosewinkel, Dieter. 2001. *Einbürgern und Ausschliessen: Die Nationalisierung der Staatsangehörigkeit vom Deutschen Bund bis zur Bundesrepublik Deutschland*. Göttingen: Vandenhoeck and Ruprecht.

———. 2002. "Citizenship and Naturalization Politics in Germany in the Nineteenth and Twentieth Centuries." In *Challenging Ethnic Citizenship: German and Israeli Perspectives on Immigration*, edited by Daniel Levy and Yfaat Weiss, 59–81. New York: Berghahn Books.

Gramsci, Antonio. 1971. *Selections from the Prison Notebooks*. Translated by Quinton Hoare and Geoffrey Nowell Smith. New York: International Publishers.

Grant, Susan-Mary. 1997. "Making History: Myth and the Construction of American Nationhood." In *Myths and Nationhood*, edited by Geoffrey Hosking and George Schöpflin, 88–106. New York: Routledge.

Grass, Günter. 1990. *Two States—One Nation?* Translated by Helen Wolff and Kurt Wolff. New York: Harcourt Brace Jovanovich.

Green, Simon. 2000. "Beyond Ethnoculturalism? German Citizenship in the New Millennium." *German Politics* 9 (3): 105–24.

———. 2001. "Citizenship Policy in Germany: The Case of Ethnicity over Residence." In *Towards a European Nationality: Citizenship, Immigration, and Nationality in the EU*, edited by Randall Hansen and Patrick Weil, 24–51. New York: Palgrave.

Greenfeld, Liah. 1992. *Nationalism: Five Roads to Modernity*. Cambridge: Harvard University Press.

Greiffenhagen, Martin and Silvia Greiffenhagen. 1993. *Ein schwieriges Vaterland: Zur politischen Kultur im Vereinigten Deutschland*. Munich: List Verlag.

Greiner, Ulrich. 1992. "The Phantom of the Nation: Why We Are Not a Nation Anymore and Why We Do Not Have to Become One—A Futile Interruption in the Intellectuals' Debate about German Unity." In *When the Wall Came Down: Reactions to German Unification*, edited by Harold James and Marla Stone, 77–82. New York: Routledge.

Griffin, Larry. 2004. "'Generations and Collective Memory' Revisited: Race, Region, and Memory of Civil Rights." *American Sociological Review* 69 (August): 544–57.

Guibernau, Montserrat. 1999. "Nations without States: Catalonia, a Case Study." In *The Ethnicity Reader: Nationalism, Multiculturalism, and Migration*, edited by Montserrat Guibernau and John Rex, 133–53. Malden, Mass.: Blackwell Publishers.

Gumbert, Edgar B., ed. 1986. *In the Nation's Image: Civic Education in Japan, the Soviet Union, the United States, France, and Britain*. Atlanta, Ga.: Center for Cross-Cultural Education, Georgia State University.

Habermas, Jürgen. 1992a. "Further Reflections on the Public Sphere." In *Habermas and the Public Sphere*, edited by Craig Calhoun, 421–61. Cambridge: MIT Press.

———. 1992b. "Yet Again: German Identity—A Unified Nation of Angry DM-Burghers?" In *When the Wall Came Down: Reactions to German Unification*, edited by Harold James and Marla Stone, 86–102. New York: Routledge.

Hahn, Carole L. 1998. *Becoming Political: Comparative Perspectives on Citizenship Education*. Albany: State University of New York Press.

Hall, Stuart. 1988. "The Toad in the Garden: Thatcherism among the Theorists." In *Marxism and the Interpretation of Culture*, edited by Lawrence Grossberg and Cary Nelson, 35–73. Urbana: University of Illinois Press.

———. 1989. "Rassismus als Ideologischer Diskurs." *Das Argument: Zeitschrift für Philosophie und Sozialwissenschaften* 178: 913–21.

———. 1994. "Cultural Studies: Two Paradigms." In *Culture/Power/History: A Reader in Contemporary Social Theory*, edited by Nicolas Dirks, Geoff Eley, and Sherry Ortner, 520–38. Princeton: Princeton University Press.

———. 1996. "Ethnicity: Identity and Difference." In *Becoming National*, edited by Geoff Eley and Ronald Suny, 337–49. New York: Oxford University Press.

Hamilton, Stephen F. 1990. *Apprenticeship for Adulthood: Preparing Youth for the Future*. New York: Free Press.

Händle, Christa. 1999. "Politische Bildung in der Schule." In *Aufgaben Politischer Bildung in der Sekundarstufe 1: Studien aus dem Projekt Civic Education*, edited by Christa Händle, Detlef Oesterreich, and Luitgard Trommer, 13–67. Opladen: Leske and Budrich.

Händle, Christa, Detlef Oesterreich, and Luitgard Trommer. 1999a. *Aufgaben Politischer Bildung in der Sekundarstufe 1: Studien aus dem Projekt Civic Education*. Opladen: Leske and Budrich.

———. 1999b. "Concepts of Civic Education in Germany Based on a Survey of Expert Opinion." In *Civic Education across Countries: Twenty-Four National Case Studies from the IEA Civic Education Project*, edited by Judith Torney-Putna, John Schwille, and Jo-Ann Amadeo, 257–84. Amsterdam: International Association for the Evaluation of Educational Achievement.

Hansen, Randall, and Patrick Weil. 2001. "Introduction: Citizenship, Immigration and Nationality: Towards a Convergence in Europe?" In *Towards a European Nationality: Citizenship, Immigration and Nationality Law in the EU*, edited by Randall Hansen and Patrick Weil, 1–23. New York: Palgrave.

Harnischmacher, Robert, ed. 1993. *Angriff von Rechts: Rechtsextremismus und Neonazismus unter Jugendlichen Ostberlins*. Rostock: Hanseatischer Fachverlag für Wirtschaft.

Haydu, Jeffrey. 1998. "Making Use of the Past: Time Periods as Cases to Compare and as Sequences of Problem-Solving." *American Journal of Sociology* 104 (2): 339–71.

Hedetoft, Ulf. 1993. "National Identity and Mentalities of War in Three EC Countries." *Journal of Peace Research* 30 (August): 281–300.

Heiderich, Rolf, and Gerhart Rohr. 2000. *Ausländerfragen Kontrovers: Ist das Boot voll?* Munich: Olzog Verlag Gmbh.

Heitmeyer, Wilhelm. 1988. *Rechtsextremistische Orientierungen bei Jugendlichen*. 2nd ed. Weinheim: Juventa.

———. 1999. "Sozialräumliche Machtversuche des Ostdeutschen Rechtsextremismus." In *Rechtsextremistische Jugendliche—Was Tun?* edited by Peter E. Kalb, Karin Sitte, and Christian Petry, 47–79. Weinheim: Beltz Verlag.

Heitmeyer, Wilhelm, Heike Buhse, Joachim Liebe-Freund, Kurt Möller, Joachim Müller, Helmut Ritz, Gertrud Siller, and Johannes Vossen. 1992. *Die Bielefelder Rechtsextremismus-Studie: Erste Langzeituntersuchung zur Politischen Sozialisation männlicher Jugendlicher*. Munich: Juventa Verlag.

Held, David. 1996. "The Decline of the Nation State." In *Becoming National: A Reader*, edited by Geoff Eley and Ronald Suny, 407–16. New York: Oxford University Press.

Hell, Julia. 1997. *Post-Fascist Fantasies: Psychoanalysis, History, and the Literature of East Germany (Post-Contemporary Interventions)*. Durham, N.C.: Duke University Press.

Hermand, Jost, and James Steakley. 1996. *Heimat, Nation, Fatherland*. New York: Peter Lang.

Hobsbawm, E. J. 1990. *Nations and Nationalism since 1780: Programme, Myth, Reality*. Cambridge: Cambridge University Press.

Hogwood, Patricia. 2000. "Citizenship Controversies in Germany: The Twin Legacy of Voelkish Nationalism and the Alleinvertretungsanspruch." *German Politics* 9 (December): 125–44.

Holzer, Werner. 1992. "The Eternal German Riddle." In *Meet United Germany: Perspectives 1992/93*, edited by Susan Stern, 341–46. Frankfurt: Frankfurter Allgemeine Zeitung.

Homola, Victor. 2001. "Germany: Jewish Leader Cites Extremists." *New York Times*, November 21, A8.

Hopf, Christel, Marlene Silzer, and Joerg M. Wernich. 1999. "Ethnozentrismus und Sozialisation in der DDR." In *Rechtsextremistische Jugendliche— Was Tun?* edited by Peter E. Kalb, Karin Sitte, and Christian Petry, 80–121. Weinheim: Beltz Verlag.

Hops, Bernd. 2001. "Die Stunde der Patrioten." *Der Tagesspiegel*, March 20, 5.

Hroch, Miroslav. 1996. "From National Movement to the Fully Formed Nation: The Nation-Building Process in Europe." In *Mapping the Nation*, edited by Gopal Balakrishnan, 78–97. New York: Verso.

Hufer, Klaus-Peter. 2001. *Argumentationstraining gegen Stammtischparolen: Materialien und Anleitungen für Bildungsarbeit und Selbstlernen*. Schwalbach: Wochenschau Verlag.

Huyssen, Andreas. 1995. "The Inevitability of Nation: Germany after Unification." In *The Identity in Question*, edited by John Rajchman, 73–83. New York: Routledge.

Ignatieff, Michael. 1993. *Blood and Belonging: Journeys into the New Nationalism*. New York: Farrar, Straus and Giroux.

Isoplan, Institut für Entwicklungsforschung, Wirtschafts- und Sozialplanung GmbH. 2002. *Ausländer in Deutschland: Vierteljährlich Erscheinender Informationsdienst zu aktuellen Fragen der Ausländerarbeit*. No. 1. Saarbrücken: Isoplan GmbH.

James, Harold. 2000. *A German Identity: 1770 to the Present Day*. London: Phoenix Press.

James, Harold, and Marla Stone, eds. 1992. *When the Wall Came Down: Reactions to German Unification*. New York: Routledge.

Jaschke, Hans-Gerd. 2001. *Rechtsextremismus und Fremdenfeindlichkeit: Begriffe, Positionen, Praxisfelder*. Wiesbaden: Westdeutscher Verlag.

Jenks, Christopher, ed. 1993a. *Cultural Reproduction*. New York: Routledge.

———. 1993b. "Introduction: The Analytic Bases of Cultural Reproduction Theory." In *Cultural Reproduction*, edited by Christopher Jenks, 1–16. New York: Routledge.

Joppke, Christian. 1999a. "How Immigration Is Changing Citizenship: A Comparative View." *Ethnic and Racial Studies* 22 (4): 629–52.

———. 1999b. *Immigration and the Nation-State: The United States, Germany, and Great Britain*. New York: Oxford University Press.

———. 2003. "Citizenship between De- and Re-Ethnicization." *Archives Européennes de Sociologie* 44 (3): 429–58.

———. 2004. "Citizenship without Identity." *Canadian Diversity* 3 (2): 85–87.

———. 2005a. "Exclusion in the Liberal State: The Case of Immigration and Citizenship Policy." *European Journal of Social Theory* 8 (1): 43–61.

———. 2005b. *Selecting by Origin: Ethnic Migration in the Liberal State*. Cambridge: Harvard University Press.

Kane, Ann. 1997. "Theorizing Meaning Construction in Social Movements: Symbolic Structures and Interpretation during the Irish Land War." *Sociological Theory* 15 (3): 249–76.

Kant, Immanuel. 1994. "Excerpt from the *Theory of Right*, Part II: Public Right." In *Citizenship: Critical Concepts*, Vol. 1, edited by Bryan S. Turner and Peter Hamilton, 295–98. New York: Routledge.

Kastoryano, Riva. 2002. *Negotiating Identities: States and Immigrants in France and Germany*. Translated by Barbara Harshav. Princeton, N.J.: Princeton University Press.

Kennedy, Michael D. 1999. "The Liabilities of Liberalism and Nationalism after Communism: Polish Businessmen in the Articulation of the Nation." In *Intellectuals and the Articulation of the Nation*, edited by Ronald Grigor Suny and Michael D. Kennedy, 345–82. Ann Arbor: University of Michigan Press.

———. 2002. *Cultural Formations of Postcommunism: Emancipation, Transition, Nation and War*. Minneapolis: Minnesota University Press.

Kennedy, Michael D., and Ronald Grigor Suny. 1999. Introduction. In *Intellectuals and the Articulation of the Nation*, edited by Ronald Grigor Suny and Michael D. Kennedy, 1–51. Ann Arbor: University of Michigan Press.

Koopmans, Ruud, and Paul Statham. 1999. "Challenging the Liberal Nation-State? Postnationalism, Multiculturalism, and the Collective Claims Making of Migrants and Ethnic Minorities in Britain and Germany." *American Journal of Sociology* 105 (November): 652–96.

Kreutzberger, Wolfgang. 1983. *Rechtsradikalismus in der Bundesrepublik: Versuch einer Zwischenbilanz*. Frankfurt: Materialis Verlag.

Kreutzner, Gabriele. 1989. "On Doing Cultural Studies in West Germany." *Cultural Studies* 3 (2) (May).

Krupa, Matthias. 2001. "Gewaltbereitschaft von Rechtsextremisten wächst." *Berliner Zeitung*, March 30, 6.

Kuhn, Hans-Werner, Peter Massing, and Werner Skuhr. 1993. *Politische Bildung in Deutschland: Entwicklung—Stand—Perspektiven.* 2nd ed. Opladen: Leske and Budrich.

Kymlicka, Will. 1995. *Multicultural Citizenship: A Liberal Theory of Minority Rights.* Oxford: Clarendon Press.

Laclau, Ernesto, and Chantal Mouffe. 1985. *Hegemony and Socialist Strategy: Towards A Radical Democratic Politics.* New York: Verso.

Lamont, Michèle. 2000. *The Dignity of Working Men: Morality and the Boundaries of Race, Class, and Immigration.* Cambridge: Harvard University Press.

Landler, Mark, and Jere Longman. 2006. "Germans' Main Objective Is a Good Time for All." *New York Times*, June 9.

LeCompte, Margaret D., and Jean J. Schensul. 1999. *Analyzing and Interpreting Ethnographic Data.* Walnut Creek, Calif.: Altamira Press.

Leitfragen Politik: Orientierungswissen politische Bildung. 1998. Stuttgart: Ernst Klett Verlag.

Lepsius, M. Rainer. 2004. "The Nation and Nationalism in Germany." *Social Research* 71 (fall): 481–500.

Levy, Daniel. 1999. "Remembering the Nation: Ethnic Germans and the Transformation of National Identity in the Federal Republic of Germany." Ph.D. diss., Columbia University.

Levy, Daniel, and Yfaat Weiss, eds. 2002. *Challenging Ethnic Citizenship: German and Israeli Perspectives on Immigration.* New York: Berghahn Books.

Linke, Uli. 1997. "Gendered Difference, Violent Imagination: Blood, Race, Nation." *American Anthropologist* 99 (3): 559–73.

Lister, Ruth, Noel Smith, Sue Middleton, and Lynne Cox. 2003. "Young People Talk about Citizenship: Empirical Perspectives on Theoretical and Political Debates." *Citizenship Studies* 7 (2): 235–53.

Ludvig, Alice. 2004. "Why Should Austria Be Different from Germany? The Two Recent Nationality Reforms in Contrast." *German Politics* 13 (3): 499–515.

Maier, Charles S. 1988. *The Unmasterable Past: History, Holocaust, and German National Identity.* Cambridge: Harvard University Press.

Majer-O'Sickey, Ingeborg. 2006. "Out of the Closet? German Patriotism and Soccer Mania." *German Politics and Society* 24 (autumn): 82–97.

Mandel, Ruth. 1989. "Turkish Headscarves and the 'Foreigner Problem': Constructing Difference through Emblems of Identity." *New German Critique* 46 (winter): 27–46.

———. 2008. *Cosmopolitan Anxieties: Turkish Challenges to Citizenship and Belonging in Germany*. Durham: Duke University Press.

Manji, Irshad. 2005. "Why Tolerate the Hate?" *New York Times*, August 9.

Mannheim, Karl. 1952. "The Problem of Generations." In *Essays on the Sociology of Knowledge*, edited by Paul Kecskemeti, 276–320. New York: Oxford University Press.

Marcuse, Harold. 2001. *Legacies of Dachau: The Uses and Abuses of a Concentration Camp*. Cambridge: Cambridge University Press.

Marshall, T. H., and Tom Bottomore. 1992. *Citizenship and Social Class*. Chicago: Pluto Press.

McLaren, Lauren M. 1999. "Explaining Right-Wing Violence in Germany: A Time-Series Analysis." *Social Science Quarterly* 80 (March): 166–80.

Merkens, Hanns. 1999. *Schuljugendliche in beiden Teilen Berlins seit der Wende: Reaktionen auf den sozialen Wandel*. Aachen: Schneider Verlag Hohengehren.

Miller, Cynthia L. 1999. "Rethinking Citizenship Frameworks: Education for Citizenship Practice, Not Citizenship Status." *Education in Russia, the Independent States and Eastern Europe* 17 (spring): 19–31.

Miller, Cynthia L., and Douglas Ready. 2002. "Social-Class and Right-Wing Radicalism among Vocational Youth in Contemporary Germany." Paper presented at the American Sociological Association Meetings, April 2002, Chicago.

Miller, Tobias. 2000. "Im Sozialkunde-Lehrplan fehlt das Thema 'Rechtsextremismus.'" *Berliner Zeitung*, December 8, 22.

Miller-Idriss, Cynthia. 2002. "Challenge and Change in the German Vocational System since 1990." *Oxford Review of Education* 28 (4): 473–90.

———. 2005. "Citizenship Education and Political Extremism in Germany: An Ethnographic Account." In *Political and Citizenship Education: International Perspectives*, edited by Stephanie Wilde, 101–22. Wallingford, UK: Symposium Press.

———. 2006a. "Everyday Understandings of Citizenship in Germany." *Citizenship Studies* 10 (5) (November): 541–70. http://www.informaworld .com.

———. 2006b. "Dismantling the Nation, Debunking Pride: Discourse and Practice in German Civics Classrooms." In *Citizenship Education: Theory-Research-Practice*, edited by Anne Sliwka, Martina Diedrich, and Manfred Hofer, 19–26. Münster: Waxmann Verlag GmbH.

Molnár, Virág. 2004. "Cultural Politics and Modernist Architecture: The Tulip Debate in Post-War Hungary." Unpublished manuscript.

Mommsen, Hanns. 1983. "History and National Identity: The Case of Germany." *German Studies Review* 6 (3): 559–82.

Morley, David, and Kevin Robing. 1990. "No Place like *Heimat*: Images of Home(land) in European Culture." *New Formations*, no. 12 (winter): 10.

Morrow, Raymond Allan, and Carlos Alberto Torres. 1995. "The Two Gramscis and Education: Technical Competence versus Political Consciousness." In *Social Theory and Education: A Critique of Theories of Social and Cultural Reproduction*, edited by Raymond Allan Morrow and Carlos Alberto Torres, 249–81. Albany: State University of New York Press.

Moses, Dirk. 1999. "The Forty-Fivers: A Generation between Fascism and Democracy." *German Politics and Society* 17 (1): 94–126.

Münz, Rainer, and Ralf Ulrich. 1998. "Zuwanderung und Staatsbürgerschaft: Was will die Mehrheit der Deutschen?" *Migration und Bevölkerung* 7: 1–2.

———. 1999. "Immigration and Citizenship in Germany." *German Politics and Society* 17 (53): 1–33.

O'Brien, Peter. 1992. "German-Polish Migration: The Elusive Search for a German Nation-State." *International Migration Review* 26 (2): 373–87.

Oesterreich, Detlef. 2002. *Politische Bildung von 14-Jährigen in Deutschland: Studien aus dem Projekt Civic Education*. Opladen: Leske and Budrich.

Oesterreich, Detlef, Christa Händle, and Luitgard Trommer. 1999. "Eine Befragung von Experten und Expertinnen zur politischen Bildung in der Sekundarstufe 1." In *Aufgaben politischer Bildung in der Sekundarstufe 1: Studien aus dem Projekt Civic Education*, edited by Christa Händle, Detlef Oesterreich, and Luitgard Trommer, 131–208. Opladen: Leske and Budrich.

Olick, Jeffrey K. 1998. "What Does It Mean to Normalize the Past? Official Memory in German Politics since 1989." *Social Science History* 22 (winter): 548–71.

———. 1999. "Genre Memories and Memory Genres: A Dialogical Analysis of May 8, 1945 Commemorations in the Federal Republic of Germany." *American Sociological Review* 64 (3): 381–402.

Oschlies, Renate. 2001. "Hinter die 'Ideologische Kostümierung' Schauen." *Berliner Zeitung*, 6.

Parade, Heidi. 2001. "Ungebetene Mitstreiter." *Der Tagesspiegel*, March 23, 5.

Paul, Gerhard. 1995. "Rechtsextremismus im Vereinten Deutschland." In *Gewalt unter Jugendlichen, Rechtsextremismus und Fremdenfeindlichkeit: Analysen und Konsequenzen für die pädagogische Arbeit*, edited by Friedrich Ebert Stiftung, 33–46. Erfurt: Friedrich Ebert Stiftung.

Peck, Jeffrey. 1996. "Rac(e)ing the Nation: Is There a German 'Home'?" In *Becoming National*, edited by Geoff Eley and Ronald G. Suny, 481–92. New York: Oxford University Press.

Pfahl-Traughber, Armin. 1999. *Rechtsextremismus in der Bundesrepublik*. Munich: C. H. Beck Verlag.

————. 2000. "Die Entwicklung des Rechtsextremismus in Ost- und West-deutschland." *Aus Politik und Zeitgeschichte: Beilage zur Wochenzeitung das Parlament* B39 (September 22): 3–13.

Phillips, David, ed. 2000a. *Education in Germany since Unification.* Oxford Studies in Comparative Education. Oxford: Symposium Books.

————. 2000b. *Post-National Patriotism and the Feasability of Post-National Community in United Germany.* Westport, Conn.: Praeger Publishers.

Phoenix TV. 2004. "Proud of Germany—How Much Patriotism Does a Country Need?"

Piesche, Peggy. 2002. "Black and German? East German Adolescents before 1989: A Retrospective View of a 'Non-Existent Issue' in the GDR." In *The Cultural After-Life of East Germany: New Transnational Perspectives.* AICGS Harry and Helen Gray Humanities Program, Series 13, edited by Leslie A. Adelson, 37–59. Washington: American Institute for Contemporary German Studies.

Pilcher, Jane. 1994. "Mannheim's Sociology of Generations: An Undervalued Legacy." *British Journal of Sociology* 45 (September): 481–95.

Popkewitz, Thomas S., and Marie Brennan, eds. 1998. *Foucault's Challenge: Discourse, Knowledge, and Power in Education.* New York: Teachers College Press.

Poutrus, Patrice G., Jan C. Behrends, and Dennis Kuck. 2000. "Historische Ursachen der Fremdenfeindlichkeit in den Neuen Bundesländern." *Aus Politik und Zeitgeschichte: Beilage zur Wochenzeitung das Parlament* B39 (September 22): 15–21.

Preuss, Ulrich K. 2003. "Citizenship and the German Nation." *Citizenship Studies* 7 (1): 37–55.

Probst, Lothar, ed. 1999. *Differenz in der Einheit: Über die kulturellen Unterschiede der Deutschen in Ost und West.* Berlin: Christoph Links Verlag.

Pufendorf, S. 1994. "On the Duties of Citizens." In *Citizenship: Critical Concepts.* Vol. 1, edited by Bryan S. Turner and Peter Hamilton, 316–17. New York: Routledge.

Putnam, Robert. 1993. *Making Democracy Work: Civic Traditions in Modern Italy.* Princeton, N.J.: Princeton University Press.

Putz, Ulrike. 2000. "Ein stolzer Deutscher aus der Karibik." *Berliner Zeitung,* November 23, 23.

Rathenow, Hanns-Fred, and Annegret Ehmann. 2000. "Education on National Socialism and the Holocaust." In *Learning from History: The Nazi Era and the Holocaust in German Education,* edited by Annette Brinkmann, Annegret Ehmann, Sybil Milton, Hanns-Fred Rathenow, and Regina Wyrwoll, 22–54. Bonn: Press and Information Office of the Federal Government.

Räthzel, Nora. 1990. "Germany: One Race, One Nation?" *Race and Class* 32 (3): 31–48.

Rippberger, Susan J., and Kathleen A. Staudt. 2003. *Pledging Allegiance: Learning Nationalism at the El Paso-Juarez Border.* New York: Routledge-Falmer.

Rippl, Susanne, and Christian Seipel. 1999. "Gender Differences in Right-Wing Extremism: Intergroup Validity of a Second-Order Construct." *Social Psychology Quarterly* 62 (December): 381–93.

Rojahn, Christoph. 1996. *Extreme Right-Wing Violence in Germany: The Political and Social Context.* London: Research Institute for the Study of Conflict and Terrorism.

Rothenberg, Bess. 2002. "'Typically German?' National Character and the Eye of the Beholder." Ph.D. diss., University of Virginia.

Rotte, Ralph. 2000. "Immigration Control in United Germany: Toward a Broader Scope of National Politics." *International Migration Review* 34 (summer): 357–89.

Rudolph, Hermann. 1983. "Wie sieht das Selbstverständnis der DDR-Gesellschaft aus?" In *Die Identität der Deutschen*, edited by Werner Weidenfeld, 193–209. Bonn: Schriftenreihe der Bundeszentrale für politische Bildung.

———. 2001. "Patrioten auf der Pirsch." *Der Tagesspiegel*, March 20, 1.

Said, Edward. 1993. *Culture and Imperialism.* New York: Vintage Books.

Salecl, Renata. 1994. "The Ideology of the Mother Nation in the Yugoslav Conflict." In *Envisioning Eastern Europe: Postcommunist Cultural Studies*, edited by Michael D. Kennedy, 87–101. Ann Arbor: University of Michigan Press.

Sammartino, Annemarie. 2004. "Migration and Crisis: The Symbolic Geography of the Weimar Republic." Ph.D. diss., University of Michigan.

Sandel, Michael. 1992. "Post-National Democracy vs. Electronic Bonapartism." *New Perspectives Quarterly* 9 (4): 4–8.

Sassen, Saskia. 1999. *Guests and Aliens.* New York: New Press.

Saussure, Ferdinand de. 1966. *Course in General Linguistics.* New York: McGraw Hill.

Schäuble, Wolfgang. 2001. "Es muss nicht gleich Stolz sein." *Süddeutsche Zeitung*, December 1, 9.

Schnabel, Kai Uwe. 1993. "Ausländerfeindlichkeit bei Jugendlichen in Deutschland: Eine Synopse empirischer Befunde seit 1990." *Zeitschrift für Pädagogik* 39 (5): 799–822.

Schnabel, Kai Uwe, and Dietrich Goldschmidt. 1997. "Ausländerfeindlichkeit bei Auszubildenden—Ein Handlungsfeld für Berufsschullehrer?" *Zeitschrift für Berufs- und Wirtschaftspädagogik* 93 (6): 607–29.

Schneider, Jens. 2001. *Deutsch Sein: Das Eigene, das Fremde und die Vergangenheit im Selbstbild des Vereinten Deutschlands*. Frankfurt am Main: Campus Verlag.

Schröder, Richard. 1999. "Warum sollten wir eine Nation sein? Von einigen gemeinsamen Aufgaben der Deutschen." In *Differenz in der Einheit: Über die kulturellen Unterschiede der Deutschen in Ost und West*, edited by Lothar Probst, 29–38. Berlin: Christoph Links Verlag.

Schubarth, Wilfried, and Richard Stöss, eds. 2001. *Rechtsextremismus in der Bundesrepublik Deutschland: Eine Bilanz*. Opladen: Leske and Budrich.

Schuman, Howard, and Cheryl Rieger. 1992. "Historical Analogies, Generational Effects, and Attitudes Toward War." *American Sociological Review* 3 (June): 315–26.

Schuman, Howard, and Jacqueline Scott. 1989. "Generations and Collective Memories." *American Sociological Review* 54 (June): 359–81.

Schweigler, Gebhard Ludwig. 1975. *National Consciousness in Divided Germany*. London: Sage Publications.

Schweikert, Klaus. 1999. *Aus einem Holz? Lehrlinge in Deutschland: Eine Ost-West-Längsschnittuntersuchung: Berichte zur beruflichen Bildung*. Bonn: Bundesinstitut für Berufsbildung.

Schwennicke, Christoph. 2001. "Zahl rechtsextremistische Straftaten drastisch angestiegen." *Süddeutsche Zeitung*, March 3.

Sekretariat der Ständigen Konferenz der Kultusminister der Länder in der Bundesrepublik Deutschland. 1999. *Handreichungen für die Erarbeitung von Rahmenlehrplänen der Kultusministerkonferenz (KMK) für den berufsbezogenen Unterricht in der Berufsschule und ihre Abstimmung mit Ausbildungsordnungen des Bundes für anerkannte Ausbildungsberufe*. Bonn.

Senatsverwaltung für Schule, Jugend und Sport. 1999. *Rahmenplan für Unterricht und Erziehung in der Berliner Schule (Berufsschule, Berufsfachschule), Fächer: Sozialkunde, Wirtschafts- und Sozialkunde, Gültig ab Schuljahr 1999/2000*. Berlin: Berliner Institut für Lehrerfort- und Weiterbildung und Schulentwicklung (BIL).

Senatsverwaltung für Stadtentwicklung. 2000. *Vierteljahresbericht über die Entwicklung der Berliner Bauwirtschaft, 3/2000*. Berlin: Senatsverwaltung für Stadtentwicklung.

Senders, Stefan. 1996. "Laws of Belonging: Legal Dimensions of National Inclusion in Germany." *New German Critique* 67 (winter): 147–76.

Sephocle, Marilyn. 1999. "Afro-Germans and National Identity." In *Who Is a German? Historical and Modern Perspectives on Africans in Germany*, edited by Leroy T. Hopkins Jr., 43–54. Washington: American Institute for Contemporary German Studies, Johns Hopkins University.

Sewell, William H. 1980. *Work and Revolution in France: The Language of Labor from the Old Regime to 1848*. New York: Cambridge University Press.

Sheehan, James. 1992. "National History and National Identity in the New Germany." *German Studies Review* 15 (winter): 163–74.

Smith, Anthony. 1983. *Theories of Nationalism.* 2nd ed. London: Duckworth.

———. 2008. "The Limits of Everyday Nationhood." *Ethnicities* 8 (4): 563–73.

Smith, Dorothy E. 1987. *The Everyday World as Problematic: A Feminist Sociology.* Boston: Northeastern University Press.

Somers, Margaret. 1993. "Citizenship and the Place of the Public Sphere: Law, Community, and Political Culture in the Transition to Democracy." *American Sociological Review* 58: 587–620.

———. 1994. "Rights, Relationality, and Membership: Rethinking the Making and Meaning of Citizenship." *Law and Social Inquiry* 19 (1): 63–112.

———. 1995. "What's Political or Cultural about the Political Culture Concept? Toward an Historical Sociology of Concept Formation." *Sociological Theory* 13 (2): 113–44.

Soysal, Yasemin. 1994. *Limits of Citizenship: Migrants and Postnational Membership in the New Europe.* Chicago: University of Chicago Press.

———. 1996. "Changing Citizenship in Europe: Remarks on Postnational Membership and the National State." In *Citizenship, Nationality, and Migration in Europe,* edited by David Cesarini and Mary Fulbrook, 17–29. New York: Routledge.

Spillman, Lynn. 1996. "'Neither the Same Nation Nor Different Nations': Constitutional Conventions in the United States and Australia." *Comparative Studies in Society and History* 38 (January): 149–81.

———. 1997. *Nation and Commemoration: Creating National Identities in the United States and Australia.* Cambridge: Cambridge University Press.

Staab, Andreas. 1998. *National Identity in Eastern Germany: Inner Unification or Continued Separation?* Westport, Conn.: Praeger Publishers.

Statistische Bundesamt Deutschland. 2007. "Population Statistics." http://www.destatis.de.

Statistische Landesamt Berlin. 2000. "Zehn Jahre Berliner Einheit-Daten und Analysen zum Vereinigungsprozess." *Statistische Monatsschrift* 1–6: 45.

Steinmetz, George. 1993. *Regulating the Social: The Welfare State and Local Politics in Imperial Germany.* Princeton, N.J.: Princeton University Press.

———. 1997. "Social Class and the Reemergence of the Radical Right in Contemporary Germany." In *Reworking Class,* edited by John Hall, 335–68. Ithaca, N.Y.: Cornell University Press.

———. 1999. "Introduction: Culture and the State." In *State/Culture: State-Formation after the Cultural Turn,* edited by George Steinmetz, 1–50. Ithaca, N.Y.: Cornell University Press.

Stern, Die. 2004. Interview by Birgit Lahann and Karin Rocholl. May 19, 224.

Stierstorfer, Klaus, ed. 2003. *Deutschlandbilder im Spiegel anderer Nationen: Literatur, Presse, Film, Funk, Fernsehen.* Reinbek: Rowohlt Taschenbuch.

Storz, Henning, and Carolin Reisslandt, eds. 2002. *Staatsbürgerschaft im Einwanderungsland Deutschland: Handbuch für die interkulturelle Praxis in der sozialen Arbeit, im Bildungsbereich, im Stadtteil.* Opladen: Leske and Budrich.

Straughn, Jeremy Brooke. 2001. "Homeland Dilemmas after State Socialism: The Politics of Narrative and Nation-Building in the Former GDR." Ph.D. diss., University of Chicago.

———. 2005. "'Taking the State at Its Word': The Arts of Consentful Contention in the German Democratic Republic." *American Journal of Sociology* 110 (6): 1598–1650.

Süddeutsche Zeitung. 2001. "Stolzträger." March 21, 9.

Suny, Ronald Grigor, and Michael D. Kennedy, eds. 1999a. *Intellectuals and the Articulation of the Nation.* Ann Arbor: University of Michigan Press.

———. 1999b. "Toward a Theory of National Intellectual Practice." In *Intellectuals and the Articulation of the Nation,* edited by Ronald Grigor Suny and Michael D. Kennedy, 383–417. Ann Arbor: University of Michigan Press.

Swidler, Ann. 1986. "Culture in Action: Symbols and Strategies." *American Sociological Review* 51: 273–86.

Tagesspiegel, Der. 2001a. "Bundeswehr: Mehr rechtsextreme Delikte." March 11.

———. 2001b. "CSU: Rau fehlt der Nationalstolz." March 20, 1.

———. 2001c. "Die Gewaltbereitschaft in Deutschland nimmt zu." March 11.

Taylor, M. E. 1981. *Education and Work in the Federal Republic of Germany.* London: Anglo-German Foundation for the Study of Industrial Society.

Thelen, Kathleen. 2004. *How Institutions Evolve: The Political Economy of Skills in Germany, Britain, the United States, and Japan.* Cambridge: Cambridge University Press.

Ulrich, Bernd. 2004. "Kann man dieses Land lieben?" *Der Tagesspiegel,* May 25, 1.

Urry, John. 1999. "Mediating Global Citizenship." *Iichiko Intercultural* 11 (June): 3–26.

Vastano, Stefano. 1992. "Germany United and Divided: Interview with Gregor Gysi." In *When the Wall Came Down: Reactions to German Unification,* edited by Harold James and Marla Stone, 149–51. New York: Routledge.

Verheyen, Dirk. 1999. *The German Question: A Cultural, Historical, and Geopolitical Exploration*. Boulder, Colo.: Westview Press.

Walzer, Michael. 1995. "The Civil Society Argument." In *Theorizing Citizenship*, edited by Ronald Beiner, 153–74. Albany: State University of New York Press.

Watts, Meredith W. 2001. "Aggressive Youth Cultures and Hate Crime: Skinheads and Xenophobic Youth in Germany." *American Behavioral Scientist* 45 (December): 600–615.

Weaver, Bradden. 1995. "Rightist Violence as a Youth Phenomenon in United Germany." In *Dimensions of German Unification: Economic, Social, and Legal Analyses*, edited by A. Bradley Shingleton, Marian J. Gibbon, and Kathryn S. Mack, 143–56. Boulder, Colo.: Westview Press.

Wegner, Gregory Paul. 1996. "In the Shadow of the Third Reich: The 'Jugendstunde' and the Legitimation of Anti-Fascist Heroes for East German Youth." *German Studies Review* 19 (1) (February): 127–46.

———. 2002. *Anti-Semitism and Schooling under the Third Reich*. New York: Routledge-Falmer.

Weil, Patrick. 1996. "Nationalities and Citizenships: The Lessons of the French Experience for Germany and Europe." In *Citizenship, Nationality and Migration in Europe*, edited by David Cesarani and Mary Fulbrook, 74–87. New York: Routledge.

Weis, Lois, and Michelle Fine. 2000. *Speed Bumps: A Student-Friendly Guide to Qualitative Research*. New York: Teachers College Press.

Welzer, Harald, Sabine Moller, and Karoline Tschuggnall. 2002. *Opa war kein Nazi: Nationalsozialismus und Holocaust im Familiengedächtnis*. Frankfurt am Main: Fischer Taschenbuch Verlag.

White, Jenny B. 1997. "Turks in the New Germany." *American Anthropologist* 99 (4): 754–69.

Wieviorka, Michel. 1996. "The Seeds of Hate." *Unesco Courier* 3 (March): 10–13.

Wildenthal, Lora. 2002. *German Women for Empire, 1884–1945*. Durham, N.C.: Duke University Press.

Williams, Raymond. 1985. *Keywords: A Vocabulary of Culture and Society*. Rev. ed. New York: Oxford University Press.

Willis, Paul. 1977. *Learning to Labor: How Working Class Kids Get Working Class Jobs*. New York: Columbia University Press.

Willms, Johannes. 2001. *Die deutsche Krankheit: Eine kurze Geschichte der Gegenwart*. Munich: Carl Hanser Verlag.

Wippermann, Wolfgang. 1999. "Das Blutrecht der Blutsnation: Zur Ideologie- und Politikgeschichte des ius sanguinis in Deutschland." In *Blut oder Boden: Doppelpass, Staatsbürgerrecht und Nationsverständnis*, edited by Jochen Baumann, Andreas Dietl, and Wolfgang Wippermann, 10–48. Berlin: Elephanten Press.

Wragg, E. C. 1999. *An Introduction to Classroom Observation.* 2nd ed. New York: Routledge.

Wren, Karen. 2001. "Cultural Racism: Something Rotten in the State of Denmark?" *Social and Cultural Geography* 2 (2): 141–62.

Wuthnow, Robert. 1987. *Meaning and Moral Order: Explorations in Cultural Analysis.* Berkeley: University of California Press.

Zimmer, Oliver. 1998. "In Search of National Identity: Alpine Landscape and the Reconstruction of the Swiss Nation." *Comparative Studies in Society and History* 40 (October): 637–65.

Zubrzycki, Geneviève. 2006. *The Crosses of Auschwitz: Nationalism and Religion in Post-Communist Poland.* Chicago: University of Chicago Press.

Foreigners (*cont.*)
ralization of, 33, 37–38, 103; economic interests of, 111, 160; in
German population, 4, 33; German terms for, 11–12; integration
of, 178; prejudice against, 97, 108–
10, 141; semantic terms for, 12. *See
also* Immigration; Violence
France, 147; headscarf affair in, 2–3,
179

Generations, 13–16, 26, 44; differences between, 7, 17, 26, 41–44, 66,
75, 83, 88–90, 93–94, 136, 148–49,
167, 170–78, 187; "45ers," 15–17, 51,
54, 68; immigrants and, 36; interaction between, 17, 122, 171, 176;
re-imagining of nation by, 27, 173;
"68ers," 15–17, 51, 54, 64–68; social
change and, 13–14, 170; transformations of, 27; younger Germans,
5, 7, 16, 18, 44, 87. *See also* Students' views; Teachers
German Democratic Republic
(GDR), 33–35, 48–49. *See also*
National identity
German General Social Survey. *See*
ALLBUS
Germanness, 3–4, 10–13, 59, 67, 71,
80, 128–29, 143–47; blood-based
understanding of, 39–48, 130–31,
149, 172–73; criteria for, 102, 133,
152–67, 173–77; cultural understanding of, 47–48, 78–79, 172. *See
also* Foreigners; National identity;
Students' views; Teachers
Germany, 3–5, 31, 46–49. *See also*
History; National identity
Globalization, 2, 28, 170
Guest workers, 4, 36, 110–11
Guilt, 10, 46, 53–59, 67–69, 79,
82–89, 138

Historikerstreit, 54
History, legacy of World War II

and Holocaust, 5, 17, 40, 48–51,
54–62, 67–69, 82–84, 138, 172,
175. *See also* Guilt; Shame;
Taboo
Hitler, Adolf, 134
Holocaust: legacy of World War II
and, 5, 17, 40, 48–51, 54–62, 67–69,
82–84, 138, 172, 175; TV specials
on, 54, 142
Hooligans, 98, 120; neo-Nazis, 5, 97,
102–4; skinheads, 5, 97–98, 129.
See also Right wing
Hotel and cooking trades, 7, 185–86.
See also Apprenticeship; Voca-
tional schools
Huguenots, 111, 131

Identity. *See* Collective identity;
National identity
Imagined communities, 3, 6, 23–
24, 28, 44, 168, 173. *See also*
National identity; Nationhood;
Re-imagining nations
Immigration, 2–3, 8–12, 16–20, 28,
36–38, 48, 108, 131, 171. *See also*
Citizenship, Foreigners
Information technology trade,
7–8, 19, 99, 150, 186–88. *See also*
Apprenticeship; Vocational
schools
Interviews, x, 7–8, 21, 66, 85, 163,
191–93; with focus groups, 7,
19–20, 119, 189; follow-up, 19, 196;
life narrative and, xi, 196; participant compensation for, 195; semistructured, 189. *See also* Qualitative
research design
Islam, 2–4, 141, 153

Jus sanguinis, 12–13, 31–33, 36–40, 45,
59, 150, 172. *See also* Citizenship;
Germanness; National identity
Jus soli, 12–13, 31, 35, 38, 156, 167,
178. *See also* Citizenship; Germanness

Some portions of this book were adapted from my earlier publications. I am grateful to the publishers of the following pieces for granting me permission.

"Citizenship Education and Political Extremism in Germany: An Ethnographic Analysis," in *Political and Citizenship Education: International Perspectives*, ed. Stephanie Wilde, 101–22 (Oxford: Symposium Books, 2005); "Everyday Understandings of Citizenship in Germany," *Citizenship Studies* 10 (5) (November 2006): 541–70 (please refer to the journal's website: http://www .informaworld.com); "Dismantling the Nation, Debunking Pride: Discourse and Practice in German Civics Classrooms," in *Citizenship Education: Theory-Research-Practice*, ed. Anne Sliwka, Martina Diedrich, and Manfred Hofer, 19–26 (Münster: Waxmann Verlag GmbH, 2006).

Cynthia Miller-Idriss is an assistant professor of international education and educational sociology, Steinhardt School of Culture, Education and Human Development, New York University.

Library of Congress Cataloging-in-Publication Data

Miller-Idriss, Cynthia.
Blood and culture : youth, right-wing extremism, and national belonging in contemporary Germany / Cynthia Miller-Idriss.
p. cm. — (Politics, history, and culture)
Includes bibliographical references and index.
ISBN 978-0-8223-4527-5 (cloth : alk. paper)
ISBN 978-0-8223-4544-2 (pbk. : alk. paper)
1. Nationalism—Germany. 2. National characteristics, German.
3. Citizenship—Germany. 4. Right-wing extremists—Germany.
5. Germany—Ethnic relations.
I. Title. II. Series: Politics, history, and culture.
DD76.M545 2009
320.540943083'5—dc22   2009008987